"It is my pleasure to endorse and recommend to you: Creating Trauma-Informed Classrooms: A Compassionate Approach to Supporting Students and Educators. In this book, Glenys Oberg provides a well-researched, yet extremely practical, educator resource for teachers and student support personnel working with trauma-impacted children and young people. Supported by case studies and ideas for practical strategies, this book will be equally as helpful for pre-service teachers during their studies and practicums. A wonderful and helpful contribution to the growing evidence and resource base for trauma-informed education."

Dr Judith Howard, *Associate Professor, Queensland University of Technology, Australia; Author of* Trauma-aware education: Essential information and guidance for educators, education sites and education systems

"As a Clinical Psychologist with over 25 years' experience, I have worked alongside teachers navigating the unseen weight of trauma in classrooms. This powerful book offers not only understanding but practical, compassionate tools grounded in neuroscience and lived school experience. It validates the emotional labour of teaching while guiding educators towards sustainable, trauma-informed practice. A must-read for anyone committed to creating safe, healing spaces for both students and staff."

Dr Rita Princi-Hubbard, *PhD, M.Psych(Clin), B.Psych(Hons), MAPS, FCCLP; Australia*

"I am pleased to offer my enthusiastic recommendation for Glenys's work, *Creating Trauma-Informed Classrooms: A Compassionate Approach to Supporting Students and Educators.* In this insightful book, Glenys provides a clear and comprehensive overview of the research on trauma and its impact on learners in school settings. Through the thoughtful use of case studies, she effectively bridges the gap between theory and the practical implementation of trauma-informed care in schools. Most importantly, the book highlights the critical importance of creating emotional safety for students by fostering a school environment that not only understands trauma but responds to it with compassion and intention."

Dr Rachel Leslie, *Academic, teacher, and Guidance Officer; University of Southern Queensland, Australia*

Creating Trauma-Informed Classrooms

This transformative guide empowers educators to create a compassionate and nurturing environment for students impacted by trauma, presenting teachers with the knowledge and practical strategies to support their students' emotional well-being and academic success.

Understanding the effects of trauma on students' learning and behaviour is essential. To achieve this, this book places emphasis on empathy, understanding, and resilience as the cornerstones of trauma-informed care. The chapters show educators how to promote emotional regulation, foster resilience, and celebrate students' unique strengths. From building positive teacher-student relationships to implementing mindfulness practices and restorative techniques, the author provides practical tools and reflective exercises to create an inclusive and safe classroom environment. Through heart-warming stories and expert insights, teachers can gain a deeper understanding of their students' experiences, enabling them to respond with compassion and sensitivity. This book also encourages reflective practice and collaboration with families and communities, ensuring educators receive ongoing support in their journey to provide trauma-informed care.

Whether a seasoned educator or a new teacher, this handbook equips educators to make a profound difference in their students' lives and ensures that all students feel seen and valued in the classroom.

Glenys Oberg is a lecturer in the School of Education at the University of Queensland, Australia, and an experienced teacher educator specialising in trauma-informed practice. She holds a PhD in Education and works closely with schools to promote compassionate, research-informed approaches to student well-being.

Creating Trauma-Informed Classrooms

A Compassionate Approach to Supporting Students and Educators

Glenys Oberg

Routledge
Taylor & Francis Group
LONDON AND NEW YORK

Designed cover image: Getty Images

First published 2026
by Routledge
4 Park Square, Milton Park, Abingdon, Oxon OX14 4RN

and by Routledge
605 Third Avenue, New York, NY 10158

Routledge is an imprint of the Taylor & Francis Group, an informa business

© 2026 Glenys Oberg

The right of Glenys Oberg to be identified as author of this work has been asserted in accordance with sections 77 and 78 of the Copyright, Designs and Patents Act 1988.

All rights reserved. No part of this book may be reprinted or reproduced or utilised in any form or by any electronic, mechanical, or other means, now known or hereafter invented, including photocopying and recording, or in any information storage or retrieval system, without permission in writing from the publishers.

Trademark notice: Product or corporate names may be trademarks or registered trademarks, and are used only for identification and explanation without intent to infringe.

British Library Cataloguing-in-Publication Data
A catalogue record for this book is available from the British Library

ISBN: 978-1032-879208 (hbk)
ISBN: 978-1032-879185 (pbk)
ISBN: 978-1003-535386 (ebk)

DOI: 10.4324/9781003535386

Typeset in Optima
by codeMantra

Contents

	Introduction	1
1	The Foundations of Trauma-Informed Care	3
2	Impact of Trauma on Learning and Behaviour	22
3	Creating Emotional Safety and Positive Teacher-Student Relationships	39
4	Cultivating Empathy, Compassion, and Self-Care in Teachers	59
5	Establishing a Supportive School Culture	78
6	Identifying and Addressing Signs of Trauma in Students	100
7	Trauma-Informed Communication and Crisis Intervention	119
8	Adapting the Curriculum and Instruction for Trauma Sensitivity	138
9	Fostering Emotional Regulation and Resilience in Students	155
10	Mindfulness and Relaxation Techniques in the Classroom	179
11	Peer Support, Social Connections, and Restorative Practices	201
12	Integrating Indigenous Perspectives and Understanding Intergenerational Trauma	222
13	Trauma-Informed Professional Development and Reflective Practice	244
	Conclusion: A Compassionate Commitment to Change	264
	Index	271

Introduction

There's a certain heaviness that settles in at the end of a school day – not the tiredness that comes from standing too long or raising your voice too often, but the weight of the unspoken. The lingering tension from a student who refused to make eye contact. The gnawing worry about the one who hasn't smiled in weeks. The quiet ache of knowing you did your best, and still, it might not have been enough.

Every teacher has felt it. That sense that something deeper is happening in the room, just beneath the surface of the lesson. That there are stories sitting in front of us that we do not know, and wounds we were never trained to see.

We enter this profession because we care – about learning, about children, about shaping the future. But caring in classrooms is not a simple act. It's complex, constant, and often overwhelming. And in a world that increasingly expects teachers to be counsellors, social workers, advocates, and role models, we are being asked to give more of ourselves than ever before – without always being given the tools to carry that load well.

This is not a book of easy answers. It does not promise that by following the five steps, you will fix every challenge. It does not pretend that trauma can be neatly resolved within the four walls of a classroom. What it does offer is something more grounded: a way of seeing, understanding, and responding to the emotional realities of students in a way that is both compassionate and sustainable.

Trauma-informed education is not a program. It's not a poster on the wall or a one-off PD session. It is a way of being in the classroom – a commitment to building safety, not just enforcing compliance; to noticing before reacting; to holding space without losing yourself in it. It means shifting the question from "What's wrong with this student?" to "What has this student experienced – and what do they need now?"

This work matters. Not just for the students who come to school carrying more than anyone knows, but for the educators who are trying to support them without burning out. Because when teachers aren't safe – emotionally, professionally, or personally – students aren't either. And no amount of curriculum planning or behaviour management will compensate for a classroom that doesn't feel human.

Throughout this book, you'll encounter strategies, stories, and reflections that aim to make trauma-informed practice more than just a theory. These pages are written with teachers in mind – those who are still learning, those who are exhausted, and those who are determined to keep showing up.

You don't have to do this work perfectly. But you do deserve to do it with clarity, community, and care. Let this book be part of that.

Trauma-Informed Care in Education

Brain Science
Understanding how trauma affects cognitive development and learning processes in students

Emotional Safety
Creating supportive classroom environments where students feel secure and valued

Practical Strategies
Specific techniques to help students overcome adverse experiences and thrive academically

This guide explores how trauma affects learning and behavior, offering practical strategies for creating supportive educational environments that environments that help students thrive despite adverse experiences.

Figure 0.1 Trauma-Informed Care in Education: Core Principles and Applications

The Foundations of Trauma-Informed Care

Introduction

Trauma has a profound impact on the lives of students, shaping not only their emotional well-being but also their ability to learn and thrive in the classroom. As educators, it is our responsibility to create an environment that acknowledges and addresses the potential impacts of trauma, fostering a sense of safety and belonging for all students. This foundational chapter sets the stage for embracing a trauma-informed approach in our classrooms. In this chapter, we will give a brief overview of the core principles and values of trauma-informed care, exploring the significance of compassion, empathy, and understanding in our teaching practices. These topics will be described in further detail throughout the book. By acknowledging that many of our students may have experienced trauma, we gain insight into their unique challenges and needs. Armed with this understanding, we can create a safe and supportive learning environment that nurtures their emotional well-being and facilitates academic growth.

As educators, our role extends beyond imparting knowledge; we have the power to be agents of healing and resilience in our students' lives. This chapter will equip us with the knowledge and tools to recognise trauma-related behaviours and respond with sensitivity rather than judgement. We will explore the transformative shift from asking "What's wrong with you?" to "What happened to you?" – a shift that lays the foundation for building trust and rapport with our students. Together, we will explore the power of compassion and empathy in fostering a positive teacher-student relationship. By adopting a strengths-based perspective, we will be able to view our students through a lens of resilience and potential, inspiring them to overcome their challenges.

DOI: 10.4324/9781003535386-2

With this chapter, we embark on a journey to build a trauma-informed classroom where every student feels understood, validated, and valued. Through compassionate teaching, we can create an environment that empowers our students to heal, learn, and thrive.

Understanding Trauma

Trauma is a complex and deeply impactful experience that can significantly shape individuals' lives, particularly students within educational settings. In this section, we will explore the multifaceted nature of trauma, its diverse forms, and its far-reaching effects on students' emotional well-being and learning.

Defining Trauma and Its Forms

Trauma can be defined as the emotional and psychological response to distressing or life-threatening events that surpass an individual's capacity to cope (Bryce, 2017; Felitti et al., 1998; Howard, 2019). It can manifest as acute trauma, resulting from a single distressing incident, or complex trauma, which emerges from prolonged or repetitive adverse experiences (Spinazzola et al., 2021). Acute trauma may include natural disasters, accidents, or violence, while complex trauma is often associated with chronic abuse, neglect, or ongoing exposure to trauma-inducing environments. Furthermore, trauma can be cumulative, where repeated exposure to distressing experiences intensifies the psychological impact, leading to more complex behavioural and emotional responses (Felitti et al., 1998).

The Neurobiological Impact of Trauma

Understanding the neurobiological impact of trauma is essential for educators seeking to support trauma-impacted students effectively. Traumatic experiences trigger the brain's primal survival response, commonly known as the fight-flight-freeze response (Van der Kolk, 2003). During such events, the amygdala, the brain's emotional centre, becomes hyperactive, leading to an increase in stress hormones like cortisol and adrenaline. This heightened state can impair higher cognitive functions such as attention, memory, and problem-solving, and inhibit effective learning and emotional regulation. Chronic activation of the stress response system may lead to long-term changes in brain structures like the hippocampus, which is critical for learning and memory, making it difficult for trauma-impacted students to retain information or concentrate in class (Evans & Coccoma, 2014).

Manifestation of Trauma in Behaviours and Emotions

Trauma can significantly influence students' behaviours and emotions, often leading to observable signs that educators must recognise and address sensitively (Collier et al., 2020). In response to trauma, students may display heightened anxiety, hypervigilance, or emotional dysregulation, as they attempt to navigate the lingering sense of threat. These students may be constantly scanning their environment for potential dangers, making it challenging to focus on schoolwork. Some students may exhibit avoidant behaviours, attempting to escape situations reminiscent of past trauma triggers, while others might display aggressive or withdrawn behaviours as a way to cope with overwhelming emotions.

Educators may notice changes in academic performance, absenteeism, or social withdrawal, which can be indicators of underlying trauma-related struggles. Additionally, trauma-impacted students might demonstrate difficulties with trust, struggling to form meaningful connections with peers and teachers due to previous betrayal or harm (Bryce, 2017; Felitti et al., 1998; Howard, 2019; McCarthy et al., 2016). Students with trauma histories may experience difficulties interpreting social cues, often misreading neutral or friendly behaviours as hostile. This can further complicate peer interactions and create challenges in the classroom.

By understanding the manifestation of trauma in behaviours and emotions, educators can provide a supportive and validating environment for students to heal and flourish. Recognising these signs allows teachers to respond with empathy, compassion, and patience, fostering a sense of safety and trust that is crucial for trauma-impacted students' growth. Research shows that trauma-sensitive interventions, such as offering predictable routines and allowing students choices, can significantly reduce stress and promote a sense of control in students' lives (Perry & Daniels, 2016). By recognising and acknowledging trauma-related signs, educators can create a nurturing and supportive learning environment that promotes healing, resilience, and academic success for all students.

Principles of Trauma-Informed Care

Trauma-informed care is founded upon essential principles that guide educators in creating a nurturing and healing environment for trauma-impacted students. These principles help educators respond to trauma in ways that promote resilience and foster a positive learning environment. In this section, we introduce the key principles of trauma-informed care: safety, trustworthiness, choice, collaboration, and empowerment.

Safety

The principle of safety emphasises the importance of establishing a physically and emotionally secure learning environment for all students. Trauma-impacted students are particularly sensitive to triggers that can activate their fight-flight-freeze response, which may cause distress or hinder learning (Van der Kolk, 2003). By cultivating a sense of safety – both physical and emotional – educators lay the foundation for students' well-being and academic success. This includes providing predictable routines, clear boundaries, and a supportive atmosphere where students feel protected, respected, and understood. Creating a trauma-sensitive environment with consistent, safe spaces and calming areas can help reduce anxiety and increase engagement (Horner et al., 2010).

Trustworthiness

Building trust is central to trauma-informed care. Many trauma-impacted students have experienced betrayal or breaches of trust, so it is essential that educators consistently demonstrate reliability, honesty, and transparency in their actions. By being clear about classroom expectations, following through on promises, and addressing students' concerns in an open manner, educators can cultivate a positive, trusting relationship with their students (Sciaraffa et al., 2018). This trust allows for better communication and enables students to feel safe enough to express their emotions and engage in learning without fear of judgement or rejection.

Choice

Providing students with choices within appropriate boundaries is a crucial element of trauma-informed care. Students who have experienced trauma often feel a lack of control over their lives, which can lead to feelings of helplessness or disengagement. By offering them choices in learning activities, classroom tasks, and social interactions, educators can promote a sense of agency and autonomy, encouraging students to take ownership of their learning (Record-Lemon & Buchanan, 2017). This approach fosters self-efficacy, empowering students to feel more capable and confident in their decisions.

Collaboration

Collaboration between educators, students, and families is a cornerstone of trauma-informed education. Trauma impacts not only the student but also their broader social environment. By engaging parents and caregivers as partners in the educational journey, educators can strengthen the support network surrounding trauma-impacted students, ensuring a consistent and unified approach to addressing their needs (Perry & Daniels, 2016). Collaborative efforts within the school community – between teachers, counsellors, and administrators – also ensure that trauma-sensitive practices are applied consistently across settings, promoting a stable and safe environment for the student.

Empowerment

Trauma-informed care aims to empower students by recognising their resilience and inherent strengths. Rather than focusing solely on deficits or challenges, educators can adopt a strengths-based perspective, identifying and celebrating the capabilities and achievements of trauma-impacted students (Woodbridge et al., 2016). By acknowledging students' successes and encouraging their personal growth, teachers help to instil a sense of self-worth and empowerment. This shift in perspective supports the development of resilience, enabling students to navigate their trauma while building confidence in their abilities to succeed in school and beyond (Bonanno & Diminich, 2013).

By integrating these principles – safety, trustworthiness, choice, collaboration, and empowerment – educators can create a trauma-informed classroom where students feel secure, supported, and valued. Through this compassionate approach, teachers foster an environment that not only enhances students' emotional well-being but also facilitates academic success and personal growth (Figure 1.1).

The Principles of Trauma-Informed Care

Trustworthiness
Building reliable, consistent consistent relationships with with clear boundaries.

Choice
Offering options to restore sense of control.

Collaboration
Sharing power and decisions decisions with students.

Safety
Creating physical and emotional security for all students.

Empowerment
Building on strengths and developing new skills.

Figure 1.1 The Principles of Trauma-Informed Care

Creating a Safe and Supportive Learning Environment

Establishing a safe and supportive learning environment is paramount in trauma-informed care (Dorado et al., 2016). Educators must be attentive to their classroom's physical layout, ensuring it promotes safety and minimises potential triggers. This may include designated calming spaces, comfortable seating arrangements, and visually appealing classroom decor.

Equally important is the emotional climate of the classroom. By cultivating a culture of respect, kindness, and empathy, educators foster an inclusive and supportive environment where all students feel valued and heard. Implementing trauma-sensitive practices, such as offering opportunities for movement breaks or utilising grounding techniques during stressful situations, can further enhance emotional well-being.

Moreover, educators play a critical role as role models in demonstrating respectful and compassionate behaviour. By engaging in active listening, validating students' feelings, and modelling healthy emotional expression, teachers create a secure space where students can feel comfortable and understood.

Shifting to a Trauma-Informed Mindset

Embracing a trauma-informed mindset involves moving away from a deficit-based approach, which may focus on students' challenges, and adopting a strengths-based perspective that recognises their resilience and potential. Instead of asking "What's wrong with you?" educators reframe their thinking to "What happened to you?" This transformation fosters an attitude of non-judgement and curiosity, allowing educators to understand and respond to students' behaviours and emotions with empathy (Van der Kolk, 2003).

A trauma-informed mindset emphasises the importance of addressing the root causes of behaviours and considering the impact of past trauma on students' present experiences. This approach helps educators avoid punitive measures and, instead, respond with compassion and appropriate support.

By shifting to a trauma-informed mindset, educators not only create a more compassionate and understanding learning environment but also inspire students to view themselves through a lens of strength and resilience. This mindset serves as the cornerstone of trauma-informed care, laying the foundation for a transformative and healing educational experience for all students (Bonanno & Diminich, 2013; Mohr & Rosen, 2017).

The Power of Compassion and Empathy

Impact of Compassion and Empathy in the Teacher-Student Relationship

Compassion and empathy are potent tools in the educator's arsenal, with the power to transform the teacher-student relationship into a source of healing and growth. When educators demonstrate genuine care and understanding, students feel seen, valued, and supported, which creates a positive emotional climate in the classroom. This emotional connection is particularly important for trauma-impacted students, as it fosters a sense of safety and belonging, essential for their emotional well-being and academic success.

By fostering a compassionate learning environment, educators create space for students to express their emotions openly and authentically. This emotional safety promotes trust and encourages students to share their thoughts and concerns without fear of judgement. When students feel heard and validated, their overall well-being improves, leading to increased engagement and improved academic performance. Furthermore, empathy plays a critical role in building strong connections with students. By putting themselves in their students' shoes, educators gain insight into their experiences and perspectives. Empathy allows teachers to understand the impact of trauma on students' lives, enabling them to respond with sensitivity and tailored support

(Sciaraffa et al., 2018). Research shows that students who feel understood by their teachers are more likely to engage positively in the classroom and develop stronger relationships with peers and educators (Pappano, 2014).

The "What's Wrong with You?" vs. "What Happened to You?" Mindset Shift

A transformative mindset shift occurs when educators move from a deficit-based approach, asking "What's wrong with you?", to a strengths-based perspective, inquiring "What happened to you?" This shift reframes students' behaviours and struggles as understandable reactions to their life experiences, including trauma. Trauma-informed educators recognise that behaviours are often driven by unmet needs and unresolved trauma rather than intentional defiance.

By understanding the impact of past trauma on students' present behaviours, educators avoid making assumptions about students' motivations. Instead, they approach students with curiosity and empathy, seeking to uncover the underlying reasons behind their actions. This shift fosters an environment of non-judgement, allowing educators to respond to challenging behaviours with compassion and appropriate support. The "What happened to you?" mindset not only promotes a sense of safety and trust between educators and students but also conveys that educators genuinely care about students' well-being and are committed to providing support without blame or punishment (Van der Kolk, 2003). This transformation helps build stronger teacher-student relationships, where students feel understood and valued, creating an environment conducive to both emotional healing and academic success (Figure 1.2).

Practical Strategies for Cultivating Compassion and Empathy

Cultivating compassion and empathy in the classroom requires intentional and consistent efforts. Educators can employ several practical strategies to create a supportive and empathetic learning environment:

The Mindset Shift

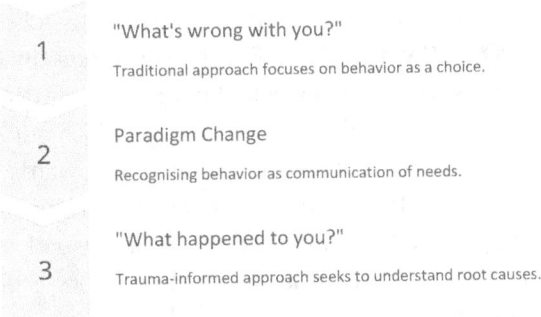

Figure 1.2 The Mindset Shift: From "What's Wrong?" to "What Happened?"

1. **Active Listening**: Engaging in active listening allows educators to fully understand students' perspectives. By giving undivided attention, validating emotions, and responding thoughtfully, educators demonstrate empathy and build trust with students. This can be particularly important for students who have experienced trauma, as they may feel disconnected from adults in their lives.
2. **Promoting Emotional Literacy**: Teaching emotional literacy equips students with the language and skills to identify and express their feelings. This empowers students to communicate their emotions effectively, enabling educators to offer appropriate support (Woodbridge et al., 2016). Building emotional literacy helps students understand their own emotions and the emotions of others, which can improve social interactions and reduce conflict.
3. **Modelling Compassion**: As role models, educators can demonstrate compassion in their interactions with students and colleagues. Displaying kindness, patience, and understanding fosters a culture of compassion in the classroom. By showing how to handle challenging situations with empathy, teachers encourage students to do the same in their own interactions.
4. **Trauma-Informed Practices**: Integrating trauma-informed practices into teaching allows educators to respond sensitively to students' trauma-related needs. Providing calming strategies, offering choices, and

maintaining a predictable routine all contribute to supporting students' emotional well-being (Evans & Coccoma, 2014). These strategies help students feel more in control and less anxious in the classroom environment.
5. **Encouraging Empathy Exercises**: Engaging students in empathy exercises, such as perspective-taking activities or literature discussions, helps them develop empathy skills. These activities teach students to understand diverse experiences and show empathy towards others, which enhances their ability to form positive peer relationships.
6. **Creating a Supportive Community**: Building a sense of community and belonging in the classroom fosters empathy among students. Encouraging collaboration, mutual support, and peer-to-peer understanding strengthens the overall classroom dynamic, helping to create a supportive and inclusive environment where every student feels valued.
7. **Reflective Practice**: Encouraging educators to engage in reflective practice allows them to assess their own biases and assumptions. By recognising their own triggers, educators can respond more empathetically to students' needs. Reflective practice can also help educators adapt their teaching to better meet the emotional and academic needs of their students (Bonanno & Diminich, 2013).

By embracing compassion and empathy in the classroom, educators empower students to navigate their trauma and challenges with resilience. A nurturing and empathetic learning environment lays the foundation for healing, growth, and academic success for all students. Through compassion, educators become agents of positive change, inspiring students to view themselves through a lens of strength and worthiness, helping them to thrive despite the challenges they face.

Self-Care for Educators

Educators play a pivotal role in fostering a compassionate and trauma-informed learning environment. However, to effectively support students' well-being, it is essential for educators to prioritise their own self-care and well-being (Oberg et al., 2023). In this section, we will discuss the importance of educator self-care, provide strategies for managing stress and preventing burnout, and encourage educators to prioritise their emotional needs to better support their students.

Stress the Importance of Educator Self-Care and Well-Being

Educators often devote significant time and energy to meet the diverse needs of their students, sometimes neglecting their own well-being in the process. Neglecting self-care can lead to increased stress, emotional exhaustion, and ultimately, burnout. It is crucial for educators to recognise that taking care of their own well-being is not a selfish act but rather an essential component of their ability to effectively support their students (Herman et al., 2018). Research shows that educators who practice self-care are better equipped to maintain the empathy, compassion, and resilience needed to create a nurturing and supportive learning environment (Bonanno & Diminich, 2013).

Prioritising self-care allows educators to foster a positive mindset and build emotional resilience, enabling them to remain effective in the classroom even when facing challenging circumstances. By modelling self-care, educators also demonstrate the importance of personal well-being to their students, teaching them the value of setting healthy boundaries and prioritising their own mental and emotional health.

Strategies for Managing Stress and Preventing Burnout

Managing stress and preventing burnout are critical aspects of self-care for educators. Implementing practical strategies can help educators sustain their well-being and continue to be effective in the classroom:

1. **Establish Boundaries**: Set clear boundaries between work and personal life. Avoid overextending yourself by scheduling regular breaks and downtime to recharge. Maintaining these boundaries helps prevent emotional overload.
2. **Practice Mindfulness**: Incorporate mindfulness practices, such as meditation or deep breathing exercises, into daily routines. Mindfulness is known to reduce stress, improve emotional regulation, and enhance focus, all of which are essential for managing classroom challenges (Evans & Coccoma, 2014).

3. **Engage in Physical Activity**: Regular physical activity, such as exercise or yoga, releases endorphins, which help reduce stress and promote overall well-being. Physical movement also improves mental clarity and energy levels, making it easier to manage the demands of teaching.
4. **Seek Social Support**: Connect with colleagues, friends, or support groups to share experiences and alleviate feelings of isolation. Building a strong social support network can provide emotional validation and stress relief (Perry & Daniels, 2016).
5. **Prioritise Sleep**: Ensure sufficient restorative sleep each night, as inadequate sleep can contribute to increased stress, emotional exhaustion, and difficulty concentrating. Consistent sleep routines are critical for maintaining both physical and emotional health.
6. **Practice Gratitude**: Cultivate a gratitude practice by regularly reflecting on the positive aspects of work and life. Practising gratitude helps shift focus towards positive experiences, reducing feelings of overwhelm and fostering a more balanced perspective (Record-Lemon & Buchanan, 2017).
7. **Time Management**: Use effective time management techniques to prioritise tasks and minimise feelings of being overwhelmed. This includes setting realistic goals, breaking tasks into manageable steps, and recognising when to delegate responsibilities.

Encourage Educators to Prioritise Their Emotional Needs

Educators often invest significant emotional energy in supporting their students, which can take a toll on their emotional well-being. It is essential for educators to recognise and validate their own emotional needs and not ignore their personal feelings in the process of caring for others. By acknowledging their emotions and seeking appropriate support when necessary, educators can create a healthier emotional space for themselves.

Engaging in reflective practices, such as journaling or seeking supervision, allows educators to process their emotions and gain insights into their experiences. This practice encourages self-awareness and helps educators understand their emotional triggers, enabling them to respond with more empathy and patience when interacting with students (Madigan & Kim, 2021). Reflective practice can also support educators in identifying areas where they may need further support or self-care interventions.

Educators are better positioned to support their students when they prioritise their own emotional needs. Acknowledging and addressing their emotions enables educators to respond with compassion and understanding, contributing to a healthier classroom environment where both students and teachers thrive. This emotional resilience empowers educators to foster a safe and compassionate learning space for students, where healing and academic growth can occur.

Self-care is an integral aspect of trauma-informed care for educators. By prioritising their well-being, educators can sustain their ability to support students effectively (Madigan & Kim, 2021). Managing stress, preventing burnout, and attending to their emotional needs are essential components of self-care, allowing educators to maintain the compassion and empathy needed to create a supportive foundation for their students' growth and well-being. As compassionate role models, educators inspire students to prioritise their own self-care, fostering a classroom culture rooted in well-being and resilience.

Framework for Trauma-Informed Classroom

Creating a trauma-informed classroom requires translating the core principles of trauma-informed care into everyday practice. By applying these principles in day-to-day teaching, educators can foster a safe and nurturing learning environment that supports both the emotional well-being and academic growth of all students.

Establishing Safety and Trust

Prioritising students' sense of safety is foundational. Many trauma-impacted students are sensitive to unpredictable environments, making it essential for educators to provide consistency and clear expectations. Honest communication and reliable routines help build trust and promote a stable atmosphere in which students feel comfortable to participate and take learning risks (Herrenkohl et al., 2019).

Cultivating Empathy and Understanding

Educators who listen actively and respond with empathy foster a classroom culture that affirms students' experiences. By adopting a strengths-based perspective, educators can recognise and nurture students' unique abilities, resilience, and potential, rather than focusing solely on deficits or challenges (Sciaraffa et al., 2018). This approach fosters a culture of empathy, allowing students to feel seen and understood, which is essential for their emotional healing and academic progress.

Promoting Choice and Agency

Trauma-impacted students often feel a lack of control in their lives, so offering choices helps restore a sense of agency. Encouraging student participation in decision-making processes, such as selecting projects or setting classroom norms, cultivates a collaborative and supportive learning environment where students feel respected and in control of their educational experience (Record-Lemon & Buchanan, 2017).

Collaboration and Support

Building a trauma-informed classroom involves collaboration between educators, students, families, and support staff. Engaging parents and caregivers as partners in the educational process strengthens the support network for trauma-impacted students, ensuring that their emotional and academic needs are met consistently across environments (Perry & Daniels, 2016). Collaboration also extends to other professionals within the school, such as counsellors and administrators, who can provide additional insights and resources to ensure a unified, holistic approach to supporting students.

Implementing Trauma-Informed Strategies

Educators can integrate specific trauma-informed strategies into their teaching practices to create a more supportive environment for trauma-affected students. These strategies may include mindfulness activities, visual schedules, or sensory-friendly spaces designed to help students regulate and re-engage (Evans & Coccoma, 2014). A visually appealing and well-organised classroom environment, with designated calming spaces, also contributes to a sense of safety and stability for students who may feel overwhelmed by sensory stimuli or chaotic surroundings. By incorporating these strategies, educators help students manage anxiety and focus on learning.

Compassionate Role Modelling

The role of educators as compassionate role models cannot be overstated. By embodying the principles of trauma-informed care, educators set an example for students to follow. Demonstrating empathy, active listening, and emotional regulation, educators foster an environment where students feel valued, respected, and understood (Van der Kolk, 2003). Educators who model self-care and emotional resilience also show students the importance of managing their own well-being, which helps them build the skills they need to navigate trauma and other challenges in a healthy way.

Embracing a Trauma-Informed Approach

Embracing a trauma-informed approach in education is vital for supporting students' emotional well-being and academic success. By integrating the core principles of trauma-informed care – safety, trustworthiness, choice, collaboration, and empowerment – educators can create a transformative learning environment that nurtures and uplifts all students (Horner et al., 2010).

Compassion, empathy, and understanding are at the heart of trauma-informed care. Recognising the impact of trauma on students' lives and shifting from a deficit-based to a strengths-based mindset enables educators to respond to their students' needs with sensitivity and care. A trauma-informed mindset encourages educators to ask, "What happened to you?" rather than "What's wrong with you?" – a critical shift in perspective that promotes healing and fosters strong, trusting relationships (Pappano, 2014).

Educators play a crucial role in modelling self-care, empathy, and emotional resilience. By prioritising their own well-being, educators become better equipped to support their students effectively. Creating a safe and nurturing learning environment not only helps students feel secure but also inspires them to flourish emotionally and academically.

The call to action for educators is clear: embrace trauma-informed practices in your classrooms. By implementing the framework and strategies outlined, educators have the power to foster a culture of compassion, healing, and growth. Together, we can create trauma-informed classrooms that empower every student to thrive and reach their full potential.

What Is Contained in the Rest of the Book

This book offers a comprehensive exploration of trauma-informed care in educational settings, providing educators with both the theoretical knowledge and practical strategies needed to support trauma-impacted students. Each chapter builds upon the foundational principles of trauma-informed care introduced in Chapter 1, guiding educators through key concepts, practical applications, and reflective questions to enhance their teaching practice.

In **Chapter 2**, we explore the impact of trauma on learning and behaviour. Educators will learn how trauma disrupts cognitive development, affecting memory, attention, and executive functioning, as well as how it manifests in common trauma-induced behaviours like aggression, withdrawal, and hypervigilance. This chapter provides strategies for identifying and managing trauma triggers in the classroom.

Chapter 3 focuses on creating emotional safety and fostering positive teacher-student relationships. It discusses the importance of emotional safety as a foundation for learning and offers practical methods for building trust, empathy, and consistency with students.

In **Chapter 4**, the focus shifts to cultivating empathy, compassion, and self-care in teachers. It highlights the importance of educator well-being, providing self-care strategies to prevent burnout, maintain emotional resilience, and sustain empathy in the classroom.

Chapter 5 covers how to establish a supportive school culture that embraces trauma-informed care. It emphasises the importance of collaboration with families, communities, and school staff to create a trauma-sensitive environment and provides strategies for fostering holistic support.

In **Chapter 6**, educators are guided in recognising signs of trauma in students and applying trauma-informed approaches to address challenging behaviours. This chapter includes practical strategies for identifying emotional, behavioural, and physical indicators of trauma and offers non-punitive responses.

Chapter 7 introduces trauma-informed communication and crisis intervention, offering strategies for effective communication and techniques for de-escalating crises in the classroom. Educators will learn how to manage crisis situations with sensitivity to trauma.

Chapter 8 explores how to adapt curriculum and instruction to meet the needs of traumatised students. It includes guidance on differentiated instruction, universal design for learning (UDL), and ways to ensure trauma-sensitive teaching approaches are integrated into the curriculum.

Chapter 9 focuses on fostering emotional regulation and resilience in students. It provides educators with tools to teach emotional regulation skills and promote resilience through coping strategies, problem-solving, and building a growth mindset.

Chapter 10 introduces mindfulness and relaxation techniques and explains their benefits for trauma-affected students. This chapter provides guidance on integrating mindfulness practices and relaxation techniques into daily classroom routines to support emotional regulation.

Chapter 11 discusses the role of peer support, social connections, and restorative practices in the trauma-informed classroom. It offers strategies for fostering peer support systems and implementing restorative practices as alternatives to punitive discipline.

Chapter 12 integrates Indigenous perspectives and addresses intergenerational trauma, highlighting the historical and ongoing impacts of colonisation on Indigenous students. This chapter provides strategies for creating culturally safe and inclusive learning environments.

Finally, **Chapter 13** highlights the importance of continuous professional development and reflective practice in sustaining trauma-informed care. It offers guidance on how educators can engage in ongoing learning and reflection to improve their trauma-informed approaches over time.

Each chapter in this book concludes with a case study that brings the theory to life, offering real-world examples of how trauma-informed practices can transform the classroom. Additionally, educators will find practical strategies and reflective questions at the end of each chapter, providing actionable steps and opportunities for self-reflection as they work towards creating a trauma-sensitive learning environment. These tools are designed to help educators apply what they've learned in their own classrooms and foster a culture of compassion, healing, and growth for all students.

References

Bonanno, G. A., & Diminich, E. D. (2013). Annual Research Review: Positive adjustment to adversity—trajectories of minimal–impact resilience and emergent resilience. *Journal of Child Psychology and Psychiatry, 54,* 378–401. https://doi.org/10.1111/jcpp.12021

Bryce, I. (2017). *Cumulative harm and resilience framework: An assessment, prevention, and intervention resource for helping professionals*. Cengage.

Collier, S., Bryce, I., Trimmer, K., & Krishnamoorthy, G. (2020). Evaluating frameworks for practice in mainstream primary school classrooms catering for children with developmental trauma: An analysis of the literature. *Children Australia, 45*(4), 258–265. https://doi.org/10.1017/cha.2020.53

Dorado, J. S., Martinez, M., McArthur, L. E., & Leibovitz, T. (2016). Healthy Environments and Response to Trauma in Schools (HEARTS): A whole-school, multi-level prevention and intervention program for creating trauma-informed, safe and supportive schools. *School Mental Health, 8*, 163–176. https://doi.org/10.1007/s12310-016-9177-0

Evans, A., & Coccoma, P. (2014). *Trauma-informed care: How neuroscience influences practice*. Routledge.

Felitti, V., Anda, R., Nordenburg, D., Williamson, D., Spitz, A., Edwards, V., Koss, M., & Marks, J. (1998). Relationship of childhood abuse and household dysfunction to many of the leading causes of death in adults: The adverse childhood experiences (ACE) study. *American Journal of Preventive Medicine, 14*(4), 245–258. https://doi.org/10.1016/S0749-3797(98)00017-8

Herman, K. C., Hickmon-Rosa, J. E., & Reinke, W. M. (2018). Empirically derived profiles of teacher stress, burnout, self-efficacy, and coping and associated student outcomes. *Journal of Positive Behavior Interventions, 20*(2), 90–100.

Herrenkohl, T., Hong, S., & Verbrugge, B. (2019). Trauma-informed programs based in schools: Linking concepts to practices and assessing the evidence. *American Journal of Community Psychology, 64*(3–4), 373–388. https://doi.org/10.1002/ajcp.12362

Horner, R. H., Sugai, G., & Anderson, C. M. (2010). Examining the evidence base for school-wide positive behavior support. *Focus on Exceptional Children, 42*(8), 1–14.

Howard, J. (2019). A systemic framework for trauma-informed schooling: Complex but necessary! *Journal of Aggression, Maltreatment, and Trauma, 28*(5), 545–565. https://doi.org/10.1080/10926771.2018.1479323

Madigan, D. J., & Kim, L. E. (2021). Does teacher burnout affect students? A systematic review of its association with academic achievement and student-reported outcomes. *International Journal of Educational Research, 105*, 101714. https://doi.org/10.1016/j.ijer.2020.101714

McCarthy, M., Taylor, P., Norman, R., Pezzullo, L., Tucci, J., & Goddard, C. (2016). The lifetime economic and social costs of child maltreatment in Australia. *Children and Youth Services Review, 71*, 271–226. https://doi.org/10.1016/j.childyouth.2016.11.014

Mohr, D., & Rosén, L. A. (2017). The impact of protective factors on posttraumatic growth for college student survivors of childhood maltreatment. *Journal of Aggression, Maltreatment & Trauma, 26*(7), 756–771.

Oberg, G., Carroll, A., & Macmahon, S. (2023). Compassion fatigue and secondary traumatic stress in teachers: How they contribute to burnout and how they are related to trauma-awareness. In Frontiers in Education (Vol. 8, p. 1128618). Frontiers. https://doi.org/10.3389/feduc.2023.1128618

Pappano, L. (2014). "Trauma-sensitive" schools. *Harvard Education Letter, 30*(1), 1–4.

Perry, D. L., & Daniels, M. L. (2016). Implementing trauma-informed practices in the school setting: A pilot study. *School Mental Health, 8*, 177–188. https://doi.org/10.1007/s12310-016-9182-3

Record-Lemon, R. M., & Buchanan, M. J. (2017). Trauma-informed practices in schools: A narrative literature review. *Canadian Journal of Counselling and Psychotherapy, 51*(4). 286–305. https://cjc-rcc.ucalgary.ca/article/view/61156

Sciaraffa, M. A., Zeanah, P. D., & Zeanah, C. H. (2018). Understanding and promoting resilience in the context of adverse childhood experiences. *Early Childhood Education Journal, 46*(3), 343–353. https://doi.org/10.1007/s10643-017-0869-3

Spinazzola, J., Van der Kolk, B., & Ford, J. D. (2021). Developmental trauma disorder: A legacy of attachment trauma in victimized children. *Journal of Traumatic Stress, 34*(4), 711–720. https://doi.org/10.1002/jts.22697

Van der Kolk, B. A. (2003). The neurobiology of childhood trauma and abuse. *Child and Adolescent Psychiatric Clinics, 12*(2), 293–317.

Woodbridge, M. W., Sumi, W. C., Thornton, S. P., Fabrikant, N., Rouspil, K. M., Langley, A. K., & Kataoka, S. H. (2016). Screening for trauma in early adolescence: Findings from a diverse school district. *School Mental Health, 1*, 1–17. https://doi.org/10.1007/s12310-015-9169-5

Impact of Trauma on Learning and Behaviour

Introduction to the Impact of Trauma on Learning and Behaviour

Trauma has profound and far-reaching effects on a child's development, shaping both their ability to learn and how they behave in the classroom. Understanding these impacts is critical for educators as it equips them to create a learning environment that is responsive to the needs of all students, particularly those who have experienced trauma. Trauma can stem from various adverse experiences, such as abuse, neglect, exposure to violence, or the loss of a loved one, each of which can significantly disrupt a child's sense of safety and stability. These disruptions often lead to changes in brain development and functioning, which inevitably manifest in the classroom (Felitti et al., 1998).

From a learning perspective, trauma can interfere with essential cognitive functions that are crucial for academic success, such as memory, attention, and executive functioning. Children affected by trauma often find it challenging to concentrate, retain information, and process new material. These are not isolated difficulties but persistent challenges that can make it hard for students to keep up with their peers academically. Over time, this struggle can lead to frustration, diminished self-esteem, and a growing sense of disengagement from the learning process (Blair & Raver, 2015). Without support, these students may begin to fall behind, widening the achievement gap and potentially setting the stage for long-term educational struggles.

In terms of behaviour, trauma can trigger a wide range of responses that are frequently misunderstood or misinterpreted as disciplinary issues. For instance, a student who is often disruptive, aggressive, or disengaged may be acting out as a response to the trauma they have experienced. The fight, flight, or freeze response – a natural reaction to perceived threats – can be easily activated in the classroom, causing students to respond in ways that may seem disruptive or inappropriate (Perry, 2006). However, these behaviours are typically survival strategies that the student has developed to cope with overwhelming emotions and a sense of danger. Recognising the connection between trauma and behaviour is essential for educators to respond with compassion and understanding, rather than resorting to punitive measures that may exacerbate the problem.

This chapter will explore the specific ways in which trauma impacts cognitive development and behaviour. It will delve into the neurological mechanisms behind these changes, providing insights into how trauma alters brain functioning and, in turn, affects learning and behaviour. Educators will also be guided on how to identify the signs of trauma in students and how to support them in a way that promotes healing and growth. By acknowledging the profound effects of trauma and learning to recognise its manifestations, educators can create a more inclusive and compassionate classroom environment where all students have the opportunity to thrive both academically and emotionally.

Trauma's Effect on Cognitive Development

Trauma has a profound impact on cognitive development, especially in children whose brains are still in the critical stages of growth and maturation. The cognitive functions affected by trauma – such as memory, attention, and executive function – are essential for successful learning and academic achievement. It is crucial for educators to understand these impacts and adapt their teaching strategies accordingly. This section explores how trauma influences these key cognitive processes, highlighting the challenges that students with a history of trauma may face in the classroom. (Figure 2.1).

Memory and Information Processing

Memory is a fundamental cognitive function that enables students to retain and retrieve information, an essential process for effective learning. Trauma, however, can severely disrupt memory processes, particularly working

Impact of Trauma on the Brain

1. Amygdala
Becomes hyperactive, triggering fight-flight-freeze freeze responses.

Hippocampus
May shrink, affecting memory formation and recall.

Prefrontal Cortex
Underdeveloped, limiting executive function and self-regulation.

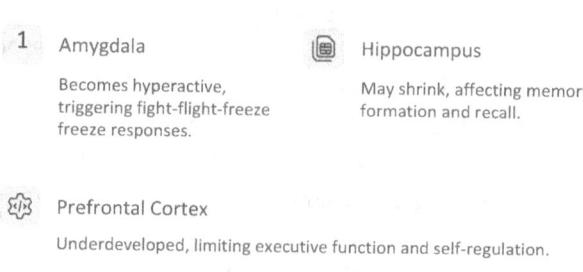

Figure 2.1 Impact of Trauma on Brain Development

memory, which is critical for holding and manipulating information over short periods. The hippocampus, a region of the brain responsible for memory formation and retrieval, is highly sensitive to stress. Chronic exposure to traumatic stress can impair the hippocampus's ability to function properly, leading to difficulties in both encoding new information and recalling previously learned material (McEwen, 2012).

For students affected by trauma, these memory impairments may manifest as forgetfulness, difficulty following instructions, and challenges in retaining information from one day to the next. For instance, a student may struggle to recall what was taught in the previous lesson or find it hard to remember new vocabulary or mathematical formulas. These memory challenges can result in significant academic struggles, as students may fall behind in the curriculum or struggle during tests and exams. Moreover, these difficulties can be misinterpreted by teachers as a lack of effort or interest, further complicating the student's educational experience.

The disruption of memory processes is not just a result of damage to memory-related brain structures but also a consequence of the body's overall stress response. When a child is in a state of chronic stress, their body consistently produces high levels of stress hormones like cortisol. While these hormones are useful in short bursts – such as during an immediate threat – prolonged exposure can damage areas like the hippocampus, leading to deficits in both short-term and long-term memory. This is especially concerning in the classroom, where learning depends heavily on the ability to retain and build upon prior knowledge (Anda et al., 2006).

To support students with trauma-induced memory deficits, educators can implement strategies such as using visual aids, breaking down information into smaller, more manageable chunks, and frequently reviewing past material to reinforce learning. Additionally, creating a calm and structured classroom environment can help reduce stress levels, which may improve memory function over time.

Attention and Concentration

Attention and concentration are other critical cognitive functions that are often compromised in children who have experienced trauma. Trauma can make it difficult for children to sustain attention, as their brains remain in a heightened state of arousal and vigilance, constantly on alert for potential threats. This heightened state is largely due to an overactive amygdala, the brain's fear centre, which leaves the child in a state of hypervigilance (Perry, 2006).

In the classroom, this hypervigilance can result in distractibility, impulsivity, and an inability to focus on academic tasks. Students may appear restless, struggle to sit still, or have difficulty completing assignments that require sustained attention. These attention deficits are often misinterpreted as symptoms of attention deficit hyperactivity disorder (ADHD), although they may stem from trauma rather than a neurodevelopmental disorder (Evans & Coccoma, 2014). Understanding this distinction is critical, as the interventions that are effective for ADHD may not be appropriate for trauma-affected students.

For example, a student who has experienced trauma may find it difficult to focus during a quiet reading session because their brain is constantly scanning the environment for danger. In such cases, traditional approaches to managing attention deficits – such as strict behavioural interventions or medication – might not address the underlying issue. Instead, trauma-sensitive strategies that reduce stress and create a sense of safety can help mitigate attention difficulties and improve the student's ability to focus. These strategies may include providing clear and consistent instructions, using calming techniques such as deep breathing exercises, and allowing for movement breaks to help students reset their focus.

Additionally, trauma can impair the brain's ability to filter out irrelevant stimuli, making it difficult for students to concentrate in typical classroom environments where distractions are common. For example, a student might be easily distracted by noises outside the classroom, the movements of other students, or even their own internal worries. Educators can support these students by minimising environmental distractions, using visual or auditory signals to capture attention, and incorporating activities that help students practice focusing on specific tasks.

Executive Function

Executive function refers to higher-order cognitive processes such as planning, organising, problem-solving, and regulating emotions. These skills are essential for academic success and social functioning, but they are often impaired in children who have experienced trauma. The prefrontal cortex, the brain region responsible for executive function, is particularly vulnerable to the effects of chronic stress. Trauma can disrupt the development of this area, leading to difficulties with impulse control, flexible thinking, and goal-directed behaviour (Blair & Raver, 2015).

In the classroom, deficits in executive function can manifest as disorganised work habits, difficulty starting or completing tasks, and challenges in adapting to new or unexpected situations. Students may struggle with time management, have trouble setting and achieving goals, or become easily frustrated when tasks are complex or require sustained effort. For instance, a student might find it difficult to follow a multi-step assignment or may procrastinate on starting a project because they feel overwhelmed by the planning required.

These challenges can lead to academic underachievement and behavioural issues, as students may act out due to their inability to manage the demands placed on them. For example, a student who lacks impulse control might frequently interrupt the teacher or classmates, not out of disrespect but because they struggle to regulate their actions. Similarly, a student who has difficulty with flexible thinking might become distressed when a lesson plan is changed or when they are asked to approach a problem in a new way.

Educators can support students with impaired executive function by providing clear, structured routines, breaking tasks into smaller, manageable steps, and offering frequent feedback and reinforcement. Additionally, teaching coping strategies and problem-solving skills can help students develop their executive function capabilities, enabling them to better manage both academic and social challenges (Brown et al., 2015). Using checklists, graphic organisers, and visual schedules can help students stay organised, while role-playing problem-solving scenarios can build the cognitive flexibility and resilience needed for success in both school and life

Understanding Trauma Triggers and Responses

Trauma triggers and the responses they elicit are crucial elements in understanding the behaviours and learning challenges exhibited by students who have experienced trauma. A trauma trigger is any stimulus – whether internal or external – that causes a person to recall a traumatic event, leading to a range of physiological and emotional responses. These triggers can be anything from a specific sound, smell, or sight to a particular situation or phrase that reminds the individual of their past trauma. For educators, understanding and identifying these triggers is essential for creating a supportive classroom environment that minimises retraumatisation and promotes positive learning experiences.

Identifying Triggers

Identifying trauma triggers in students can be challenging, as triggers vary widely from person to person and are often not immediately apparent. Common triggers might include loud noises, sudden movements, certain smells, or specific times of the day that correspond with a past traumatic event. For example, a student who has experienced domestic violence may react negatively to loud voices or unexpected noises like a door slamming. Similarly, a student who has experienced the loss of a loved one may find particular dates or anniversaries especially triggering (Pappano, 2014).

In the classroom, these triggers can lead to sudden changes in a student's behaviour, such as becoming withdrawn, agitated, or overly vigilant. Educators may observe that a student who was previously engaged in a task suddenly becomes distracted or distressed when exposed to a particular stimulus. Recognising these patterns is key to identifying the specific triggers affecting individual students. Teachers can collaborate with school counsellors, psychologists, and the students themselves to better understand what might be causing these responses. By identifying and mitigating triggers, educators can help create a classroom environment that feels safer and more predictable for students who have experienced trauma (Evans & Coccoma, 2014).

Physiological Responses

When a trauma trigger is activated, it can lead to a range of physiological responses as the body prepares to deal with what it perceives as a threat.

This response is primarily driven by the activation of the autonomic nervous system, particularly the sympathetic nervous system, which triggers the "fight, flight, or freeze" response. During this response, the body releases stress hormones like cortisol and adrenaline, which prepare the body to confront the threat, escape from it, or freeze in place (Perry, 2006).

In the classroom, these physiological responses can manifest in various ways. A student might become physically agitated, showing signs such as an increased heart rate, sweating, or shaking. Others may experience overwhelming fear or panic, leading to behaviours like crying, yelling, or attempting to leave the room. Some students may exhibit a freeze response, becoming unresponsive or appearing to "zone out." It is important to remember that these reactions are automatic and not within the student's conscious control – they are survival mechanisms conditioned by their traumatic experiences.

Understanding these physiological responses is crucial for educators, as they help explain why a student might suddenly behave in a way that seems disproportionate to the situation at hand. Recognising that these behaviours are rooted in trauma, rather than intentional disobedience, can guide teachers in responding with empathy and appropriate support, rather than resorting to punitive measures (SAMHSA, 2014).

Behavioural Responses

The behavioural responses that arise from trauma triggers can be complex and varied, making them difficult for educators to interpret. Some students may react aggressively, lashing out at peers or authority figures – behaviours that can be easily misunderstood as deliberate misbehaviour, rather than a response to a trigger. Other students may withdraw completely, refusing to participate in classroom activities, or become hyperactive and distractible, struggling to focus due to their heightened state of arousal (Van der Kolk, 2005).

It is essential for educators to understand these behaviours as trauma responses rather than simply disciplinary issues. For example, a student who suddenly becomes defiant or disruptive may be doing so because they are re-experiencing a past trauma through a current trigger. Similarly, a student who withdraws or disengages may be trying to protect themselves from a perceived threat. Educators can support these students by creating a calm and predictable environment, using de-escalation techniques, and providing safe spaces where students can go if they feel overwhelmed.

Trauma-Related Behaviors in the Classroom

Hypervigilance	Scanning for threats, startling easily, difficulty focusing
Withdrawal	Avoiding participation, seeming "checked out," isolation
Aggression	Verbal outbursts, physical reactions, defiance
Perfectionism	Fear of mistakes, excessive self-criticism, work avoidance
People-pleasing	Excessive compliance, difficulty expressing needs

Figure 2.2 Table Outlining Common Trauma-Linked Behaviours in Students

Additionally, behavioural responses to trauma triggers can include less visible actions, such as self-harm or other risky behaviours. These actions may be the student's way of coping with overwhelming emotions or attempting to regain a sense of control. It is critical for educators to be vigilant for signs of these behaviours and respond with interventions that prioritise the student's safety and well-being (Blodgett & Lanigan, 2018).

By understanding and identifying trauma triggers and the resulting physiological and behavioural responses, educators can respond more effectively and compassionately. This understanding allows teachers to create a trauma-sensitive environment that supports the emotional and academic needs of all students, fostering a space where healing and learning can occur simultaneously (Figure 2.2).

The Link between Trauma and Challenging Behaviours

Trauma is often at the root of many challenging behaviours exhibited by students in the classroom. Behaviours such as aggression, defiance, withdrawal, and disengagement are not random acts of disobedience but are deeply connected to the student's past traumatic experiences. Understanding this link is essential for educators, as it shifts the perspective from viewing these behaviours as purely disciplinary issues to recognising them as survival strategies that students have developed in response to trauma.

Aggression and Acting Out

One of the most visible and disruptive behaviours linked to trauma is aggression. Students who have experienced trauma, particularly those exposed to violence or abuse, may exhibit aggressive behaviours as a way to assert control in situations where they feel threatened. This aggression may manifest in physical altercations, verbal outbursts, or defiant behaviour towards authority figures. Often, these students are not acting out of malice but are responding to perceived threats – whether real or imagined – that trigger their fight response (Perry, 2006).

Aggression in trauma-affected students often stems from a state of hyperarousal, where the student feels a constant need to defend themselves from potential harm. This state is the result of the body's chronic activation of the stress response system, which is designed to protect against danger. However, when this system is overactivated due to repeated trauma, students may perceive threats even in safe environments, such as the classroom. For example, a student who becomes aggressive after being accidentally bumped by a peer may not only be reacting to the immediate situation but also to unresolved trauma involving physical harm.

In addition to physical aggression, trauma-affected students may also engage in verbal aggression, such as shouting or making threatening statements. These behaviours are often defensive mechanisms intended to create distance between themselves and others, particularly when they feel emotionally vulnerable or overwhelmed. For these students, an aggressive outburst is a way to regain a sense of control and power in a situation that feels threatening.

Educators must recognise that aggressive behaviour is often a protective response, and traditional punitive approaches may not be effective. Rather than punishment, which can exacerbate feelings of fear and helplessness, a more effective strategy is de-escalation and building trust. Educators can use calming techniques, such as speaking softly or offering the student a break from the situation, to reduce anxiety and prevent the aggressive behaviour from escalating.

Establishing a predictable and structured classroom environment is also key to minimising aggression in trauma-affected students. Predictability helps reduce the sense of threat that triggers the fight response. By establishing clear routines, providing advance notice of changes, and ensuring consistent classroom expectations, educators can create a more secure environment, reducing the likelihood of aggressive reactions.

In addition, teaching students alternative ways to express their emotions and resolve conflicts is highly beneficial. Social-emotional learning (SEL) programmes that focus on emotional regulation, communication skills, and conflict resolution can equip trauma-affected students with healthier coping strategies. For example, role-playing exercises that allow students to practice responding to conflict in non-aggressive ways can help them develop the skills needed to manage their emotions effectively and reduce their reliance on aggression as a means of coping.

Withdrawal and Disengagement

On the opposite end of the behavioural spectrum, trauma can lead to withdrawal and disengagement. Students who have experienced neglect, emotional abuse, or loss may respond to trauma by retreating into themselves. This behaviour is often linked to the freeze response, where the student becomes emotionally numb or detached as a way of coping with overwhelming feelings. In the classroom, this may manifest as a student who avoids eye contact, refuses to participate in activities, or appears to be daydreaming or zoning out during lessons (Van der Kolk, 2005).

Withdrawal and disengagement are often attempts by the student to protect themselves from further emotional pain. For some students, the classroom environment may trigger memories of trauma, whether through interactions with peers, academic subjects, or the overall school atmosphere. In response, they may withdraw as a means of creating psychological distance from what they perceive as threatening or overwhelming.

This withdrawal can be particularly problematic in an educational setting, where active engagement is key to learning. Disengaged students may fail to complete assignments, avoid participating in group activities, and show little interest in academic or social aspects of school life. Over time, this lack of engagement can lead to poor academic performance, social isolation, and a diminished sense of self-worth.

For educators, the challenge is to gently re-engage these students without forcing them out of their protective shell too quickly. Building a trusting relationship is the first step, which involves creating a classroom atmosphere that is non-threatening and supportive, where the student feels valued and understood. Teachers can offer low-pressure opportunities for participation, such as allowing the student to work individually or in a small group where they feel more comfortable.

Providing a safe space within the classroom where the student can retreat when feeling overwhelmed can also be helpful. This space might include calming sensory materials, such as soft textures or soothing visuals, that can help the student regain a sense of calm and control. Over time, as the student feels safer in the classroom, they may become more willing to engage with peers and participate in learning activities.

Activities that promote self-expression, such as art, writing, or music, can also be effective in helping withdrawn students process their emotions and reconnect with their surroundings. These activities offer a non-verbal outlet for expression, which can feel less intimidating than direct communication. Gradually increasing the student's involvement in these activities can help rebuild their confidence and connection with the classroom community.

Attention-Seeking and Hyperactivity

Attention-seeking behaviours and hyperactivity are also common in students who have experienced trauma. (Figure 2.3). These behaviours can be a way for students to seek validation, reassurance, or simply to ensure that they are noticed in an environment where they may feel invisible or unimportant. Hyperactivity, in particular, may stem from the body's heightened state of arousal following trauma, where the student remains in a constant state of alertness and cannot easily calm down (Pappano, 2014).

For instance, a student who frequently interrupts the teacher or is constantly moving around the classroom may be attempting to manage feelings of anxiety or fear by keeping themselves occupied. While these behaviours may be challenging for educators, it is important to understand that they are often driven by a need for stability and reassurance. Attention-seeking is not

Adverse Childhood Experiences (ACEs)

Adverse Experiences
Abuse, neglect, household dysfunction, community violence.

Neurological Effects
Stress response activation, brain architecture changes.

Learning Impacts
Attention difficulties, memory problems, executive function challenges.

Behavioral Manifestations
Withdrawal, aggression, hypervigilance, emotional dysregulation.

Figure 2.3 Adverse Childhood Experiences and Their Impact

always about disrupting the class, but rather about seeking connection and validation in a way that feels safe to the student.

Hyperactivity can also be a manifestation of the body's ongoing response to trauma. When a student has been exposed to chronic stress, their brain may become conditioned to operate in a state of heightened arousal, making it difficult for them to sit still, focus, or regulate their energy levels. In a classroom setting, this may look like constant fidgeting, difficulty staying seated, or frequent shifting between tasks without completing them.

To support students who exhibit attention-seeking behaviours and hyperactivity, educators can implement strategies that provide structure and opportunities for positive attention. Establishing consistent routines can give students a sense of predictability and security, reducing their anxiety and decreasing the need for attention-seeking behaviour. Additionally, offering regular positive feedback and reinforcement for appropriate behaviour can help students feel noticed and valued in a constructive way.

For hyperactive students, incorporating movement breaks into the classroom routine can be beneficial. These breaks allow students to release excess energy in a controlled manner, which can help them refocus when they return to their work. Activities such as stretching, brief physical exercises, or even sensory-based tasks like using stress balls or fidget toys can help hyperactive students manage their energy levels and improve their concentration

Case Study: Addressing Trauma-Induced Learning and Behavioural Challenges

Student Background

Sarah is a nine-year-old student in Year 4 who frequently displays challenging behaviours in the classroom. Her teacher, Ms. Patel, noticed that Sarah often becomes agitated and distracted, especially during group activities or when there are loud noises in the classroom. After consulting with the school counsellor and reviewing her background, Ms. Patel discovered that Sarah had experienced traumatic events early in life, including a house fire and subsequent displacement. These traumatic experiences left Sarah feeling unsafe in unpredictable environments, leading to her heightened sensitivity to noise and sudden changes in routine.

Application of Strategies

Ms. Patel recognised that Sarah's behavioural issues were likely linked to trauma triggers related to loud noises and chaotic environments. To create a more trauma-sensitive environment, Ms. Patel decided to implement strategies that directly addressed Sarah's specific triggers. She began by making small adjustments to the classroom setting, such as creating a quieter and more structured seating arrangement for Sarah, allowing her to work in a space farther from noisy areas like the door or windows.

To further support Sarah, Ms. Patel introduced a calm-down kit that included noise-cancelling headphones and a visual schedule to help Sarah prepare for transitions between activities. By providing Sarah with these tools, Ms. Patel aimed to reduce the impact of noise-related triggers and help her feel more in control of her environment. In addition, Ms. Patel incorporated frequent movement breaks and allowed Sarah to step away from group activities when she felt overwhelmed, giving her space to self-regulate.

Outcomes and Reflections

After several weeks of using these trauma-informed strategies, Ms. Patel noticed significant improvements in Sarah's behaviour.

The calm-down kit helped Sarah cope with noise-related stress, reducing her outbursts and improving her concentration during lessons. The use of the visual schedule provided Sarah with a sense of predictability, which made transitions smoother and less anxiety-inducing. Ms. Patel reflected on how understanding Sarah's trauma triggers and implementing small but meaningful changes in the classroom environment not only supported Sarah but also contributed to a calmer and more organised classroom for all students.

Chapter 2 Summary: Impact of Trauma on Learning and Behaviour

In Chapter 2, we explore the profound impact that trauma has on a child's cognitive development and classroom behaviour. Trauma, often stemming from adverse experiences such as abuse, neglect, or loss, can significantly disrupt cognitive functions crucial for learning, including memory, attention, and executive functioning. These disruptions often manifest as difficulties in concentration, retention of information, and problem-solving, leading to academic challenges and a widening achievement gap. Trauma can also trigger behavioural responses such as aggression, withdrawal, or hyperactivity, which are frequently misunderstood as disciplinary issues rather than trauma responses.

This chapter delves into the specific ways that trauma influences cognitive development, including the effects on memory, attention, and executive function. It examines how trauma alters brain functioning, leading to common classroom challenges like difficulty focusing or regulating emotions. The chapter also addresses the role of trauma triggers – stimuli that can cause trauma-impacted students to re-experience traumatic stress – and their resulting physiological and behavioural responses. Educators are guided through strategies to identify and mitigate these triggers in the classroom, fostering a more supportive learning environment.

By understanding the neurological and behavioural effects of trauma, educators are better equipped to create trauma-sensitive classrooms that promote healing, academic engagement, and emotional well-being. The chapter emphasises the importance of compassion, structured routines, and trauma-informed strategies to help students overcome the barriers posed by their traumatic experiences, ultimately allowing them to thrive both academically and emotionally.

Creating Trauma-Informed Classrooms

Guiding Questions

1. **How does trauma impact cognitive development?**
   Consider how trauma affects key cognitive functions such as memory, attention, and executive functioning. How do these impairments manifest in a student's learning and classroom behaviour?

2. **What are trauma triggers and how can they be identified?**
   Reflect on the different types of trauma triggers (e.g., sounds, environments, actions) that students may face. What steps can educators take to identify and mitigate these triggers?

3. **How do physiological responses to trauma affect learning?**
   Explain the fight, flight, or freeze response in the context of trauma and how it influences a student's ability to engage in classroom activities.

4. **What strategies can help students manage trauma-related behaviours?**
   Identify two trauma-informed strategies that can be used to address challenging behaviours like aggression, withdrawal, or hyperactivity. How do these strategies foster a supportive learning environment?

Teachers Toolbox

Teachers' Toolbox for Chapter 2

STRATEGY	DESCRIPTION
SUPPORTING MEMORY AND INFORMATION PROCESSING	Use visual aids like diagrams and charts to reinforce lessons. Break tasks into smaller steps, such as providing step-by-step written instructions, and use mnemonic devices to help students retain information. Review material frequently, using retrieval practice to reinforce learning.
ENHANCING ATTENTION AND CONCENTRATION	Use clear, consistent instructions and provide visual schedules to guide transitions. Incorporate grounding techniques like deep breathing exercises before starting a task. Reduce distractions by seating students away from busy areas and using fidget tools or stress balls for students needing sensory input.
SUPPORTING EXECUTIVE FUNCTION	Implement structured routines with a daily agenda visible in the classroom. Use checklists or graphic organisers to help students plan tasks, and provide regular verbal cues to keep them on track. Offer frequent feedback and use positive reinforcement to encourage progress.

(Continued)

(Continued)

STRATEGY	DESCRIPTION
ADDRESSING AGGRESSION AND ACTING OUT	Use de-escalation techniques such as speaking in a calm, low tone, maintaining neutral body language, and offering the student a chance to take a break or use a calm corner to prevent further escalation. Introduce emotional regulation strategies, such as teaching students to use a "feelings chart" to identify their emotions.
RE-ENGAGING WITHDRAWN AND DISENGAGED STUDENTS	Build trust through one-on-one interactions and offer low-pressure participation options, like working individually or in small groups. Create a calm space in the classroom where students can retreat when overwhelmed, using sensory materials such as soft cushions or calming visuals to help them relax. Encourage non-verbal self-expression through activities like art projects or journaling.
MANAGING ATTENTION-SEEKING AND HYPERACTIVITY	Establish consistent routines with predictable transitions, giving advance notice when changes occur. Provide movement breaks throughout the day, incorporating brief physical activities like stretching or using a sensory circuit. Use positive reinforcement to acknowledge appropriate behaviour, offering specific praise such as "I noticed you stayed focused for the entire activity – great job!"

References

Anda, R. F., Felitti, V. J., Bremner, J. D., Walker, J. D., Whitfield, C., Perry, B. D., Dube, S. R., & Giles, W. H. (2006). The enduring effects of abuse and related adverse experiences in childhood. *European Archives of Psychiatry and Clinical Neuroscience, 256*(3), 174–186.

Blair, C., & Raver, C. C. (2015). School readiness and self-regulation: A developmental psychobiological approach. *Annual Review of Psychology, 66*(1), 711–731.

Blodgett, C., & Lanigan, J. D. (2018). The association between adverse childhood experiences (ACE) and school success in elementary school children. *School Psychology Quarterly, 33*(1), 137–146.

Brown, F., Anderson, J. L., & De Pry, R. L. (2015). *Individual positive behavior supports: A standards-based guide to practices in school and community settings.* Brookes.

Evans, A., & Coccoma, P. (2014). *Trauma-informed care: How neuroscience influences practice.* Routledge.

Felitti, V., Anda, R., Nordenburg, D., Williamson, D., Spitz, A., Edwards, V., Koss, M., & Marks, J. (1998). Relationship of childhood abuse and household dysfunction to many of the leading causes of death in adults: The adverse childhood experiences

(ACE) study. *American Journal of Preventive Medicine, 14*(4), 245–258. https://doi.org/10.1016/S0749-3797(98)00017-8

McEwen, B. S. (2012). Brain on stress: How the social environment gets under the skin. *Proceedings of the National Academy of Sciences, 109*(Supplement_2), 17180–17185.

Pappano, L. (2014). "Trauma-sensitive" schools. *Harvard Education Letter, 30*(1), 1–4.

Perry, B. D. (2006). Applying principles of neurodevelopment to clinical work with maltreated and traumatized children: The neurosequential model of therapeutics. In N. Boyd Webb (Ed.), *Working with traumatized youth in child welfare* (pp. 27–52). Guilford Press.

SAMHSA (Substance Abuse and Mental Health Services Administration). (2014). *SAMHSA's concept of trauma and guidance for a trauma-informed approach.* U.S. Department of Health and Human Services.

Van der Kolk, B. A. (2005). Developmental trauma disorder: Toward a rational diagnosis for children with complex trauma histories. *Psychiatric Annals, 35*(5), 401–408.

Creating Emotional Safety and Positive Teacher-Student Relationships

Introduction to Emotional Safety and Positive Teacher-Student Relationships

Creating emotional safety in the classroom is foundational to any trauma-informed approach to education. Emotional safety refers to an environment where students feel secure, respected, and understood – where they are free from the fear of being judged, humiliated, or harmed. For students who have experienced trauma, establishing a sense of emotional safety is crucial, as it directly affects their ability to engage in learning and develop trusting relationships. Without this sense of security, students are likely to remain in a heightened state of anxiety, making it difficult for them to focus, process information, or connect with others.

In trauma-informed classrooms, emotional safety must be built through both the physical and emotional environment. Teachers play a key role in creating this safe space, as they set the tone for the classroom culture and model the behaviours that foster trust and inclusivity. Physical aspects of the classroom, such as calming decor, quiet corners, or predictable routines, contribute to creating a safe space for students. However, the most significant contributor to emotional safety is the relationship between the teacher and the student. This relationship, characterised by trust, empathy, and consistency, can provide students with a sense of stability that helps them feel secure enough to engage and thrive.

Positive teacher-student relationships are at the heart of trauma-informed education. For trauma-affected students, the teacher often becomes a key figure who provides the secure attachment they may have missed in other areas of their lives. Building trust with students, especially those who have experienced betrayal or neglect, requires a deliberate and consistent effort. Teachers must demonstrate reliability, openness, and a genuine interest in their students' well-being. When students trust that their teacher will respond to their needs with care and understanding, they are more likely to feel comfortable expressing themselves and taking risks in their learning.

Trust, however, cannot exist without empathy. Empathy is the ability to understand and share the feelings of another person, and it is essential for building strong, positive relationships with students. Trauma-impacted students often struggle with emotional regulation and may exhibit challenging behaviours as a result. In these moments, teachers must be able to respond with empathy – seeing the behaviour as a communication of unmet needs or past trauma, rather than simply as defiance or misbehaviour. This perspective shift allows teachers to respond in ways that de-escalate situations and build stronger connections with their students.

In addition to trust and empathy, consistency is another vital component of building emotional safety and positive relationships. Trauma often leaves students feeling uncertain and distrustful of adults, particularly if they have experienced instability at home. For these students, the classroom needs to be a place of predictability where routines are clear and expectations are consistent. Teachers can provide this sense of consistency through daily routines, clear communication, and by being dependable in their interactions with students. When students know what to expect from their teacher, they are less likely to feel threatened or anxious and more likely to engage meaningfully in classroom activities.

By creating an emotionally safe environment and nurturing positive, trusting relationships, teachers can help trauma-affected students feel secure enough to take risks, express themselves, and fully participate in learning. This chapter will explore how educators can cultivate emotional safety and develop strong teacher-student relationships, providing the foundation for both academic success and emotional healing.

Emotional Safety

Emotional safety refers to the creation of an environment where individuals feel secure, valued, and free from emotional harm or fear of rejection. In the context of trauma-informed education, it involves ensuring that students, particularly those who have experienced trauma, are able to express themselves without fear of judgement, exclusion, or further trauma. Emotional safety forms the cornerstone of trauma-informed practices because it directly addresses the feelings of vulnerability, fear, and hypervigilance that many trauma-affected students experience (Cavanaugh, 2016).

For students, especially those who have been exposed to adverse childhood experiences (ACEs) or ongoing trauma, emotional safety is crucial. It helps mitigate the effects of their traumatic experiences by providing a consistent, supportive environment that fosters trust and healing. Without emotional safety, students may remain in a state of heightened arousal or stress, which hinders their ability to focus, learn, and build healthy relationships (Pickens & Tschopp, 2017).

Emotional Safety's Impact on Learning and Relationships

Emotional safety is essential for students' readiness to engage in learning. When students feel emotionally safe, their brains are better able to shift from survival mode (fight, flight, or freeze responses) to learning mode. Research indicates that students in emotionally safe environments exhibit greater attention, cognitive processing, and memory retention, all critical for academic success (Karris, 2022). Conversely, when emotional safety is compromised, the amygdala – the brain's emotional centre – becomes hyperactive, making it difficult for students to concentrate on academic tasks or retain new information (van der Kolk, 2005).

Emotionally safe environments also foster meaningful connections between students and their peers, as well as between students and teachers. Building trust is an essential component of trauma-informed care, and it begins with creating an emotionally safe space where students feel they belong and are supported. This sense of safety encourages students to engage more fully in learning activities, participate in classroom discussions, and develop positive peer relationships (Cavanaugh, 2016). Teachers who actively listen, validate students' emotions, and demonstrate empathy help create a climate that fosters mutual respect and emotional safety.

The Role of the Classroom Environment in Promoting Emotional Safety

A trauma-informed classroom is designed to be both physically and emotionally safe, with every element intentionally aimed at reducing anxiety and promoting a sense of calm and predictability. The physical setup of the classroom plays a significant role in fostering emotional safety. Simple changes, such as creating designated calm areas, using soft lighting, and incorporating soothing visuals, can help make the space feel less intimidating for trauma-affected students. Such areas allow students to retreat when they feel overwhelmed, providing them with a quiet space where they can regulate their emotions and re-engage with their learning on their own terms (Rodaughan et al., 2024).

Beyond the physical environment, the emotional climate established by the teacher is paramount. Teachers play a pivotal role in creating emotional safety by setting clear expectations, maintaining consistent routines, and modelling respectful and compassionate behaviour. These actions help reduce the unpredictability that many trauma-affected students fear. Predictable routines and consistent responses to behaviour provide students with the stability they need to feel emotionally secure. Additionally, trauma-informed teachers use non-punitive discipline strategies, such as restorative justice practices or de-escalation techniques, to ensure that students feel supported rather than punished when they struggle with emotional regulation (Cavanaugh, 2016).

Teachers can further promote emotional safety by using trauma-sensitive language that avoids blame or judgement. For example, instead of asking "What's wrong with you?" teachers can shift to "What happened to you?" This shift acknowledges the role of trauma in shaping students' behaviour and fosters a more supportive, understanding environment (Pickens & Tschopp, 2017). In addition, building strong relationships with students through active listening and validation of their emotions creates an environment of trust and emotional safety, which is foundational for trauma-informed education.

Positive Teacher-Student Relationships

The Significance of Building Trust through Consistency, Reliability, and Transparency

Building trust is at the heart of fostering positive teacher-student relationships, particularly in trauma-informed classrooms. Students who have experienced trauma often struggle to trust adults due to past experiences of instability, neglect, or betrayal. As a result, establishing trust requires teachers to be consistent, reliable, and transparent in their interactions with students. Trust allows students to feel safe in the classroom, which is essential for their emotional and academic development. In a trauma-informed setting, trust is not just about fulfilling promises or being dependable; it also involves creating an environment where students know that their emotional needs will be met with understanding and care (Cavanaugh, 2016).

Consistency is crucial in building this trust. For trauma-impacted students, unpredictable environments can trigger anxiety or fear, leading to difficulties in concentrating and engaging with their learning. A consistent classroom routine, with clear expectations and predictable responses from the teacher, helps to reduce this anxiety. When students know what to expect, they feel more secure and are better able to focus on academic tasks rather than worrying about potential disruptions or surprises (Pickens & Tschopp, 2017). Additionally, maintaining consistent behaviour management strategies ensures that students understand the boundaries within the classroom, which fosters a sense of safety.

Reliability is another key factor in building trust. Trauma-affected students may have experienced adults who were unreliable or even harmful, leading to feelings of abandonment or betrayal. Teachers who are reliable – who follow through on their commitments and are present when students need support – help to rebuild that lost sense of trust. Students begin to believe that their teacher will be there for them, both emotionally and academically, which encourages them to engage more fully in the classroom environment (Rodaughan et al., 2024).

Transparency also plays a critical role in trust-building. When teachers are open and honest with their students, they model the type of communication that builds mutual respect and understanding. Being transparent might involve explaining why certain rules or routines are in place or sharing how decisions are made within the classroom. For trauma-impacted students, who may have experienced environments where decisions were made without explanation or where they felt powerless, transparency can empower them and create a stronger sense of belonging and participation in their learning journey (van der Kolk, 2005).

The Importance of Attachment Theory in Understanding the Role of Relationships in a Student's Social and Emotional Development

Attachment theory offers a valuable lens through which to understand the importance of teacher-student relationships, particularly for trauma-impacted students. First developed by John Bowlby, attachment theory posits that children form emotional bonds, or attachments, with their caregivers, which serve as the foundation for their social and emotional development. When these attachments are secure, children develop a sense of trust, safety, and confidence in exploring the world around them. However, for children who have experienced trauma, these attachments may be disrupted or insecure, which can negatively impact their ability to form healthy relationships later in life, including relationships with teachers and peers (Bowlby, 1969).

In a classroom setting, teachers often serve as surrogate attachment figures for trauma-impacted students, particularly when secure attachments were not formed in the home environment. Teachers who are consistent, empathetic, and responsive can help students develop secure attachments, which in turn supports their social and emotional development. A secure attachment with a teacher allows students to feel safe in the classroom, which is essential for emotional regulation, resilience, and academic engagement. When students feel that their teacher cares for them and is invested in their success, they are more likely to take risks in their learning and to seek help when needed (Pickens & Tschopp, 2017).

Insecure attachments, on the other hand, may cause students to act out in ways that seem puzzling or disruptive. For example, a student with an insecure attachment may test boundaries or reject the teacher's attempts to build a connection, as they may expect relationships to be inconsistent or harmful, based on their past experiences. Understanding attachment theory helps educators to interpret these behaviours not as defiance or misbehaviour but as a reflection of unmet emotional needs. By responding with patience, consistency, and care, teachers can begin to address the underlying attachment issues and help students feel more secure in their relationships (Sweetman, 2022).

The Teacher's Role as a Secure Base for Trauma-Impacted Students

In attachment theory, the concept of a "secure base" refers to the role of the caregiver (or in this case, the teacher) as a source of safety and support from which children can explore the world and return to when they feel threatened or overwhelmed. For trauma-impacted students, the teacher often becomes this secure base within the school environment. By providing consistent emotional support, setting clear boundaries, and offering a predictable environment, teachers help students develop the confidence they need to engage with their learning and navigate social relationships (Karris, 2022).

A teacher who serves as a secure base not only provides emotional safety but also models appropriate ways to manage emotions and resolve conflicts. Trauma-affected students may not have had the opportunity to learn these skills in their home environments, and the classroom becomes a key setting for their social and emotional development. Teachers who demonstrate empathy, patience, and active listening can help students learn to regulate their emotions and communicate their needs effectively. These skills are critical for both academic success and future social relationships (Rodaughan et al., 2024).

One of the ways teachers can act as a secure base is by creating an environment where students feel comfortable taking risks in their learning. For trauma-affected students, the fear of failure or rejection may be heightened, making them reluctant to participate in classroom activities or engage with challenging material. However, when teachers provide reassurance, offer constructive feedback, and celebrate efforts rather than just outcomes, they create a supportive space where students feel safe enough to try new things. This sense of safety is crucial for both emotional healing and academic growth (Cavanaugh, 2016).

Additionally, the teacher's role as a secure base extends beyond emotional support to the development of a growth mindset in students. Trauma-affected students often struggle with low self-esteem and may believe that their abilities are fixed or that they are incapable of success. Teachers who encourage a growth mindset – emphasising that abilities can be developed through effort and perseverance – help students reframe their negative self-perceptions and build confidence in their ability to succeed. This not only improves their academic outcomes but also supports their long-term emotional resilience (van der Kolk, 2005).

Practical Strategies for Establishing Emotional Safety

Creating a classroom environment where trauma-affected students feel emotionally safe is essential for their academic success and emotional well-being. Trauma-affected students often struggle with heightened anxiety, feelings of unpredictability, and mistrust in relationships due to past experiences. By incorporating trauma-informed practices, educators can establish emotional safety, which helps students feel secure enough to engage in learning and develop healthy relationships. In this section, we will explore practical strategies for creating a predictable and structured classroom environment, building trust, and showing empathy.

Creating a Predictable and Structured Classroom Environment

Trauma-affected students often experience heightened anxiety when faced with unpredictable environments. They may be hypersensitive to sudden changes, loud noises, or disruptions, which can trigger feelings of insecurity or fear. One of the most effective ways to mitigate this anxiety is by creating a classroom environment that is predictable, structured, and consistent. When students know what to expect, they feel more in control and are better able to focus on their learning rather than being preoccupied with potential threats.

Emotional Safety and Positive Teacher-Student Relationships

1. **Establish Clear Routines**

    A consistent daily routine provides students with a sense of stability and security. Begin each day with a clear agenda that outlines the day's activities, including any changes to the usual schedule. This can be displayed on a whiteboard or projector so that students can see it as soon as they arrive in class. For example, you might write:

    - 8:30–9:00: Reading
    - 9:00–10:00: Maths
    - 10:00–10:30: Recess
    - 10:30–11:30: Science
    - 11:30–12:30: Group Work

    Students feel more secure when they know what to expect and can anticipate transitions throughout the day. Providing students with this kind of structure can help reduce anxiety, as they know what will happen next and can mentally prepare for each task.

2. **Use Visual Schedules**

    Visual schedules can be particularly helpful for younger students or students who struggle with reading. Create visual aids that show each part of the day with simple images or icons. For example, you could use a book icon for reading time, a pencil for writing activities, and a playground for recess. Visual schedules help students follow along with the day's events and provide a sense of stability.

3. **Prepare Students for Changes**

    Despite efforts to maintain consistency, there will be times when the routine needs to change – whether due to special events, substitute teachers, or classroom disruptions. To help trauma-affected students feel less anxious about these changes, prepare them in advance whenever possible. For instance, if you know a school assembly will replace a regular lesson, notify the students the day before or as soon as you know. You might say, "Tomorrow we'll have an assembly at 9:00, so our reading time will be shorter. We'll still have maths after the assembly." By preparing students for change, you help them feel more in control and reduce their anxiety about the unknown.

4. **Create a Calming Classroom Environment**

    The physical environment of the classroom also plays a significant role in creating emotional safety. Consider designing a calm, soothing space with soft lighting, neutral colours, and quiet areas where students can retreat if they feel overwhelmed. A "calm corner" with soft seating, sensory tools (such as stress balls or fidget toys), and calming visuals (like nature scenes) can provide students with a space to self-regulate when they feel anxious or overstimulated. Ensure that the classroom environment is orderly and free from clutter, as chaotic spaces can heighten feelings of stress.

Approaches to Building Trust

Building trust is at the heart of creating emotional safety for trauma-affected students. Trust is built through consistent actions, open communication, and following through on promises. Trauma-impacted students may be wary of adults and may test boundaries to see if they can rely on their teacher. Establishing a trusting relationship requires intentionality and patience.

1. **Open Communication**

    Open communication is key to building trust with trauma-affected students. Teachers should create an environment where students feel comfortable expressing their thoughts and emotions. This can be fostered through regular check-ins where students have the opportunity to share how they are feeling or any concerns they have. For example, at the start of each day, you might have a short "circle time" where students can share something they're looking forward to or something that's worrying them. Encouraging students to communicate openly helps them feel heard and valued.

2. **Set Clear Expectations**

    Trauma-affected students benefit from knowing exactly what is expected of them in the classroom. Clear expectations help reduce feelings of uncertainty and provide students with a framework for behaviour. When setting expectations, it's important to communicate them in a positive, supportive manner. For example, instead of saying, "Don't shout in class," frame the expectation positively by saying, "We use quiet voices in the classroom so everyone can focus on their work." Reinforce these expectations consistently and offer gentle reminders as needed.

In addition to behavioural expectations, it is helpful to set clear academic expectations. Break tasks into smaller steps and explain the process for completing assignments. This helps students feel more in control and less overwhelmed by large or complex tasks.

3. **Follow Through on Promises**

   One of the most effective ways to build trust is by following through on promises. Trauma-affected students may have experienced adults in their lives who were unreliable or who made promises that weren't kept. To counter this, it is essential for teachers to be reliable and to deliver on what they say. If you promise a student you will speak to them after class about an issue, make sure you do so. If you promise the class an extra ten minutes of free time if they complete a task, follow through on that promise. Consistency and reliability help students understand that they can count on you, which is critical for building trust.

4. **Offer Choices**

   Providing students with choices helps build trust by giving them a sense of control over their learning. For trauma-affected students, having a say in their daily activities can help mitigate feelings of powerlessness. For example, during independent reading time, you might allow students to choose between several different books or offer them the choice to read independently or with a partner. When students feel that their voice matters, they are more likely to trust their teacher and engage in learning.

Techniques for Showing Empathy

Empathy is one of the most powerful tools a teacher can use to create emotional safety in the classroom. By showing empathy, teachers demonstrate that they understand and care about their students' experiences and emotions. Trauma-affected students often feel misunderstood or isolated, and empathy helps bridge that gap, fostering a connection between teacher and student.

1. **Active Listening**

   Active listening involves giving students your full attention when they are speaking and responding in a way that shows you have understood them. This means not interrupting, maintaining eye contact, and acknowledging their feelings. For example, if a student expresses frustration about an assignment, you might say, "I can see that this task is really frustrating for you. Let's see if we can break it down into smaller steps to make it more manageable." By listening actively, you show students that their thoughts and emotions matter, which helps to build trust and emotional safety.

2. **Validate Student Experiences**

    Validation is another important aspect of showing empathy. Trauma-affected students may feel that their emotions or experiences are not valid, especially if they've been dismissed or ignored in the past. Validating their experiences means acknowledging their feelings without judgement. For example, if a student becomes upset after a loud noise in the classroom, you might say, "I understand why that noise upset you – it was sudden, and loud noises can feel overwhelming. It's okay to feel that way." Validation helps students feel seen and understood, which is crucial for creating emotional safety.

3. **Maintain a Non-Judgemental Stance**

    Trauma-affected students may exhibit challenging behaviours, such as outbursts, withdrawal, or defiance. It is important for teachers to respond to these behaviours in a non-judgemental way. Instead of reacting with frustration or punishment, take a moment to consider the underlying cause of the behaviour. For example, if a student lashes out at a peer, ask yourself whether this behaviour might be linked to past trauma. By approaching the situation with curiosity rather than judgement, you can respond with empathy and support rather than discipline. A non-judgemental stance helps students feel that they are accepted and supported, even when they make mistakes.

4. **Model Empathy**

    Teachers can also model empathetic behaviour by showing empathy in their interactions with other students and colleagues. When students see their teacher being empathetic to others, they learn that empathy is a valued behaviour in the classroom. This helps to create a classroom culture where students feel safe expressing their emotions and supporting one another (Figure 3.1).

Creating Emotional Safety

Predictable Routines
Visual schedules, transition warnings, consistent expectations.

Safe Physical Space
Calm corners, reduced visual clutter, comfortable seating options.

Relationship Building
Regular check-ins, positive interactions, authentic interest.

Clear Communication
Simple directions, emotional vocabulary, validation.

Figure 3.1 Strategies for Fostering Emotionally Safe Classroom Environments

Case Study and Practical Strategies

Case Study: Fostering Emotional Safety Through Predictable Routines

Student Background

Michael is a 12-year-old Year 7 student who has been struggling with the transition from primary to secondary school, where he now has multiple teachers and classes each day. He frequently experiences anxiety during transitions between subjects and often appears overwhelmed by the changes in routine and the lack of predictability in his new school environment. Michael's homeroom teacher, Mr. Smith, noticed that these feelings of anxiety seem to peak during times of transition, such as moving between classes or when there are sudden changes to the usual school schedule. Following conversations with the school counsellor, Mr. Smith learned that Michael had experienced multiple ACEs, including exposure to domestic violence and the loss of a family member, which left him highly sensitive to unpredictability and sudden changes.

Application of Strategy: Implementing Predictable Routines

Recognising that unpredictability was a key trigger for Michael's anxiety, Mr. Smith implemented a strategy focused on predictable routines to provide Michael with the emotional safety he needed to navigate the school day more confidently. Predictability is especially important for trauma-affected students like Michael because it helps reduce the sense of threat that can arise from uncertainty and change. By knowing what to expect, Michael could begin to feel more secure and less anxious about transitions.

Morning Routine with Visual Schedules

To begin, Mr. Smith introduced a morning routine that set the tone for the rest of the day. Each morning during homeroom, Mr. Smith displayed a visual schedule on the board, outlining the day's subjects, break times, and any special events or changes. The schedule was designed to be clear and easy to follow, using both text and simple icons to represent different subjects and activities. For example, an image of a book signified English, a calculator represented Maths, and a clock showed break times. By making the schedule highly visual and accessible, Mr. Smith ensured that Michael – and other students – could easily anticipate the structure of the day ahead.

This routine provided Michael with an immediate sense of control over his day. The visual schedule allowed him to mentally prepare for what was coming next, reducing his anxiety about transitions between classes. Importantly, Mr. Smith made sure to include any changes in the schedule ahead of time. For example, if a substitute teacher was scheduled to take over a lesson or if there was an upcoming school assembly, it was clearly indicated on the board. Michael found comfort in being able to see these changes in advance, which prevented him from feeling caught off guard.

Preparing for Transitions

While the visual schedule helped Michael understand the overall structure of the day, Mr. Smith recognised that transitions between classes were particularly stressful for him. To address this, Mr. Smith incorporated specific routines around these transition periods. Five minutes before each transition, Mr. Smith would give a verbal and visual cue to the class, reminding them of the upcoming change. For example, if the class was about to move from English to Maths, Mr. Smith would say, "In five minutes, we'll be finishing up with English and heading to Maths. Please make sure you've completed your notes, and I'll give you a signal when it's time to pack up."

This cue system was particularly effective for Michael, as it allowed him to anticipate the transition and begin mentally preparing for it. Knowing that a change was coming and being given specific time to wrap up his current task helped ease the anxiety that often came with transitions. Mr. Smith also used a calm-down strategy for Michael during transitions, offering him the option to take an extra minute or two before moving to the next class if he felt overwhelmed. By providing this flexibility within the predictable structure, Mr. Smith gave Michael space to regulate his emotions without feeling pressured.

Managing Unexpected Changes
One of the challenges in creating a predictable routine is that schools often require flexibility due to unexpected events, such as fire drills, last-minute schedule changes, or school-wide activities. Understanding that these unplanned disruptions could easily trigger Michael's anxiety, Mr. Smith took proactive steps to help Michael manage unexpected changes.

When a sudden change was necessary, Mr. Smith would pull Michael aside for a quick, private check-in, explaining the situation and offering reassurance. For example, if there was a surprise fire drill, Mr. Smith might quietly say, "Michael, I know we didn't plan for this, but there's going to be a fire drill in five minutes. You'll hear the alarm, but we'll all stay together, and everything will be fine. Just follow my lead." By preparing Michael individually for the change and offering a calm, reassuring presence, Mr. Smith reduced the likelihood that the unexpected event would overwhelm him.

Additionally, Mr. Smith taught Michael some self-regulation techniques he could use during times of unpredictability, such as deep breathing exercises or quietly counting to ten. These techniques gave Michael tools to calm himself when he felt anxious and empowered him to take control of his emotions in moments of uncertainty.

> **Outcomes and Reflections**
>
> The introduction of predictable routines had a profound impact on Michael's ability to manage his school day. The visual schedule helped him feel in control of his environment, reducing his anxiety about what was to come. With clear signals for transitions and extra support for unplanned changes, Michael became more engaged in his learning and was less likely to act out or disengage during the school day. The combination of routine, flexibility, and individualised support allowed Michael to regain a sense of stability that had been missing since his transition to secondary school.
>
> Mr. Smith reflected on the importance of predictability in helping trauma-affected students like Michael succeed. He noted that while many students benefit from structure, it is especially crucial for those with trauma backgrounds, as it provides the emotional safety they need to fully participate in their education. The success of this strategy also demonstrated to Mr. Smith the value of anticipating and planning for the needs of trauma-affected students, showing that small adjustments to the daily routine could have a significant impact on their well-being and academic performance.
>
> By using predictable routines and offering support during transitions, Mr. Smith was able to create a classroom environment where Michael felt safe, understood, and more confident navigating the challenges of secondary school.

Chapter 3 Summary: Creating Emotional Safety and Positive Teacher-Student Relationships

In Chapter 3, the focus is on the foundational importance of emotional safety and the role of positive teacher-student relationships in trauma-informed classrooms. Emotional safety refers to creating an environment where students feel secure, respected, and understood. This chapter highlights how essential emotional safety is for trauma-affected students, as it directly impacts their ability to engage in learning, form meaningful connections, and manage their emotions. A predictable, calm, and structured classroom environment helps reduce anxiety for students who may feel threatened by unpredictability and change. Teachers, through their actions and the overall emotional climate they create, play a pivotal role in ensuring students feel safe.

Positive teacher-student relationships are critical to trauma-informed care, especially for students who have experienced instability or neglect. Building trust with these students requires consistency, reliability, and transparency, allowing them to feel secure and supported. This chapter also explores attachment theory, demonstrating how teachers can act as surrogate attachment figures, offering the secure relationships that many trauma-affected students lack in their personal lives. By becoming a secure base, teachers provide emotional support and stability, allowing students to explore their academic potential and social relationships confidently.

This chapter outlines several practical strategies for creating emotional safety, such as maintaining predictable routines, preparing students for changes, and fostering open communication. It also emphasises empathy as a key tool in building trust and understanding, guiding teachers on how to use active listening, validate student experiences, and maintain a non-judgemental approach when addressing challenging behaviours.

By prioritising emotional safety and building positive, trusting relationships, educators can create an environment where trauma-affected students feel empowered to learn, grow, and heal emotionally.

Guiding Questions for Chapter 3

1. **What is emotional safety, and why is it a foundational aspect of trauma-informed classrooms?**
   Reflect on how emotional safety underpins students' capacity to learn, regulate, and engage. Consider the ways trauma can compromise a student's sense of safety, even in environments that appear objectively secure. How do classroom interactions, teacher tone, peer dynamics, and consistency influence a student's emotional state? Think about how you cultivate emotional safety daily—and what changes could deepen that sense of security for all learners.

2. **How can predictable routines and a structured environment help reduce anxiety for trauma-affected students?**
   Consider how routines provide a sense of order and control, especially for students whose prior experiences may have been chaotic or unpredictable. Reflect on the power of clear transitions, consistent expectations, and visual cues in reducing stress and supporting emotional regulation. How can your classroom environment and daily schedule reinforce a sense of calm, continuity, and reliability?

3. **Why is building trust important when working with trauma-impacted students, and what specific actions can teachers take to foster trust?**
   Think about the time and consistency required to earn trust from students who may have experienced relational harm. What small but meaningful gestures—like following through on promises, maintaining confidentiality, or responding calmly to distress—might build that trust over time? Reflect on how your consistency, fairness, and empathy contribute to a safe relational space where students feel genuinely supported.

4. **What role does empathy play in creating positive teacher-student relationships, and how can teachers demonstrate empathy effectively?**
   Reflect on how empathy shapes your responses to challenging behaviours and emotional outbursts. How do you demonstrate to students that you understand—not excuse—their distress or dysregulation? Consider the difference between empathy and sympathy, and how active listening, validation, and non-judgemental support can help students feel seen and understood.

5. **How does attachment theory inform our understanding of the importance of teacher-student relationships, particularly for students who have experienced trauma?**
   Revisit the core ideas of attachment theory and their relevance in the classroom. How might a teacher serve as a secure base for students with disrupted early attachments? Consider how relational consistency, attunement, and emotional availability can help students rebuild trust in others and regulate their emotions more effectively. Reflect on how understanding attachment needs can guide your practice, particularly when working with students who exhibit anxious, avoidant, or disorganised attachment behaviours.

Teachers Toolbox

Teachers' Toolbox for Chapter 3

STRATEGY	DESCRIPTION
IMPLEMENT VISUAL SCHEDULES AND ROUTINES	Use visual schedules to outline the day's activities, giving trauma-affected students a sense of structure and predictability. Include icons or images to make the schedule more accessible for younger students or those with reading difficulties.
PREPARE FOR TRANSITIONS	Use transition cues to help students anticipate changes, such as a five-minute warning before switching activities. Offer extra support during transitions by allowing students who struggle to use a calm-down space if they feel overwhelmed.
COLLABORATE WITH OTHER TEACHERS	When students have multiple teachers, collaborate with colleagues to ensure consistent routines across different classrooms. Share strategies for transitions and behaviour management, creating a unified approach for trauma-affected students.
OFFER PREDICTABLE SUPPORT	Regularly check in with trauma-affected students to offer consistent emotional support. Start the day with a brief check-in where students can share how they feel and discuss any concerns, providing reassurance throughout the day.
USE ACTIVE LISTENING AND EMPATHY	Practice active listening by giving students your full attention when they speak. Use empathetic responses like "I understand this is difficult for you" to validate their emotions and help them feel heard and supported.
PREPARE STUDENTS FOR CHANGE	When unexpected changes arise (e.g., substitute teachers, school assemblies), give students advance notice and provide them with time to process the information. Offer reassurance and a clear explanation of what will happen.
TEACH SELF-REGULATION STRATEGIES	Teach trauma-affected students self-regulation techniques, such as deep breathing or mindfulness exercises, that they can use when they feel anxious or stressed. Incorporate these practices into the daily routine.
DEVELOP PERSONALISED SUPPORT PLANS	Create individualised support plans for trauma-affected students, identifying specific triggers and coping strategies. Involve the student in the process, allowing them to have agency over how they can manage stress or anxiety in the classroom.

References

Bowlby, J. (1969). *Attachment and loss: Vol. 1.* Attachment. Basic Books.

Cavanaugh, B. (2016). Trauma-informed classrooms and schools. *Beyond Behavior, 25*(2), 41–46. https://doi.org/10.1177/107429561602500206

Karris, S. W. (2022). *The impact of trauma on learning and behaviors in the classroom and how a trauma-informed classroom helps* [Master's thesis, Bethel University]. Spark Repository. https://spark.bethel.edu/etd/778

Pickens, I. B., & Tschopp, N. (2017). *Trauma-informed classrooms.* National Council of Juvenile and Family Court Judges.

Rodaughan, J., Murrup-Stewart, C., & Berger, E. (2024). Aboriginal practitioners' perspectives on culturally informed practice for trauma healing in Australia. *The Counseling Psychologist, 52,* 1113–1141. https://doi.org/10.1177/00110000241268798

Sweetman, N. (2022). What Is a Trauma Informed Classroom? What Are the Benefits and Challenges Involved? In *Frontiers in Education* (Vol. 7, p. 914448). Frontiers Media SA. https://doi.org/10.3389/feduc.2022.914448

Van der Kolk, B. A. (2005). Developmental trauma disorder: Toward a rational diagnosis for children with complex trauma histories. *Psychiatric Annals, 35*(5), 401–408.

4 Cultivating Empathy, Compassion, and Self-Care in Teachers

Introduction to Empathy, Compassion, and Self-Care

In trauma-informed education, the qualities of empathy and compassion are not only desirable – they are essential. Increasingly, teachers find themselves supporting students shaped by adverse experiences, including abuse, neglect, and poverty, all of which can profoundly impact a student's ability to engage in learning. Empathy allows educators to "walk in another's shoes" (Wiggins & McTighe, 2005), understanding and resonating with their students' emotional states, while compassion moves them to take action, fostering environments that promote healing and support.

Building on earlier chapters, we see that trauma can fundamentally alter students' emotional and behavioural regulation, often leading to behaviours that might initially seem challenging. Children who experience trauma are likely to display signs such as reactivity, withdrawal, or aggression, posing unique challenges for educators untrained in trauma-informed approaches (Foreman & Bates, 2021). Teachers who interpret these behaviours with compassion rather than judgement contribute to an emotionally safe classroom, a cornerstone of trauma-informed care that enables students to feel secure enough to learn and build trust.

However, sustaining empathy and compassion effectively requires that teachers practice self-care. The demands of supporting trauma-impacted

DOI: 10.4324/9781003535386-5

students can lead to secondary trauma or compassion fatigue, characterised by emotional exhaustion and a diminished capacity to empathise (Miller & Flint-Stipp, 2019). Educators who frequently encounter students' trauma narratives may, without proper self-care strategies, carry these emotional burdens themselves, risking burnout.

Self-care is, therefore, a professional imperative. Practices like mindfulness, reflective exercises, and connecting with peer support networks equip teachers to manage the emotional demands of their role while maintaining the resilience needed to support students effectively (Miller & Flint-Stipp, 2019). These practices empower teachers to sustain their capacity for empathy and compassion, creating a classroom where both students and teachers can thrive. This chapter explores how empathy, compassion, and self-care intertwine in trauma-informed teaching. We will discuss the importance of these qualities, examine the risks of compassion fatigue, and provide practical self-care strategies to prevent burnout, supporting educators on their journey to become resilient, empathetic guides for their students.

Empathy and Compassion in Trauma-Informed Teaching

In trauma-informed educational settings, empathy and compassion are not just valuable qualities – they are essential foundations for effective teaching, particularly when working with students affected by adverse experiences. While empathy allows teachers to understand and connect with the emotions of their students, compassion transforms this understanding into meaningful action, motivating educators to respond thoughtfully to students' needs and vulnerabilities (Barton & Garvis, 2019). For educators, embodying empathy and compassion requires more than simply recognising trauma's impact; it demands a deliberate approach to building secure, supportive relationships that nurture students' well-being and resilience. Through this trauma-informed lens, teaching becomes a process of cultivating environments that validate students' experiences, foster trust, and alleviate the emotional burdens that students carry. Trauma-informed teaching, therefore, goes beyond managing behaviour; it is about creating spaces where healing and learning go hand-in-hand.

Defining Empathy and Compassion in Trauma-Informed Teaching

In a trauma-informed classroom, empathy and compassion are foundational elements that guide teachers' interactions and responses to students' needs. Empathy – the ability to "walk in another's shoes" – enables teachers to perceive and understand the emotions behind students' behaviours, especially when those behaviours are challenging or difficult to interpret (Wiggins & McTighe, 2005). For students affected by trauma, who may struggle with emotional regulation and trust, empathy from teachers provides reassurance that their feelings are seen, acknowledged, and valued. When educators approach situations with empathy, they shift from assigning blame to understanding the deeper context behind student behaviours, which often leads to more effective and supportive responses.

Compassion builds on empathy by encouraging teachers to take actionable steps in support of their students. Compassionate interactions involve addressing trauma-induced behaviours as indicators of unmet needs or distress, rather than as deliberate acts of defiance (Halifax, 2012). By responding compassionately, teachers create an environment where students feel genuinely cared for rather than judged or punished. This compassionate approach in trauma-informed teaching does not excuse poor behaviour; instead, it fosters a classroom climate where students feel safe to express themselves, encouraging emotional regulation and engagement. Furthermore, empathy and compassion are not only vital for supporting students but also play an essential role in helping educators avoid burnout and compassion fatigue. In high-emotion contexts, where teachers are consistently providing support, compassion enables educators to maintain a balanced emotional involvement, sustaining their own well-being as they foster supportive relationships with their students (Jiménez, 2017).

The Impact of Teacher Empathy on Student Security and Trust

Empathy in the classroom has profound implications for students' sense of security, particularly for those who have experienced trauma. When students feel understood by their teachers, they are more likely to perceive the classroom as a safe space, which is essential for both engagement and learning. Trauma-affected students often enter the classroom with heightened levels of distrust or fear, shaped by past experiences where adults may have been inconsistent or unresponsive to their needs (Brunzell et al., 2016). An empathetic response from teachers offers a new experience – one where students are seen, heard, and valued, regardless of their struggles.

Positive teacher-student relationships are central to building trust in trauma-informed settings. According to attachment theory, children form attachments based on the consistency and responsiveness of caregivers, which profoundly influences their ability to develop trust in later relationships (Bowlby, 1969). For students affected by trauma, the teacher often becomes a critical figure in restoring trust, offering the stable connection they may not have experienced elsewhere (Cavanaugh, 2016). Through empathy, teachers respond to students' distress with patience and understanding, fostering a classroom culture that prioritises emotional safety and support.

Practically speaking, empathetic teachers use behaviours that communicate acceptance and encouragement, helping students feel a sense of belonging. Simple actions, such as active listening, validating students' feelings, and responding consistently to behaviours, help students feel secure. For example, if a student reacts angrily due to feelings of anxiety or frustration, an empathetic teacher might respond with, "I can see that something is bothering you. Do you want to talk about it, or would you like a few minutes to calm down?" This approach not only addresses the immediate behaviour but also demonstrates that the teacher is willing to listen and understand rather than simply reprimand. Over time, this creates an environment where students feel safe to express themselves, an essential step towards emotional healing and academic engagement.

Empathy also allows teachers to recognise early signs of distress, providing support before behaviours escalate. In classrooms where teachers respond empathetically, students learn they can seek help without fear of judgement, a critical reassurance for students who may feel isolated due to trauma. Empathetic interactions not only reduce conflict but also build resilience, teaching students that their emotions are manageable and that there are safe, supportive ways to address them.

Compassionate Interactions and Trauma-Informed Responses

In trauma-informed teaching, compassion is essential for creating a respectful, safe atmosphere that acknowledges and validates students' past experiences. Compassionate teaching involves recognising that trauma can manifest in various behaviours, including withdrawal, defiance, or aggression, and responding to these behaviours with an understanding of their underlying causes (Downey, 2007). Instead of viewing these behaviours as disruptions, trauma-informed teachers interpret them as indicators of unaddressed trauma, adjusting their responses to support the student's emotional needs while maintaining classroom stability.

A compassionate approach requires patience and flexibility, recognising that trauma-affected students may need extra time, reassurance, or tailored support to feel comfortable in the classroom. Teachers who practise compassion are more capable of de-escalating situations, as they see challenging behaviours as opportunities to build trust rather than disruptions to be controlled. This perspective is central to trauma-informed education, allowing teachers to maintain authority while fostering an environment where students feel supported, not controlled. For instance, if a student withdraws or becomes uncharacteristically aggressive, a compassionate teacher might ask, "Is something making you feel uncomfortable today?" or allow the student a moment to reset in a designated calm space within the classroom. Such responses validate students' experiences and show that their teacher is attuned to their emotional well-being as well as their academic needs.

In addition to supporting students, compassionate teaching helps prevent compassion fatigue. By maintaining a balanced approach to compassion, teachers can empathise without becoming overwhelmed, recognising the importance of self-care and peer support. This balance allows educators to offer genuine support without risking burnout, creating a classroom climate that prioritises healing and growth. Teachers who practise compassionate interactions not only foster resilience in students but also set emotional boundaries that protect their own well-being, ensuring they can continue to support their students effectively over time.

In trauma-informed education, empathy and compassion are vital tools for both students and teachers. These qualities transform the classroom into a place of understanding, safety, and growth, where students feel secure enough to explore learning and express their emotions. By integrating empathy and compassion into their daily practice, educators create a supportive foundation that empowers students to move beyond trauma and develop the resilience needed for academic and personal success.

The Role of Self-Care in Sustaining Empathy

For teachers working within trauma-informed educational settings, self-care is not a luxury but a professional necessity. While empathy is essential for supporting trauma-affected students, it can lead to emotional exhaustion and compassion fatigue if educators do not actively manage their well-being (Miller & Flint-Stipp, 2019). Teachers who continuously pour their emotional energy into supporting students often risk burnout, which can ultimately erode their ability to remain empathetic and engaged. As a result, self-care practices become essential tools that enable educators to maintain the resilience needed to respond empathetically over time.

Self-Care as a Foundation for Empathetic Engagement

Compassion fatigue is a recognised phenomenon in helping professions, including education, where individuals are frequently exposed to others' trauma and emotional distress (Hydon et al., 2015). Left unaddressed, compassion fatigue can lead to symptoms like irritability, emotional detachment, and a diminished capacity for empathy, all of which undermine teachers' effectiveness in the classroom. For trauma-informed educators, empathy is a crucial part of creating a trusting and safe learning environment, and maintaining this empathetic approach requires teachers to prioritise their well-being. Self-care provides a foundation that allows educators to recharge, reflect, and return to their work with renewed understanding and compassion.

Practising self-care enables teachers to avoid emotional depletion, supporting both their mental health and their ability to remain engaged with students. Teachers who incorporate regular self-care into their routines can better manage the emotional demands of their roles, preventing the buildup of stress that often leads to burnout. By establishing boundaries and actively engaging in restorative activities, educators sustain their capacity to empathise with students, which is essential for fostering a trauma-informed classroom. In this way, self-care becomes integral to professional practice, allowing teachers to create an environment that supports healing and learning for students.

Key Self-Care Methods for Teachers

To manage the emotional demands of trauma-informed teaching effectively, educators need accessible and sustainable self-care strategies. Among the most effective self-care methods are mindfulness practices, reflective exercises, and developing peer support networks. Each addresses different aspects of emotional and mental well-being, providing a balanced approach to managing stress and maintaining empathy.

- **Mindfulness Practices:** Mindfulness helps teachers stay present and aware, reducing emotional reactivity and enabling them to manage stress more effectively. Techniques like deep breathing, meditation, and guided visualisation create moments of calm amid the demands of a school day. Regular mindfulness practice helps teachers regulate their emotions, which is especially useful when managing challenging behaviours associated with trauma-affected students. For example, taking a few moments to breathe deeply before addressing a disruptive behaviour can help a teacher respond with calm empathy rather than frustration, maintaining trust and safety in the classroom environment (Birnie et al., 2010).
- **Reflective Exercises:** Reflection allows teachers to process experiences, identify stressors, and develop coping strategies for emotional challenges. Reflective practices might include journaling, debriefing with colleagues, or participating in professional development focused on trauma-informed practices. By setting aside time for reflection, teachers gain insight into their emotional responses, allowing them to address the impact of their work. Regular reflection also helps teachers recognise the positive aspects of their roles, reinforcing their sense of purpose and commitment to supporting students.
- **Peer Support Networks:** Building a supportive network among colleagues is one of the most effective ways to manage the challenges of trauma-informed teaching. Peer support networks allow teachers to share

Creating Trauma-Informed Classrooms

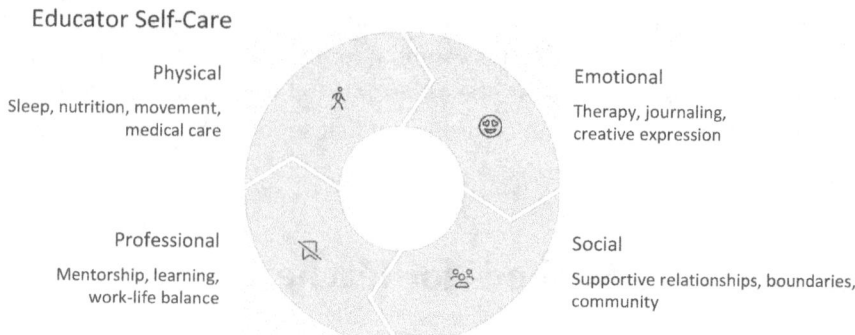

Figure 4.1 Four Domains of Self-Care Specific to Educators

experiences, discuss difficult situations, and offer mutual encouragement. In settings where secondary trauma is common, connecting with others who understand these challenges can be deeply validating and reassuring. Peer support also promotes collaborative problem-solving, as teachers exchange strategies for managing stress and supporting one another through difficult moments (Jennings et al., 2011). A supportive professional community fosters resilience, reminding educators they are not alone in their commitment to creating trauma-informed classrooms (Figure 4.1).

Modelling Self-Care and Resilience for Students

Beyond supporting personal well-being, self-care also serves as an essential model for students, demonstrating healthy ways of managing stress. In Chapter 3, the significance of educators as role models was discussed, particularly in terms of how they display resilience and emotional regulation in the classroom. For students affected by trauma, observing teachers who engage in self-care and demonstrate calm, controlled responses to stress can be both educational and reassuring. Trauma-affected students benefit from these examples of healthy coping, as they offer practical models for managing challenging emotions constructively.

When teachers prioritise self-care, they exemplify resilience, showing students that it is both necessary and acceptable to take steps to protect one's mental and emotional health. For instance, if a teacher shares that they practice mindfulness to manage stress or reflects on difficult days to find solutions, students gain valuable insight into positive coping mechanisms. In trauma-informed classrooms, where students often navigate complex emotional responses, such modelling can be particularly powerful. Students witness firsthand how adults handle stress healthily, reinforcing the idea that self-care is not only beneficial but also a fundamental part of well-being.

The Broader Impact of Self-Care on Trauma-Informed Practice

Integrating self-care into professional practice benefits not only individual teachers but also the broader effectiveness of trauma-informed education. Teachers who prioritise self-care are more likely to experience job satisfaction and less likely to feel overwhelmed by their roles, which encourages retention and long-term commitment to teaching. This consistency is particularly valuable in trauma-informed settings, where high turnover can disrupt the stability that trauma-affected students need. By sustaining themselves through self-care, teachers contribute to a more predictable and supportive school environment, benefiting students and colleagues alike.

Moreover, self-care fosters a culture of resilience within the school community. When teachers openly practise self-care, they contribute to a professional environment that values and supports emotional health. This, in turn, encourages other educators to adopt similar practices, creating a ripple effect that promotes a positive, supportive atmosphere across the school. In trauma-informed educational settings, where emotional demands are significant, this culture of resilience can be transformative, empowering teachers to maintain empathy, compassion, and dedication to their work over the long term. Through self-care, educators not only strengthen their capacity to support students but also contribute to a school environment where well-being is a shared priority, enhancing the effectiveness of trauma-informed education at every level.

Preventing Burnout and Recognising Compassion Fatigue

Teaching in trauma-informed educational settings requires a high level of emotional investment, with educators often serving as the first line of support for students impacted by adverse experiences. Over time, this intense exposure can lead to compassion fatigue – a specific form of secondary trauma resulting from sustained empathetic engagement with others' suffering. Unlike general stress or burnout, compassion fatigue arises from the cumulative emotional toll of supporting trauma-affected students and is characterised by emotional exhaustion, reduced empathy, and feelings of depersonalisation (Bride, 2007). For teachers in trauma-informed roles, recognising and addressing compassion fatigue is essential to maintain resilience and sustained compassion in the classroom.

Understanding Compassion Fatigue and Its Symptoms

Compassion fatigue manifests as a gradual depletion of emotional resources, often driven by the ongoing demands of supporting students who regularly exhibit trauma-related behaviours. This condition frequently leads to emotional exhaustion, where teachers feel drained and unable to offer the same level of empathy and support they once provided. A reduced capacity for empathy is another defining characteristic, as educators may become emotionally numb or detached in response to the relentless demands of their role. If left unchecked, this detachment can progress to depersonalisation, where teachers begin to see students not as individuals with needs but as sources of stress, a shift that can significantly disrupt classroom dynamics and the teacher-student relationship.

While burnout and compassion fatigue are related, they have distinct causes and effects. Burnout generally stems from chronic workplace stress, such as excessive workload or insufficient support, whereas compassion fatigue is specifically linked to the emotional strain of engaging with others' trauma (Figley, 1995). Understanding these differences is vital for teachers, as awareness of compassion fatigue enables them to identify early signs and take proactive steps to protect their mental health. Without intervention, compassion fatigue can lead educators to withdraw emotionally, diminishing their empathy and creating a less supportive classroom environment for students (Figure 4.2).

Preventive Strategies for Sustaining Compassion in the Classroom

To guard against compassion fatigue, teachers need a range of proactive strategies that foster emotional resilience and sustainable empathy. Key

Compassion Fatigue vs. Burnout

Compassion Fatigue
- Sudden onset
- Secondary trauma exposure
- Preoccupation with students' trauma
- Heightened anxiety
- May still find work meaningful

Burnout
- Gradual development
- Work-related stress
- Emotional exhaustion
- Cynicism and detachment
- Reduced sense of accomplishment

Figure 4.2 Signs of Compassion Fatigue vs Burnout

strategies include effective time management, setting realistic workload expectations, and accessing support services – each of which equips educators to manage the emotional demands of trauma-informed teaching more effectively.

- **Time Management:** Effective time management allows teachers to create boundaries that protect their emotional and mental energy. By structuring their day and prioritising tasks, teachers can ensure they have adequate time to recharge between emotionally demanding interactions. Allocating specific periods for tasks like lesson planning, grading, and classroom preparation helps prevent overextension, while setting aside dedicated time for relaxation and self-care reduces the risk of emotional exhaustion. Additionally, learning to delegate non-essential tasks or saying no to additional responsibilities can alleviate the pressure to be constantly available, helping teachers avoid burnout.
- **Realistic Workload Expectations:** Trauma-informed teaching often requires a greater level of emotional labour, so it is essential that educators set realistic goals for what they can achieve. Teachers who establish manageable workload expectations are less likely to feel overwhelmed or disappointed if they cannot meet every demand. This may involve adapting lesson plans to accommodate trauma-affected students' diverse needs, seeking administrative support to maintain reasonable class sizes, or advocating for limits on additional responsibilities. By adopting realistic expectations, teachers allow themselves the space to provide quality care without compromising their own well-being.
- **Accessing Support Services:** Support networks, both formal and informal, are invaluable in helping teachers manage the emotional challenges of compassion fatigue. Mental health services, such as counselling or

therapy, can provide educators with tools to process the emotional impact of their work, helping them manage stress more effectively. Schools offering Employee Assistance Programs (EAPs) or other mental health resources can be instrumental in supporting teachers' well-being. Additionally, connecting with peer support networks allows teachers to share experiences, offer encouragement, and brainstorm strategies for handling difficult situations. Such services not only provide practical assistance but also remind teachers they are not alone, helping to alleviate feelings of isolation.

A Non-Judgemental Approach to Trauma Responses

A core principle of trauma-informed teaching is the capacity to recognise and reframe students' trauma responses in a way that reduces judgement and fosters empathy. Previous chapters have emphasised the importance of identifying trauma-related behaviours – such as aggression, withdrawal, or defiance – not as disciplinary issues but as expressions of underlying distress (Foreman & Bates, 2021). For teachers, this perspective shift is essential to avoid burnout, as it allows them to respond to challenging behaviours with understanding rather than frustration, preserving their emotional resilience.

For example, a student who reacts aggressively to a perceived slight may be experiencing hyperarousal, a common trauma response. Rather than interpreting this behaviour as intentional defiance, a trauma-informed teacher recognises it as an expression of underlying anxiety or stress. By responding with empathy – perhaps by offering the student a moment to take a break or engage in a calming activity – the teacher can defuse the situation while maintaining a supportive, non-judgemental stance. This approach benefits not only the student but also the teacher, as it fosters a constructive response instead of one driven by frustration or resentment.

Reframing trauma responses also involves creating a classroom environment that minimises triggers and promotes stability. Teachers can achieve this by establishing predictable routines and setting clear expectations. By proactively addressing potential sources of stress, educators can reduce the frequency and intensity of trauma responses, ultimately lowering the risk of compassion fatigue. A supportive, non-judgemental approach creates a classroom atmosphere where both students and teachers feel respected and understood, fostering resilience on both sides.

Building a Culture of Emotional Sustainability

Preventing burnout and compassion fatigue is not solely the responsibility of individual teachers; it requires a collective commitment to emotional sustainability within the school community. Schools that prioritise teacher well-being by offering professional development on self-care and trauma-informed practices foster a culture that supports sustained compassion. Administrators play a vital role in this process by acknowledging the emotional demands of trauma-informed teaching and providing resources such as manageable class sizes, mental health support, and structured collaboration opportunities among teachers. When schools promote a culture of resilience, teachers are more likely to feel valued and supported, reducing the likelihood of burnout and compassion fatigue.

Professional development that focuses on empathy, resilience, and self-care equips teachers with skills to navigate the challenges of trauma-informed education. Workshops on managing compassion fatigue, practising mindfulness, and building peer support networks empower teachers to sustain their commitment to compassionate teaching. By investing in these resources, schools signal that teacher well-being is a priority, cultivating a compassionate and effective learning environment for both educators and students.

In trauma-informed educational settings, where emotional demands are high, a culture of resilience can have transformative effects, helping teachers maintain empathy, compassion, and dedication to their roles. When teachers are supported in caring for their well-being, they are better equipped to create stable, trusting relationships with their students, ultimately fostering a more positive and sustainable classroom environment. Through proactive strategies, non-judgemental approaches, and a collective focus on emotional sustainability, educators can effectively manage the challenges of trauma-informed teaching, ensuring they are able to support students in a way that is both compassionate and sustainable.

Case Study and Practical Strategies

Scenario

Emma is a middle school teacher with a strong commitment to her students, many of whom have faced significant adversity. While she has always enjoyed the challenge of creating a supportive classroom environment, Emma finds herself feeling increasingly overwhelmed. The daily demands of managing student trauma responses, combined with her personal standards for excellence, are beginning to take a toll on her well-being. She experiences frequent headaches, fatigue, and irritability, which are early signs of burnout and compassion fatigue. Recognising the need for change, Emma decides to develop a self-care plan based on practices outlined in professional development sessions and recent insights into self-care strategies specific to teachers.

Step 1: Setting Boundaries and Time Management

Emma's first step is to reassess her time commitments and set clearer boundaries. According to self-care strategies emphasised in wellness literature, setting boundaries and reducing work hours are essential for preventing burnout. Emma realises that she often spends extra hours at school, completing tasks she could distribute throughout the week or delegate. She starts by leaving school at a set time each day and allocating a few focused hours for grading and lesson planning over the weekend. Additionally, Emma schedules small breaks during the day to rest her mind and recharge. Implementing these time management practices helps Emma reduce the constant feeling of being on-call. She feels a sense of control over her time, which decreases her stress levels. As her physical symptoms subside, Emma notices she has more energy and patience in the classroom, allowing her to engage more positively with students.

Step 2: Incorporating Mindfulness and Reflection

Emma introduces mindfulness into her daily routine, beginning each morning with a few minutes of deep breathing to start the day with a calm mindset. Throughout the day, she practices short breathing exercises, especially before handling challenging interactions with students. These moments help Emma stay grounded and approach her students' trauma responses with empathy rather than frustration. In addition, Emma dedicates time each week to reflect on her experiences. Following guidance from mental health literature on self-care, she journals about situations that triggered stress, noting both her responses and any positive strategies she used. By reflecting on these patterns, Emma gains valuable insights into her emotional triggers and identifies opportunities to adjust her approach. This reflective practice enhances her resilience and enables her to interact with her students more compassionately and effectively, even on difficult days.

Step 3: Joining a Peer Support Group

Isolation is a common challenge for teachers experiencing compassion fatigue, as they may feel they must manage these emotions alone. Seeking connection, Emma starts a peer support group at her school, where teachers meet to discuss their challenges, share strategies, and support one another. Emma finds that being part of a peer network offers both emotional relief and practical support. She learns about new approaches to managing trauma-affected students, from classroom routines that promote stability to de-escalation techniques that help students regain control of their emotions. Emma's group provides her with a sense of community and reinforces her commitment to trauma-informed teaching. Through peer discussions, she gains confidence and feels validated in her experiences, reducing her feelings of isolation. The shared strategies also empower her to handle difficult situations more effectively, making her classroom a safer, more predictable space for students.

Implementing Trauma-Informed Strategies in the Classroom

Equipped with self-care tools, Emma revisits her trauma-informed practices in the classroom. Drawing on strategies discussed in Chapters 2 and 3, she focuses on predictable routines and structured responses to trauma-related behaviours. She establishes a consistent morning check-in where students can express their feelings and set intentions for the day. This routine helps Emma identify students who may need

> additional support, allowing her to address issues early before they escalate.
>
> Emma also incorporates calming techniques, such as a quiet corner with sensory materials and stress-relief tools, where students can go if they feel overwhelmed. By establishing this safe space, she reinforces a compassionate, non-judgemental approach to student interactions, modelling how to manage emotional responses constructively. This approach not only benefits her students but also reinforces Emma's commitment to her own well-being, as she feels empowered by her ability to create a supportive environment.

Chapter Summary

In trauma-informed education, empathy, compassion, and self-care form an essential triad that enables teachers to support students' emotional and educational needs while safeguarding their own well-being. Empathy allows teachers to connect with students on a deeper level, understanding the complex emotions and behaviours that arise from trauma. Compassion extends this understanding, encouraging teachers to act in ways that support students' healing and resilience, creating a classroom environment where students feel seen, valued, and safe. However, the sustainability of this empathetic and compassionate approach relies heavily on teachers' commitment to self-care. Regular self-care practices, including mindfulness, peer support, and boundary setting, empower educators to manage the emotional demands of their work, preventing burnout and compassion fatigue. By integrating self-care into their routines, teachers maintain the mental and emotional resilience needed to foster supportive relationships with students, enhancing their effectiveness in trauma-informed classrooms.

Together, empathy, compassion, and self-care work synergistically to build a trauma-informed approach that benefits both teachers and students. While empathy and compassion are crucial for creating safe, understanding spaces, it is sustained teacher well-being that ensures these qualities can be consistently practised. In this way, self-care becomes not only a personal priority but also a professional commitment that underpins the success of trauma-informed education.

Guiding Questions

1. **Why are empathy and compassion essential in trauma-informed education?**
   - Reflect on how empathy and compassion contribute to understanding students' trauma responses and fostering an environment that encourages healing, safety, and resilience.

2. **What self-care strategies can teachers use to maintain their well-being while supporting traumatised students?**
   - Consider practical self-care actions that teachers can adopt to protect their mental health while sustaining compassionate engagement with their students.

Teachers Toolbox

Teacher's Toolbox for Chapter 4

STRATEGY	DESCRIPTION
BUILDING EMPATHY IN THE CLASSROOM	Use perspective-taking activities and storytelling to foster empathy and understanding among students. Activities like role-playing help students and teachers understand each other's experiences, building connections and trust.
COMPASSIONATE COMMUNICATION	Practise active listening and use empathetic responses, validating students' emotions to create an open, safe classroom environment. Examples include rephrasing students' concerns to show understanding and acknowledging their feelings without judgement.
MINDFULNESS PRACTICES FOR TEACHERS	Engage in mindfulness exercises, such as daily breathing and guided visualisation, to manage stress and support emotional regulation, especially during high-stress interactions with students.

(Continued)

(Continued)

STRATEGY	DESCRIPTION
REFLECTIVE PRACTICE	Dedicate time weekly for reflection, using journalling to process responses to challenges, identify stressors, and build resilience. This self-reflective approach strengthens teachers' emotional responses and strategies for future interactions.
PEER SUPPORT NETWORKS	Join peer groups within the school or local educational community for sharing experiences and receiving support. Peer networks offer emotional reinforcement, reduce isolation, and promote shared strategies for managing compassion fatigue.
SELF-CARE BOUNDARIES AND TIME MANAGEMENT	Set boundaries around work hours to prevent burnout, using planners to prioritise tasks and designating personal time at home to recharge. This structure helps maintain personal well-being and supports sustained empathy in teaching.
MODELLING SELF-CARE AND RESILIENCE	Share self-care practices occasionally, like mindfulness or physical activity, as examples for students to follow. Demonstrating resilience through calm responses also helps students learn positive coping mechanisms implicitly.

References

Barton, G., & Garvis, S. (2019). Theorizing compassion and empathy in educational contexts: What are compassion and empathy and why are they important? In G. Barton & S. Garvis (Eds.), *Compassion and Empathy in Educational Contexts*, 3–14. Palgrave Macmillan. https://doi.org/10.1007/978-3-030-18925-9_1

Birnie, K., Speca, M., & Carlson, L. E. (2010). Exploring self-compassion and empathy in the context of mindfulness-based stress reduction (MBSR). *Stress and Health*, 26(5), 359–371. https://doi.org/10.1002/smi.1305

Bowlby, J. (1969). *Attachment and loss: Vol. 1. Attachment.* Basic Books.

Bride, B. E. (2007). Prevalence of secondary traumatic stress among social workers. *Social Work*, 52(1), 63–70. https://doi.org/10.1093/sw/52.1.63

Brunzell, T., Stokes, H., & Waters, L. (2016). Trauma-informed positive education: Using positive psychology to strengthen vulnerable students. *Contemporary School Psychology*, 20, 63–83. https://doi.org/10.1007/s40688-015-0070-x

Cavanaugh, B. (2016). Trauma-informed classrooms and schools. *Beyond Behavior, 25*(2), 41–46. https://doi.org/10.1177/107429561602500206

Downey, L. (2007). *Calmer classrooms: A guide to working with traumatized children*. State of Victoria, Child Safety Commissioner.

Figley, C. R. (1995). *Compassion fatigue: Coping with secondary traumatic stress disorder in those who treat the traumatized*. Brunner/Mazel.

Foreman, T., & Bates, P. (2021). Equipping preservice teachers with trauma informed care for the classroom. *Northwest Journal of Teacher Education, 16*(1), 2. https://doi.org/10.15760/nwjte.2021.16.1.2

Halifax, J. (2012). A heuristic model of enactive compassion. *Current Opinion in Supportive and Palliative Care, 6*(2), 228–235.

Hydon, S., Wong, M., Langley, A. K., Stein, B. D., & Kataoka, S. H. (2015). Preventing secondary traumatic stress in educators. *Child and Adolescent Psychiatric Clinics, 24*(2), 319–333. https://doi.org/10.1016/j.chc.2014.11.003

Jennings, P. A., Snowberg, K. E., Coccia, M. A., & Greenberg, M. T. (2011). Improving classroom learning environments by cultivating awareness and resilience in education (CARE): Results of two pilot studies. *The Journal of Classroom Interaction, 46*(1), 37–48. https://www.jstor.org/stable/23870550

Jiménez, J. M. (2017). *Compassion vs. empathy: Emotional leadership can be exhausting, but compassionate leadership doesn't have to be*. Retrieved from https://www.betterup.com/blog/compassion-vs-empathy

Miller, K., & Flint-Stipp, K. (2019). Preservice teacher burnout: Secondary trauma and self-care issues in teacher education. *Issues in Teacher Education, 28*(2), 28–45. https://www.proquest.com/scholarly-journals/preservice-teacher-burnout-secondary-trauma-self/docview/2339146614/se-2

Wiggins, G., & McTighe, J. (2005). *Understanding by design*. Association for Supervision and Curriculum Development.

 Establishing a Supportive School Culture

Introduction to Supportive School Cultures

Developing a supportive, trauma-informed school culture is a comprehensive, strategic approach that acknowledges the significant impact trauma can have on both students and educators. This approach prioritises creating an environment where all members of the school community feel secure, valued, and empowered. According to Cavanaugh (2016), trauma-informed practices are designed to foster settings that recognise and address the adverse effects of trauma, promoting safety, stability, and positive relationships throughout the school. This chapter presents foundational strategies that schools can adopt to build such a culture, with a focus on the collaborative roles of families, communities, and various school stakeholders.

Given the prevalence of childhood trauma, educators increasingly advocate for trauma-informed approaches that embed supportive frameworks into school policies, professional development, and daily interactions. Greig et al. (2021) highlight that cultivating a trauma-informed school culture requires systemic change and collaboration, with commitment from school leaders and educators alike towards a shared vision of strengthening student resilience and engagement.

A trauma-informed school culture is built upon several key components, including policy alignment to support trauma-sensitive practices, continuous professional development for educators, and the integration of social-emotional learning (SEL). SEL plays a central role in helping students develop emotional regulation, resilience, and social skills, which support both their academic and personal growth. Embedding SEL within a trauma-informed framework provides students with essential tools to manage emotional challenges, fostering a sense of belonging and empowerment within the school (Brunzell et al., 2021; Cavanaugh, 2016).

Additionally, the collaboration of families and communities is vital to this approach. Families and local organisations provide essential reinforcement of trauma-informed practices, helping bridge the gap between home and school. Engaging these external partners enhances the relevance and impact of school initiatives, building a broader support network that strengthens a trauma-informed approach and ultimately benefits the entire school community.

School Culture: Elements of a Supportive, Trauma-Informed Environment

In a trauma-informed school culture, prioritising safety, trust, empathy, and inclusiveness is fundamental for supporting students' holistic well-being. This approach addresses the challenges trauma-affected students often face, including difficulties with emotional regulation and engagement, by creating an environment that fosters growth and healing. A supportive school culture is built through strategic policies, professional development, and trauma-sensitive practices, all working together to nurture every student, particularly those impacted by trauma (Cavanaugh, 2016).

Defining a Trauma-Informed School Culture

A trauma-informed school culture places a high value on both physical and emotional safety. Research shows that schools adopting trauma-informed practices establish structured and predictable routines that help trauma-affected students feel secure, countering the unpredictability they may experience outside of school. Such practices aim to prevent retraumatisation and promote resilience by providing emotional stability (Brunzell et al., 2016). Additionally, school-wide behavioural expectations – such as clear, consistent rules around respect and safety – reinforce this stability, supporting students' ability to focus on learning in a secure environment (Pappano, 2014).

Trust is equally essential in a trauma-informed school setting, where teachers and staff play a pivotal role in establishing trust through consistent, transparent, and respectful interactions. Trauma often undermines students'

School-Wide Trauma-Informed Culture

Leadership
Policies, resources, modeling, professional development.

Staff
Consistent practices, collaboration, shared language.

Families
Partnership, communication, resource connection.

Students
Voice, choice, peer support, skill-building.

Figure 5.1 Visual Model of Systemic, Whole-School Implementation

capacity to trust others, making it crucial for educators to demonstrate reliability and respect in their relationships with students. The National Centre for Trauma-Informed Care (NCTIC, 2015) underscores the importance of empowering students and giving them a voice in decisions that affect them. This empowerment is especially critical for traumatised students, who may feel powerless. Teachers can cultivate trust by consistently maintaining boundaries, implementing restorative rather than punitive practices, and offering students a safe space to express themselves.

Empathy in trauma-informed practices involves viewing student behaviour as a reflection of their emotional state rather than as intentional defiance. Adopting a strengths-based perspective encourages educators to recognise students' resilience and unique capacities, focusing on their strengths rather than perceived deficits. This empathetic approach contributes to an environment where students feel valued, which in turn promotes positive engagement and self-esteem (Sciaraffa et al., 2018).

Inclusiveness is another key element, ensuring that all students, regardless of background or experience, feel a sense of belonging. A culturally responsive framework that acknowledges students' diverse backgrounds is essential to prevent retraumatisation and to foster a learning environment where students see their identities reflected positively in school practices and curricula (Sugai et al., 2012) (Figure 5.1).

Policy and Procedural Foundations

Establishing a supportive trauma-informed culture requires policies and procedures that create consistent and non-retraumatising responses to student behaviour. Non-punitive, restorative disciplinary practices replace traditional punishment, which can often alienate trauma-affected students, with approaches that encourage accountability and personal growth. The Berry Street Education Model (Brunzell et al., 2016), an Australian trauma-informed framework, highlights the importance of non-punitive methods in building resilience and helping students manage their behaviour in supportive settings.

Integrating SEL into the curriculum is also a critical aspect of trauma-informed policy. SEL programmes provide students with the tools to manage emotions, develop empathy, and form healthy relationships. By embedding SEL within the school day, trauma-affected students receive regular opportunities to practise self-regulation and build resilience – skills that are essential for academic and personal growth (Brunzell et al., 2016). Policies that focus on SEL are further strengthened by targeted behavioural interventions, creating a responsive rather than punitive environment that supports students' unique needs (Pappano, 2014).

Schools also benefit from employing screening tools and conducting regular assessments to identify students who may need additional support due to trauma-related challenges. Early identification allows educators to implement tailored interventions, ensuring that students have access to resources that help them navigate emotional and behavioural difficulties effectively (Cavanaugh, 2016). Additionally, policies should be revisited regularly to remain responsive to the evolving needs of the school community and to ensure alignment with trauma-informed principles.

Training and Development

Professional development is crucial in equipping school staff with the skills and knowledge necessary to foster trauma-informed environments. Effective training should encompass trauma awareness, empathy training, and de-escalation techniques, preparing educators to address the complexities of supporting trauma-affected students.

- **Trauma Awareness:** Trauma awareness training introduces educators to the impact of trauma on student behaviour, helping them interpret actions that might otherwise be misperceived as disruptive or defiant (Cavanaugh, 2016). By understanding trauma's effects, teachers can approach student behaviours with greater empathy and effectiveness, contributing to a supportive school culture.

- **Empathy Training:** Empathy training is particularly valuable in trauma-informed settings, where understanding and emotional connection are essential for building trust with students. Reflective practices, such as journaling or peer supervision, allow teachers to process their emotional responses, which strengthens their capacity for compassionate interactions with students (Madigan & Kim, 2021). By reflecting on their emotional triggers, educators can maintain a calm, empathetic approach, supporting a more resilient school culture.
- **De-escalation Techniques:** Training in de-escalation is essential for trauma-informed educators, as trauma-affected students may have heightened reactions to perceived threats or stressors. De-escalation training equips teachers with strategies to handle these situations calmly, ensuring emotional safety for all students. Techniques such as verbal de-escalation, active listening, and providing safe spaces are invaluable tools that allow educators to foster a non-threatening, supportive classroom environment (Brunzell et al., 2016).

Additionally, supporting educators through resources such as mentorship and access to school-based clinicians is crucial for preventing burnout and compassion fatigue. The emotional demands of working with trauma-affected students can be challenging, making it essential for schools to provide resources that support educator well-being. Mentorship programmes and workshops on stress management and resilience-building offer teachers the support they need to sustain trauma-informed care (American Counseling Association, 2011).

By equipping educators with skills in trauma awareness, empathy, and de-escalation, schools create a foundation for a trauma-informed culture that prioritises both student and educator well-being. This approach fosters a learning environment where students feel safe, supported, and empowered, while teachers feel capable and valued in their roles.

Family and Community Collaboration

Family and community collaboration is crucial for effective trauma-informed school initiatives, as it fosters a cohesive environment that addresses the comprehensive needs of trauma-affected students. By coordinating efforts among schools, families, and community organisations, students gain access to a consistent, supportive network that nurtures resilience, stability, and overall well-being. This section highlights the rationale for family and community involvement in trauma-informed practices, examines the roles and responsibilities of families and community partners, and presents practical strategies for effective collaboration.

Rationale for Collaboration

Families and communities play an essential role in trauma-informed practices by extending support beyond the classroom and creating a stable, predictable environment for students (Leslie et al., 2024a). Trauma often disrupts a child's sense of safety, making stable support across home and school environments particularly valuable. For trauma-affected students, consistency between home and school fosters a much-needed sense of security and predictability (Cavanaugh, 2016). Research indicates that these students often experience heightened emotional responses linked to stress or anxiety, and consistent trauma-sensitive practices across both settings can help regulate these responses and encourage positive behavioural and emotional outcomes.

Community support is also indispensable, as it provides students and their families with access to resources that may be unavailable within the school alone, such as mental health services, family counselling, and after-school programmes. The Berry Street Education Model, a trauma-informed approach widely adopted in Australia, emphasises community involvement in creating an extended network of support that helps address students' social, emotional, and academic challenges (Brunzell et al., 2016). By forming partnerships with community organisations, schools can extend trauma-informed care beyond the school setting, fostering a stronger sense of belonging for students and reinforcing positive behavioural and academic outcomes within their communities.

Key Roles and Responsibilities

In trauma-informed frameworks, families and caregivers are seen as integral components of the support network for trauma-affected students. Their role extends beyond academic support, as they are encouraged to engage in open communication with the school, participate in trauma-informed training, and offer feedback on the support their child receives. Maintaining transparent communication between families and educators ensures that families are informed about trauma-sensitive practices within the school, enabling them to reinforce similar approaches at home. This consistent support system across home and school benefits students, who respond well when principles of trauma-informed care are upheld in different aspects of their lives.

Shared responsibility between families and educators is fundamental to creating a trauma-informed culture. Families can support trauma-sensitive practices in the home by establishing predictable routines and providing safe spaces for emotional regulation. For instance, if a school adopts non-punitive disciplinary practices, parents can adopt similar approaches at home, promoting consistent responses to behaviour that acknowledge the impact of trauma. Research shows that family involvement in school activities, such as attending trauma-informed information sessions or volunteering, strengthens connections within the school community and facilitates a more integrated approach to trauma-informed care (Cavanaugh, 2016).

Community organisations bring expertise and resources that complement the school's trauma-informed practices. Mental health organisations, for example, can offer counselling services, crisis intervention, and resources for managing trauma symptoms, which are essential for students requiring support beyond what the school can provide. The Substance Abuse and Mental Health Services Administration (SAMHSA) advocates for trauma-informed schools to incorporate "family and community supports," ensuring that students and families have continuous access to trauma-sensitive resources within and beyond the school. Additionally, cultural organisations can offer culturally relevant, trauma-informed practices that validate students' identities, particularly for students from minority backgrounds who may have experienced culturally specific trauma.

Practical Aspects of Community Involvement

Effective community involvement requires schools to establish clear, accessible pathways for collaboration with external organisations. Partnerships with mental health agencies, for example, can provide on-site counselling services or facilitate referral systems, making it easier for families to access essential support. These partnerships enable schools to offer comprehensive trauma-informed care tailored to individual students' needs. Research indicates that collaborations with mental health agencies improve outcomes for trauma-affected students by providing timely, professional support that schools often cannot manage alone (Evans et al., 2014).

In addition to mental health services, schools can work with community organisations to host workshops and training sessions that educate both parents and staff on trauma-sensitive practices. Topics might include understanding trauma responses, fostering resilience, and promoting healthy coping mechanisms. These workshops not only equip families with skills to support their children but also create opportunities for community members to connect and reinforce a trauma-informed approach across the wider community (NCTIC, 2015).

Volunteering programmes and mentorship initiatives provide additional avenues for community engagement. Schools can invite community members to contribute as tutors, mentors, or after-school programme facilitators, offering students extra support and positive role models. Local artists or athletes, for instance, could volunteer to engage students in creative or athletic activities, which provides trauma-affected students with valuable outlets for self-expression and confidence building (Bowman-Perrott et al., 2013).

Community involvement can also extend to providing practical support for families experiencing financial hardship or other stressors that might compound trauma. By collaborating with local charities, food banks, and housing support services, schools can ensure that vulnerable families have access to critical resources. Alleviating these basic stressors supports a trauma-informed framework by reducing pressures that may interfere with students' ability to focus and thrive in school (Cavanaugh, 2016). Meeting fundamental needs, such as food security or stable housing, can significantly reduce stress, allowing students to engage more positively in academic and social settings.

Engagement Strategies

Engaging families and communities in trauma-informed practices is essential for creating a cohesive support network for trauma-affected students. Structured engagement methods, clear communication, and strategic utilisation of community resources contribute to fostering resilience and stability. Teachers play a vital role in facilitating these connections within their classrooms, directly involving families and community resources to strengthen trauma-informed support.

Methods for Engaging Families and Communities

Establishing reliable communication channels is the foundation of engaging families in trauma-informed education. Regular newsletters, emails, and classroom updates provide families with insights into trauma-informed practices, classroom activities, and resources for supporting their children. These updates can offer tips on understanding trauma-related behaviours, strategies for emotional regulation, and information about community events that support trauma-sensitive principles. Teachers can use these updates to highlight specific classroom practices, fostering transparency and building trust with families (Brunzell et al., 2016).

Teachers can also organise classroom-specific family workshops or open-house sessions that focus on trauma-informed topics. These sessions offer parents practical tools, such as guidance on creating stable routines at home or understanding classroom expectations. Hosting these sessions in accessible, community-friendly settings increases family engagement and provides opportunities for parents to ask questions or share observations about their children's needs. Workshops that incorporate interactive elements, like role-playing or group discussions, encourage family participation and reinforce the classroom's trauma-sensitive approach (Cavanaugh, 2016).

To extend engagement beyond the classroom, teachers can encourage family involvement in community outreach initiatives. For example, by organising classroom projects that reflect local themes or social issues, teachers can invite families to participate in activities that connect the school with broader community efforts. This involvement may include participation in class-led charity events, local volunteer work, or partnerships with nearby cultural organisations. Such initiatives build a sense of belonging and reinforce trauma-sensitive principles by promoting empathy, community awareness, and shared responsibility.

Communication Approaches

Culturally sensitive communication is crucial for fostering trust and inclusivity in trauma-informed classrooms. Teachers can reach out to families through a variety of methods, such as emails, phone calls, or face-to-face meetings, tailoring their approach to each family's preferences and cultural background. This personalised communication respects diverse perspectives and helps ensure that all families feel heard and valued (Sugai et al., 2012).

Regular check-ins with families, particularly for students with identified trauma-related needs, enable teachers to share progress updates and collaborate on strategies. These check-ins allow teachers to provide parents with insights into their child's emotional and academic development while also inviting families to share observations that can inform the teacher's approach. This level of transparency promotes consistency between home and school, creating a stable trauma-informed environment for students (Leslie et al., 2024b).

Teachers can also utilise digital platforms to maintain real-time communication with families. Messaging apps or dedicated portals offer convenient ways to share classroom updates, celebrate student achievements, and remind families about trauma-informed workshops or support sessions. Keeping communication warm, respectful, and inclusive strengthens teachers' connections with families, creating a sense of shared investment in trauma-informed practices.

Leveraging Community Resources

Teachers can play a vital role in connecting families with community resources by integrating these services directly into classroom initiatives. By inviting local agencies to participate in classroom activities or host informational sessions for parents, teachers help make essential resources more visible and accessible. For instance, representatives from mental health agencies or counselling services can be invited to parent-teacher meetings or other school events to discuss available support options. This approach raises awareness of community resources that families may not otherwise know about and highlights the teacher's role in creating a supportive network of care (Evans et al., 2014).

Mentorship programmes coordinated with community organisations further expand the classroom's support system. Teachers can identify students who may benefit from additional guidance and connect them with mentors through partnerships with local community centres or non-profits. Involving families in mentorship decisions helps establish a collaborative approach that benefits both students and families. Mentors who maintain regular check-ins with teachers provide continuity and ensure that classroom goals align with the support provided through mentorship.

Teachers can also support trauma-affected students by organising peer support groups or by inviting community facilitators to lead sessions within the classroom. These groups create a safe space for students to share experiences and learn from peers who may have similar backgrounds. Collaborating with local agencies to facilitate these groups ensures alignment with trauma-sensitive practices and that sessions are managed by trained professionals. This collaboration reinforces classroom efforts to foster resilience and strengthen peer support networks (SAMHSA, 2014).

Classroom-Specific Strategies for Family and Community Engagement

Teachers have a unique role in fostering family and community engagement directly within the classroom. By actively involving families in classroom routines and creating community engagement opportunities, teachers help reinforce trauma-informed practices that support students' well-being.

1. **Invite Family Participation in Classroom Routines:** Activities like "Family Story Time," where family members read to the class or share cultural stories, strengthen the classroom's community atmosphere, and make families active participants in students' learning environments.
2. **Coordinate Take-Home Resources:** Teachers can prepare take-home activities or resource packets that encourage families to practice trauma-sensitive strategies at home. For example, a "calming techniques" packet might include guided breathing exercises or activities designed to build emotional resilience.
3. **Use Home-School Journals for Ongoing Dialogue:** A home-school journal allows teachers and parents to maintain an ongoing dialogue about the student's progress and needs. By inviting parents to share

observations, teachers gain valuable insights into the student's home environment, which can inform trauma-sensitive approaches within the classroom.
4. **Invite Community Experts to Classroom Discussions:** Local mental health professionals or community workers can be invited to lead age-appropriate discussions on resilience, empathy, and well-being. These visits introduce students to trauma-sensitive concepts and make families aware of resources they can access. Teachers can further support these connections by sharing contact details for the experts, enhancing the support network that spans home, school, and community (Rodaughan et al., 2024).
5. **Encourage Collaborative Projects with a Community Focus:** Teachers can design classroom projects that involve community organisations and encourage family participation. For instance, a class project might involve assembling care packages for a local shelter or volunteering at a community garden. These projects promote empathy, strengthen family-school-community relationships, and integrate trauma-informed principles of compassion and support into students' educational experience.

Through these classroom-specific strategies, teachers actively support family and community engagement in trauma-informed practices, creating a nurturing environment that promotes students' academic and emotional well-being.

Case Study of a Successful Trauma-Informed School Culture Implementation

Rivertown Secondary School undertook a transformative journey to establish a trauma-informed culture, driven by the recognition of the profound impact of trauma on students and the urgent needs of their community. The school had observed rising behavioural issues, declining student engagement, and an increase in absenteeism. Teachers frequently reported feeling ill-equipped to manage the behavioural challenges that arose, and many students exhibited signs of distress, including anxiety, difficulty concentrating, and heightened emotional reactions. The broader community was also facing economic hardship and rising mental health concerns, which further underscored the need for a supportive, trauma-sensitive environment. In response, Rivertown implemented policy changes, staff training, community partnerships, and family engagement strategies to create a stable, nurturing school culture that prioritised emotional well-being.

Policy Changes
Rivertown's trauma-informed initiative began with a comprehensive shift in school policy to move away from traditional punitive disciplinary measures. Observing how suspensions and detentions often escalated behavioural issues and alienated students, particularly those affected by trauma, the school adopted restorative practices. These practices encouraged students to reflect on the impact of their actions and work collaboratively to resolve conflicts. By replacing punitive approaches with non-punitive, reflective methods, Rivertown sought to reduce retraumatisation and create a culture of understanding and empathy. Over time, this change led to a notable decline in behavioural incidents and a more cooperative atmosphere among students, who began to take greater responsibility for their actions. In addition, Rivertown integrated social-emotional learning (SEL) into its curriculum to provide students with tools for emotional regulation, empathy, and resilience. SEL was woven into various subjects and emphasised throughout the school day, teaching students skills to manage stress, communicate effectively, and navigate social challenges. By promoting emotional literacy as a core part of education, Rivertown cultivated a school culture where students could express their feelings constructively and support one another in positive ways. This policy shift helped create a safer, more cohesive school environment, where students were more engaged in learning and less likely to act out in disruptive ways.

Staff Training
Professional development was a critical component of Rivertown's trauma-informed transformation. The administration recognised that teachers and staff were on the front lines of supporting trauma-affected

students, yet many felt unprepared for this responsibility. To address this, Rivertown introduced extensive training on trauma awareness, empathy development, and de-escalation techniques. These sessions equipped teachers to identify signs of trauma and respond compassionately, rather than reactively, when students exhibited challenging behaviours. Staff learned strategies for building trust, validating students' emotions, and creating a supportive classroom climate. As staff grew more skilled in these approaches, the school culture began to shift significantly. Teachers reported that students displayed increased trust in adults and a greater willingness to engage in academic and social activities. Moreover, Rivertown recognised the importance of supporting staff well-being, particularly given the risk of compassion fatigue in trauma-informed settings. Teachers participated in mindfulness workshops and were encouraged to prioritise self-care, fostering a healthier, more resilient staff community. These efforts led to increased job satisfaction among staff, who felt more equipped and valued in their roles. This sense of empowerment among teachers had a ripple effect, enhancing their commitment to sustaining a trauma-sensitive environment that benefitted both students and educators alike.

Community Partnerships
Recognising that trauma-affected students' needs often extend beyond the classroom, Rivertown established partnerships with local mental health agencies and support organisations. The school connected with community resources to provide students with access to on-site counselling services and crisis intervention programmes, addressing mental health concerns that teachers could not manage alone. This collaboration with mental health professionals ensured that students received consistent, holistic support for their emotional and behavioural challenges. Additionally, Rivertown partnered with cultural organisations within the community to incorporate culturally responsive practices into its trauma-informed approach. In a community with diverse cultural backgrounds, this focus helped foster a sense of belonging among students who might otherwise feel marginalised. By celebrating cultural heritage and engaging students in community events, Rivertown reinforced the idea that each student's

background was valued and respected. These partnerships strengthened the school's trauma-informed culture, building a supportive network that extended into the community and provided families with resources they might not have accessed independently.

Family Engagement
Family engagement was a cornerstone of Rivertown's trauma-informed strategy. The school understood that consistent support across home and school environments was essential for trauma-affected students. Through regular family workshops, Rivertown offered parents guidance on supporting their children's emotional well-being and managing trauma-related behaviours. These workshops also allowed parents to learn about the school's trauma-informed practices, fostering a unified approach that reinforced emotional safety at home and at school. To facilitate ongoing communication, Rivertown implemented family check-ins, where teachers and counsellors could share updates on students' progress and collaborate with families on personalised strategies. The school also distributed newsletters highlighting updates on school initiatives and information on community resources. This proactive approach helped families feel included in their children's education, creating a support network that extended beyond the school walls. Parents reported feeling more connected to the school and better equipped to support their children's needs, contributing to a positive, community-oriented school culture.

Behavioural and Cultural Shifts

As Rivertown's trauma-informed policies, training, and partnerships took effect, the behaviour and culture within the school shifted profoundly. Students who had previously exhibited high levels of anxiety and emotional dysregulation began to engage more positively in the classroom, as they felt supported and understood. The adoption of restorative practices led to fewer behavioural incidents and a significant reduction in suspensions and detentions, as students were encouraged to take accountability for their actions through constructive means. Teachers observed a more respectful, cooperative atmosphere among students, who showed increased empathy towards one another and a willingness to resolve conflicts peacefully. The overall school culture evolved into one marked by trust, empathy, and inclusivity. With staff trained to respond compassionately to trauma, students felt safer approaching teachers for support, leading to stronger student-teacher relationships. This enhanced trust contributed to improved academic engagement, as students were more comfortable participating and taking risks in their learning. Rivertown's commitment to culturally responsive practices further strengthened the sense of belonging, particularly for students from minority backgrounds, who now saw their identities respected and valued in school settings.

Challenges and Solutions

Despite its successes, Rivertown faced several challenges in implementing a trauma-informed culture. Initially, some staff members were resistant to the shift from punitive discipline to restorative practices, fearing it would undermine classroom control. To address this, the administration held additional training sessions to clarify the benefits of restorative practices, using case studies and peer discussions to demonstrate the long-term benefits of these approaches. Teachers were encouraged to share their experiences and strategies, which gradually built buy-in and comfort with the new methods. Funding limitations also presented a challenge, particularly in securing resources for sustained training and mental health services. Rivertown sought grants and collaborated with local businesses to offset these costs, ensuring the continuity of trauma-informed initiatives. Additionally, community organisations and local government agencies contributed resources and expertise, enabling Rivertown to establish a trauma-informed culture that extended beyond the school's funding constraints.

Repercussions of the Trauma-Informed Transformation

Rivertown's commitment to a trauma-informed culture had far-reaching repercussions. Behavioural incidents and absenteeism declined, as students felt more connected and supported in their school environment. The focus on social-emotional learning translated into improved academic outcomes, with students exhibiting higher levels of engagement, focus, and resilience. The positive cultural shift within the school fostered a sense of community, where students and staff alike valued empathy, respect, and collaboration. Overall, Rivertown's success illustrates the profound impact of trauma-informed practices on school culture, student behaviour, and family engagement. Through comprehensive policy changes, dedicated staff training, community partnerships, and family involvement, Rivertown transformed its culture into one that empowers students to thrive academically and emotionally. The school's model offers valuable insights for other institutions seeking to create supportive, trauma-sensitive environments that address the holistic needs of students and foster a resilient, inclusive community.

Chapter Summary

This chapter explored the foundational elements necessary for establishing a supportive, trauma-informed school culture, emphasising the importance of policies, family and community engagement, and classroom practices. A trauma-informed school culture is built on policies that support safety, empathy, and inclusivity, with an emphasis on non-punitive disciplinary approaches and SEL. These policies provide students with structured, predictable environments where they can develop emotional regulation, resilience, and positive social skills.

Professional development for staff plays a crucial role in sustaining trauma-informed practices. By equipping educators with training in trauma awareness, empathy, and de-escalation techniques, schools ensure that classrooms are supportive spaces where trauma-affected students feel understood and secure. Teachers, in turn, can use this training to directly engage families and involve community resources, helping to create a consistent trauma-sensitive approach that extends from the classroom to the home.

Community partnerships and family engagement further reinforce trauma-informed practices. Schools that collaborate with local agencies and community organisations can offer additional support resources, such as counselling, mentorship programmes, and peer support groups, which are often beyond the capacity of school staff. Through family workshops, newsletters, and consistent communication, schools also engage families in trauma-sensitive practices, ensuring that students experience a consistent, supportive approach both in and out of school.

The chapter's case study illustrated Rivertown Secondary School's successful implementation of a trauma-informed culture, detailing the policy shifts, staff training, community partnerships, and family engagement that contributed to a positive transformation in the school's environment. Challenges, including initial staff resistance and funding limitations, were met with proactive solutions that emphasised collaboration and resilience. Rivertown's experience demonstrates the powerful impact of a trauma-informed approach, resulting in a more inclusive, empathetic, and resilient school community that fosters student well-being and engagement.

Guiding Questions

1. **What are the key policies and practices that contribute to creating a trauma-informed school culture, and how do they support student well-being?**
Reflect on how your school's current policies promote – or possibly hinder – trauma-informed practice. Are disciplinary measures aligned with restorative approaches? Do your school routines and expectations actively support emotional regulation and predictability for students? Consider how changes in policy and classroom implementation can foster a more inclusive, consistent, and healing environment for trauma-affected students.

2. **How does professional development in trauma-informed practices enhance educators' ability to support students and foster positive classroom environments?**
Think about the training and support you've received related to trauma-informed education. In what ways has it shaped your understanding of student behaviour, empathy, and classroom management? Are there areas where further development could help you feel more confident and capable in supporting students affected by trauma? Reflect on how whole-staff training can build a shared language and vision for school-wide trauma sensitivity.

3. **What role do community partnerships play in trauma-informed initiatives, and how can schools effectively collaborate with local agencies to support students?** Consider the community resources your school currently accesses – or could access – to support students and

families. Are there existing partnerships with mental health providers, cultural organisations, or local services? How can these relationships be deepened to create a more comprehensive network of support? Reflect on how leveraging external expertise can extend trauma-informed care beyond the school walls and meet students' needs more holistically.

4. **How can teachers involve families in trauma-informed practices, and why is family engagement important for sustaining a supportive school culture?**

    Examine your current communication and collaboration with families. Are there consistent, culturally responsive strategies in place to inform and involve families in trauma-sensitive approaches? What methods could help strengthen the home-school connection? Reflect on how family engagement – through dialogue, workshops, and shared routines – reinforces emotional safety and continuity of care for students navigating trauma.

Teachers Toolbox

Chapter 5 Teacher's Toolkit

STRATEGY	DESCRIPTION
POLICY ALIGNMENT AND CLASSROOM IMPLEMENTATION	Embed non-punitive, trauma-informed policies into daily classroom practices. Teachers can apply restorative approaches to discipline, encouraging students to reflect on actions and engage in conflict resolution.
FAMILY ENGAGEMENT WORKSHOPS	Organise classroom-specific family workshops focused on trauma-informed practices, where parents can learn techniques to support emotional regulation and resilience at home. Interactive formats encourage active participation and help build a shared understanding of trauma-informed practices.
REGULAR COMMUNICATION CHANNELS	Use newsletters, updates, and home-school journals to keep families informed on trauma-sensitive approaches, key classroom activities, and available support services. Ensure that communication is warm, inclusive, and culturally sensitive.

(Continued)

(Continued)

STRATEGY	DESCRIPTION
HOME-SCHOOL JOURNALS FOR DIALOGUE	Provide a home-school journal for ongoing communication with families. This tool allows parents to share observations from home, enabling teachers to better understand each student's needs and foster consistency across school and home environments.
COMMUNITY EXPERT SESSIONS	Invite mental health professionals or community service representatives into the classroom for sessions with students and families. These sessions raise awareness of local resources and help families access additional support.
STUDENT AND FAMILY PROJECT COLLABORATION	Design classroom projects that include family and community participation, such as service projects with local charities or cultural events. These initiatives promote community cohesion and reinforce trauma-sensitive principles, encouraging empathy and responsibility.
DIGITAL PLATFORMS FOR REAL-TIME UPDATES	Use digital platforms or messaging apps to provide real-time updates to families, sharing student achievements and reminders about trauma-informed events or workshops. This approach strengthens family engagement by making communication accessible and immediate.
RESOURCE PACKS FOR HOME USE	Provide take-home resource packs with calming activities, resilience-building exercises, or family discussion prompts. This allows trauma-sensitive practices to continue at home, reinforcing the skills learned in the classroom.
PEER MENTORSHIP COORDINATION	Collaborate with community organisations to establish mentorship programmes for trauma-affected students. These mentors can support both academic and emotional development, complementing classroom-based trauma-sensitive practices.
LOCAL SERVICE PARTNERSHIP INTEGRATION	Partner with local counselling and mental health services to provide accessible resources for families directly through the school, either through referrals or informational sessions on campus.

References

American Counseling Association. (2011). *Vicarious trauma*. Fact Sheet #9. Retrieved from https://static1.squarespace.com/static/60773266d31a1f2f300e02ef/t/65b235e7149f36190739ffef/1706178023620/fact-sheet-9---vicarious-trauma.pdf

Bowman-Perrott, L., Davis, H., Vannest, K., Williams, L., Greenwood, C., & Parker, R. (2013). Academic benefits of peer tutoring: A meta-analytic review of single-case research. *School Psychology Review, 42*(1), 39–55. https://doi.org/10.1080/02796015.2013.12087490

Brunzell, T., Stokes, H., & Waters, L. (2016). Trauma-informed positive education: Using positive psychology to strengthen vulnerable students. *Contemporary School Psychology, 20*, 63–83. https://doi.org/10.1007/s40688-015-0070-x

Brunzell, T., Waters, L., & Stokes, H. (2021). Trauma-informed teacher wellbeing: Teacher reflections within trauma-informed positive education. *Australian Journal of Teacher Education (Online), 46*(5), 91–107. https://doi.org/10.14221/ajte.2021v46n5.6

Cavanaugh, B. (2016). Trauma-informed classrooms and schools. *Beyond Behavior, 25*(2), 41–46. https://doi.org/10.1177/107429561602500206

Evans, S. W., Stephan, S. H., & Sugai, G. (2014). Advancing research in school mental health: Introduction of a special issue on key issues in research. *School Mental Health, 6*, 63–67. https://doi.org/10.1007/s12310-014-9126-8

Greig, J, Bailey, B, Abbott, L, & Brunzell, T. (2021). Trauma-informed integral leadership: Leading school communities with a systems-aware approach. *International Journal of Whole Schooling, 17*(1), 62–97.

Leslie, R., Larsen, E., Fanshawe, M., & Brown, A. (2024a). "It is more than the average parent goes through": Using the experiences of Australian parents of dyslexic children to draw a distinction between advocacy and allyship. *Australian Journal of Learning Difficulties, 29*(1), 53–74. https://doi.org/10.1080/19404158.2024.2342523

Leslie, R., Fanshawe, M., Larsen, E., & Brown, A. (2024b). The perceptions parents of dyslexic children have on barriers to meaningful parent–school partnerships in Australia. *Exceptionality, 33*(1), 40–58. https://doi.org/10.1080/09362835.2024.2389081

Madigan, D. J., & Kim, L. E. (2021). Does teacher burnout affect students? A systematic review of its association with academic achievement and student-reported outcomes. *International Journal of Educational Research, 105*, 101714. https://doi.org/10.1016/j.ijer.2020.101714

National Center for Trauma Informed Care (NCTIC). (2015). *Trauma-informed approach and trauma-specific interventions*. Substance Abuse and Mental Health Services Administration. Retrieved from https://www.tribalyouth.org/wp-content/uploads/2021/08/samhsa_gov-Trauma-Informed_Approach_and_Trauma-Specific_Interventions.pdf

Pappano, L. (2014). Trauma-Sensitive Schools. *Harvard Education Letter, 30*(3), 1–4.

Rodaughan, J., Murrup-Stewart, C., & Berger, E. (2024). Aboriginal practitioners' perspectives on culturally informed practice for trauma healing in Australia. *The Counseling Psychologist, 57*, 1113–1141. https://doi.org/10.1177/00110000241268798

Sciaraffa, M. A., Zeanah, P. D., & Zeanah, C. H. (2018). Understanding and promoting resilience in the context of adverse childhood experiences. *Early Childhood Education Journal, 46*(3), 343–353. https://doi.org/10.1007/s10643-017-0869-3

Substance Abuse and Mental Health Services Administration (SAMHSA). (2014). *Trauma-informed care in behavioral health services.* Treatment Improvement Protocol Series 57. Substance Abuse and Mental Health Services Administration. Retrieved from https://library.samhsa.gov/sites/default/files/sma14-4816.pdf

Sugai G., O'Keeffe, B. V., & Fallon, L. M. (2012). A contextual consideration of culture and school-wide positive behavior support. *Journal of Positive Behavior Interventions, 14*(4), 197–208. https://doi.org/10.1177/1098300711426334

Identifying and Addressing Signs of Trauma in Students

Introduction to Identifying and Addressing Signs of Trauma

As established in earlier chapters, a trauma-informed approach in education requires more than traditional classroom management – it involves creating spaces where students feel understood, valued, and safe. For many students, the classroom can become a vital place of stability and reassurance, especially when educators are equipped to recognise and respond sensitively to trauma-related behaviours. This chapter builds on the core principles of empathy, safety, and compassionate engagement introduced in previous chapters, offering practical guidance for identifying signs of trauma in students and understanding the underlying causes of behaviours that may initially seem challenging.

Educators today are encountering increasing numbers of students affected by adverse experiences – whether sudden and acute, such as family loss, or ongoing, such as community violence or neglect. Research suggests that a significant proportion of students have encountered trauma by the time they reach school, and the effects of these experiences are profound, often shaping students' cognitive, emotional, and social development in lasting ways (Copeland et al., 2007; Costello et al., 2002). Trauma disrupts core areas of functioning, making everyday tasks – like paying attention, following directions, or managing impulses – difficult to navigate within a classroom environment.

For trauma-affected students, common classroom dynamics can sometimes amplify stress. A structured environment, which generally supports focus and engagement, may trigger heightened responses in students whose brains are primed for survival rather than learning (Blair & Raver, 2015; McEwen, 2012).

Understanding these responses as adaptations to past experiences rather than as intentional defiance or disengagement is key to a trauma-informed approach. Educators who recognise trauma's influence on behaviour and learning can shift from a disciplinary mindset to one that seeks to uncover and address the roots of these behaviours, creating a classroom culture that prioritises healing and resilience (Brunzell et al., 2016; Perry, 2006).

The trauma-informed educator asks, "What happened to you?" rather than "What's wrong with you?" This subtle yet powerful shift encourages educators to view behaviour through a lens of empathy, recognising that students' responses often stem from coping mechanisms developed in response to adverse experiences (Cavanaugh, 2016; van der Kolk, 2005). By developing this perspective, teachers not only foster trust and connection with students but also contribute to an environment where academic engagement and emotional safety can flourish.

This chapter builds on the foundation of empathy and supportive school culture discussed in previous chapters, presenting tools and strategies for identifying trauma-related behaviours, understanding their root causes, and responding in ways that reinforce students' sense of safety and belonging. In doing so, educators can support trauma-affected students in managing and ultimately transforming their responses, allowing them to focus on their strengths and progress in both learning and personal growth. By integrating these practices, teachers help cultivate a classroom atmosphere that fosters resilience, understanding, and a deep sense of community for all students.

Recognising Trauma in Students

For educators, recognising trauma in students is a crucial component of creating a safe, supportive classroom environment. Trauma manifests through a range of indicators – emotional, behavioural, and physical – that reflect the impact of adverse experiences on a young person's cognitive and emotional development. These indicators often serve as visible signs of the underlying stress and emotional dysregulation that students experience as they attempt to navigate both past traumas and present challenges in a structured school setting. By learning to interpret these behaviours as expressions of trauma rather than deliberate disruptions, educators can respond in ways that prioritise students' needs for safety, empathy, and support, aligning with the trauma-sensitive practices discussed in earlier chapters.

Emotional Indicators

Emotional indicators of trauma often emerge as mood instability, with students exhibiting rapid shifts between emotions, sometimes triggered by seemingly minor events. Irritability and heightened sensitivity are common; many trauma-affected students operate in a state of hyperarousal, meaning they are on constant alert for potential threats. This hypervigilance is often a deeply ingrained survival mechanism resulting from prolonged exposure to stressful environments. As noted by researchers, this emotional hyperactivity can interfere with students' ability to engage fully in classroom activities and peer interactions (Dods, 2015).

Trauma can also lead to emotional numbness, where students appear detached or indifferent. In some cases, this emotional flatness is a defence mechanism developed to avoid distress, a response to an environment that previously felt unsafe or overwhelming (Spence et al., 2021). Anxiety is another prevalent emotional response among trauma-affected students, who may seem overly cautious, hesitant to participate, or fearful of new situations. This anxious state often manifests as a reluctance to engage with peers or to take academic risks, as their sense of safety feels fragile and easily compromised.

Behavioural Indicators

Behavioural indicators of trauma may include aggression and defiance, responses often misinterpreted as intentional misconduct rather than expressions of distress. Trauma can activate a student's "fight" response, which might present as outward hostility or resistance to authority figures. However, this behaviour is frequently rooted in a need for self-protection rather than wilful defiance (Bartlett et al., 2017; Dods, 2015). Educators who understand these behaviours as defensive strategies developed in response to trauma can respond with compassion and structure, reducing the likelihood of escalation.

Withdrawal is another common behaviour seen in trauma-affected students. For some, detachment or social isolation serves as a protective mechanism to avoid potential emotional harm. Students may avoid interaction with peers and may even become "invisible" in classroom settings, engaging minimally to prevent vulnerability. In other cases, students may exhibit hypervigilance, characterised by constant monitoring of their surroundings and difficulty relaxing or trusting others in their environment. This heightened state of alertness often disrupts the student's capacity to focus on academic tasks or develop meaningful connections within the classroom (McNeeley, 2005).

Physical Indicators

The physical indicators of trauma can be subtle yet telling signs of a student's distress. Somatic symptoms, such as frequent headaches, stomach aches, or other unexplained physical ailments, are common among trauma-affected students. These symptoms reflect the ways in which the body absorbs and manifests stress. For young students, this may include complaints of nausea, fatigue, or general discomfort, all of which can serve as physical outlets for emotional pain. Research suggests that these somatic complaints are often connected to the body's prolonged exposure to stress hormones, which can impair physical health and create an enduring sense of unease or discomfort (Spence et al., 2021).

Understanding these physical manifestations requires educators to consider the mind-body connection inherent in trauma. Physical symptoms should not be dismissed as mere complaints but recognised as legitimate signals of distress, potentially rooted in a student's broader history of adverse experiences. By acknowledging these physical indicators, educators can take proactive steps to create a supportive classroom environment, one that alleviates stress and encourages students to feel safe within the school setting (Figure 6.1).

The Traffic Light Model

◯ Green: Regulated

Calm, engaged, responsive. Support with positive reinforcement and continued learning.

⊗ Yellow: Escalating

Fidgeting, voice changes, withdrawal. Offer breaks, regulation tools, and connection.

ⓘ Red: Crisis

Fight, flight, freeze responses. Focus on safety, de-escalation, and minimal demands.

Figure 6.1 The Traffic Light Model of Trauma Symptoms

Neurobiological Foundations of Trauma Responses

The neurobiological impact of trauma plays a significant role in shaping the emotional, behavioural, and physical indicators described above. Trauma, particularly in early childhood, can disrupt typical brain development, altering areas responsible for emotional regulation, impulse control, and cognitive function. The brain's "fight, flight, or freeze" response, a survival mechanism activated under perceived threat, is especially relevant to understanding trauma-related behaviours. For trauma-affected students, this response is often heightened, making them more prone to intense reactions even in relatively neutral situations.

As explained in Chapter 1, prolonged activation of this stress response can rewire the brain to remain in a constant state of alertness, ready to react defensively to any perceived danger. This neurological adaptation, while protective in threatening environments, becomes maladaptive within the structured context of a classroom. For instance, a student displaying aggression may be experiencing a "fight" response, while another who withdraws might be experiencing a "freeze" reaction (Bartlett et al., 2017; Dods, 2015). By understanding the neurobiological underpinnings of these responses, educators are better equipped to respond appropriately, creating a supportive environment that de-escalates rather than exacerbates students' stress.

Recognising and interpreting these trauma indicators – emotional, behavioural, and physical – requires educators to maintain an attuned, empathetic approach, one that moves beyond surface-level behaviour to the deeper context of each student's experience. When teachers approach students' actions with an understanding of the trauma-informed framework, they reinforce a compassionate, inclusive classroom culture. By fostering this empathetic environment, educators offer trauma-affected students a pathway to resilience, validating their experiences while helping them develop coping skills that enable both personal growth and academic success.

Educator's Role in Recognising Trauma

Recognising trauma in the classroom is a fundamental skill for educators committed to creating safe, inclusive, and supportive learning environments. Trauma often manifests in behaviours that, at first glance, may appear disruptive or defiant. However, a trauma-informed educator understands that these behaviours are typically expressions of deeper emotional struggles, coping mechanisms developed in response to past experiences. Rather than viewing challenging behaviours through a disciplinary lens, educators play a critical role in observing and interpreting these behaviours non-judgementally.

Non-judgemental observation is essential to creating an environment of trust and emotional safety. When educators approach student behaviours without bias, they signal to students that the classroom is a safe space where they are accepted and understood, regardless of their actions. Instead of immediately correcting behaviours or interpreting them as signs of disrespect, trauma-informed educators take a step back, seeking to understand the underlying reasons for these actions. This approach not only fosters a deeper connection with the student but also prevents reinforcing the shame or guilt that trauma-affected students may already experience (Spence et al., 2021). By observing without judgement, educators gain insight into the complexities of students' lives and help create an atmosphere where students feel valued and supported.

A guiding question for this trauma-sensitive approach is, "What happened to you?" rather than "What's wrong with you?" This shift in perspective encourages educators to view behaviours as forms of communication rather than intentional defiance. Often, students affected by trauma are communicating their distress, fear, or need for security through actions that might seem aggressive, withdrawn, or inattentive (Dods, 2015). For instance, a student who appears hostile when asked to participate in a group activity may be expressing an underlying anxiety about social interactions, rooted in previous experiences where they felt vulnerable or unsafe. By adopting the "What happened to you?" approach, teachers can reframe their responses, offering empathy and understanding rather than punitive measures. This reframing builds on the trauma-informed practices discussed in Chapter 3, where behaviours are seen as indicators of students' needs rather than problems to be corrected.

In practice, there are several classroom situations where trauma indicators may surface, requiring the teacher's careful and compassionate interpretation. For example, during a quiet reading session, a student may become visibly agitated, unable to remain still. Rather than assuming the student is simply misbehaving, a trauma-informed educator might recognise this restlessness as a potential sign of trauma-induced anxiety or hypervigilance. In response, the teacher could offer the student a quiet sensory tool or a designated area to move freely, providing a form of support that acknowledges the student's need for physical release.

Another example may occur during group work, where a trauma-affected student withdraws, refusing to engage with their peers. Instead of labelling this as defiance or laziness, a trauma-informed educator might see this withdrawal as a protective mechanism, perhaps linked to past experiences of social exclusion or mistrust. By allowing the student a gentle pathway back into participation, such as assigning them a role with less direct interaction, the teacher respects the student's boundaries while still encouraging social engagement. These small but meaningful adjustments reflect the understanding that trauma-affected students may require alternative pathways to participation, reinforcing the classroom's role as a place of emotional safety.

The trauma-informed educator thus serves as a consistent, empathetic presence in the classroom, recognising that behaviours often communicate unspoken needs. Through non-judgemental observation and a compassionate approach to interpreting behaviours, teachers support students' emotional safety and well-being.

Understanding Challenging Behaviours through a Trauma-Informed Lens

A trauma-informed lens is essential for educators aiming to understand the challenging behaviours frequently displayed by trauma-affected students. Recognising that these behaviours often function as adaptive survival strategies, rather than as deliberate acts of disobedience, enables educators to respond with empathy and appropriate support. Bullard (2021) highlights that shifting from traditional behaviour models to a trauma-informed approach positively impacts student engagement and emotional resilience, especially for those who have encountered adverse childhood experiences (ACEs). Instead of perceiving challenging behaviours merely as disruptions, a trauma-informed approach interprets them as signals of a student's underlying need for safety, stability, or emotional expression (Bullard, 2021; Finkelhor et al., 2007)

Manifestations of Trauma as Challenging Behaviours

Trauma-related behaviours frequently emerge as survival responses, particularly within the framework of the "fight, flight, or freeze" mechanism, which may become heightened in trauma-affected students. These survival behaviours often include aggression, defiance, withdrawal, or hyperactivity. For example, a student who exhibits defiance may actually be manifesting a "fight" response, a protective mechanism shaped by past environments where they felt unsafe. Educators who understand these responses through a trauma-informed lens can move beyond punitive measures, focusing instead on addressing the underlying emotional needs that drive such behaviours (Minahan, 2019; Perry & Szalavitz, 2017).

Attachment theory provides further insight into how trauma manifests in relational dynamics within the classroom, particularly in students' interactions with authority figures and peers. Trauma, especially when experienced early in life, can disrupt a child's ability to form secure attachments, leading to attachment styles characterised by mistrust, boundary-testing, or social withdrawal. As Bullard (2021) notes, students with insecure or disorganised attachment patterns may test the reliability of their relationships with teachers, seeking to establish control or stability. This can result in behaviours like defiance, where students repeatedly challenge authority figures to gauge the consistency and safety of their environment. Alternatively, some students might withdraw from social engagement, seeing relationships as potential sources of emotional threat, a protective adaptation against previous experiences of relational instability (Bowlby, 1988).

Deconstructing Challenging Behaviours

Applying a trauma-informed lens to behaviours such as aggression, withdrawal, and hyperactivity reveals the complex neurological and psychological factors involved. Aggressive behaviour, often viewed as hostile, may represent the "fight" response, wherein students instinctively react to perceived threats, even in safe environments. Bullard (2021) discusses how trauma can prime the brain to detect threats where none objectively exist, leading to impulsive or aggressive reactions that serve as self-protective measures. This heightened vigilance often translates into reactive behaviours when students feel vulnerable or exposed, illustrating that these actions are rooted in the student's physiological responses to stress rather than a conscious choice to disrupt (Bullard, 2021; Cavanaugh, 2016).

Similarly, withdrawal and social disengagement are common trauma responses that may be misunderstood as disinterest or defiance. For some trauma-affected students, "flight" responses lead them to avoid engagement in classroom activities or isolate themselves from peers. Bullard (2021) explains that avoidance is often a defensive mechanism developed to reduce emotional exposure. By recognising this, educators can move away from punitive interpretations and engage students in ways that acknowledge and support their need for security, offering gradual pathways back to involvement in the classroom.

Hyperactivity, often mistaken for behavioural disorders, can also stem from trauma. Trauma-affected students might appear restless or inattentive, not because of a deficit in focus but due to hyperarousal – an ongoing state of heightened alertness. According to Bullard (2021), students in this state may find it difficult to sit still, focus on tasks, or follow instructions, as their nervous systems remain in constant readiness for perceived threats. Recognising hyperactivity as a manifestation of trauma rather than misconduct, educators can adopt trauma-sensitive practices, such as allowing movement breaks or providing calming tools, to help students self-regulate in safe, structured ways (Bullard, 2021).

The Role of Cognitive Impairment in Behavioural Challenges

Trauma also impacts cognitive functioning, often impairing students' ability to focus, manage impulses, and process information. This link between trauma and executive function challenges was highlighted by Bullard (2021), who observed that students with ACEs often struggle to retain new information, manage their emotions, and maintain sustained attention. These cognitive difficulties can make trauma-affected students appear inattentive or disruptive, when in reality they are grappling with the neurological impact of their experiences. As discussed in earlier chapters, the effects of trauma on executive functioning can create barriers to learning and behaviour regulation, leading to a cycle where students face continuous frustration both academically and socially (Brunzell et al., 2016; Minahan, 2019). Educators can support these students by breaking tasks into smaller steps, providing additional instructions, and offering frequent encouragement to mitigate the cognitive load and foster engagement.

Recognising Trauma Triggers

Understanding the role of trauma triggers – environmental or situational cues that evoke a traumatic memory – is essential for educators working with trauma-affected students. Bullard (2021) explains that triggers might include loud noises, sudden changes in routine, or certain physical cues, all of which can evoke intense emotional responses in students. When a student encounters a trigger, their response may seem exaggerated or inappropriate, yet it reflects a deeply rooted physiological reaction. Recognising and managing these triggers within the classroom allows educators to create a safer environment that accommodates students' trauma histories. For instance, an educator aware of a student's sensitivity to noise might use visual cues instead of loud commands to direct attention. Similarly, providing advance notice for schedule changes can help students prepare mentally, reducing their stress responses and supporting their capacity to remain engaged in learning (Bullard, 2021; Perry & Szalavitz, 2017).

In applying a trauma-informed lens, educators redefine challenging behaviours not as obstacles but as opportunities to understand students' experiences and needs. Through non-judgemental observation and empathetic responses, educators can support trauma-affected students in feeling secure and respected, which in turn fosters resilience and emotional growth. This approach aligns with Bullard's (2021) findings that trauma-informed practices benefit not only individual students but also contribute to a classroom environment marked by trust, understanding, and inclusivity, ultimately enhancing learning and well-being for all students.

Intervention Strategies for Trauma-Impacted Students

Implementing trauma-informed intervention strategies requires a holistic approach that balances the needs of the entire classroom with the specific needs of trauma-impacted students. By creating a structured, predictable classroom environment and employing individualised, compassionate intervention techniques, educators can foster a sense of safety that enables students to focus on learning. This section presents a combination of classroom-wide and individual strategies that minimise anxiety, support self-regulation, and promote respectful communication, each essential for a trauma-sensitive environment.

Classroom-Wide Approaches

A key component of trauma-informed practice is establishing a predictable, structured environment. For trauma-impacted students, unpredictability can intensify anxiety, as they may have experienced situations where uncertainty was associated with danger or emotional pain (Bullard, 2021). When routines are stable and transitions are clearly signalled, students are better able to anticipate what comes next, which helps reduce their baseline level of stress. Structured environments support all students, but for those impacted by trauma, they create a framework in which they feel more secure and ready to engage. Perry and Szalavitz (2017) highlight that predictable routines can help regulate the brain's stress response, fostering emotional stability that enhances both learning and social interactions.

A practical strategy for creating such an environment includes establishing clear daily schedules and incorporating visual cues to signal transitions. Posting a visual schedule at the front of the classroom provides students with a reliable reference point throughout the day, which can reduce anxiety related to change. Educators can further reduce stress by giving students a few minutes' notice before any deviation from the routine, using calm, clear language to explain upcoming shifts. This approach supports students' need for control and predictability, essential components of trauma-informed care (Brunzell et al., 2016).

In addition to structure, the classroom can benefit from designated calm spaces where students can take a break when overwhelmed. Such areas offer a refuge for self-regulation, helping students return to a state of calm without needing to leave the classroom entirely. These spaces can include soft seating, sensory tools like stress balls or weighted items, and calming visuals or soft lighting. The goal is to provide a non-punitive "time-out" area where students are encouraged to self-regulate without feeling isolated or shamed. This approach aligns with concepts introduced in Chapters 3 and 5, where emotionally safe classrooms are described as inclusive environments that acknowledge students' emotional needs and support them proactively (Bullard, 2021).

By incorporating these classroom-wide strategies, educators create an environment that respects students' emotional boundaries while providing tools for them to manage stress. Predictable routines, visual supports, and accessible calm spaces collectively foster a climate of emotional security, enabling students to feel more in control and ready to learn.

Individual Intervention Techniques

While classroom-wide strategies provide a foundation of support, trauma-impacted students may require specific, non-punitive interventions that address their unique behavioural challenges. These interventions often involve de-escalation techniques and choices that help students regain a sense of control over their actions, as trauma can often make students feel powerless. Offering choices within boundaries allows students to feel empowered, shifting the dynamic from one of control to collaboration. For example, if a student is struggling to engage with a task, an educator might ask, "Would you prefer to work on this now or in ten minutes?" This simple question gives the student agency, helping them manage their engagement in a way that feels respectful and empowering (Minahan, 2019).

Non-punitive responses to challenging behaviours are crucial in trauma-informed settings. De-escalation techniques, such as using a calm tone, validating the student's emotions, and encouraging deep breathing, help students manage their responses without feeling punished or singled out. For example, when a student becomes visibly upset, an educator might say, "I can see that you're feeling frustrated. Let's take a few deep breaths together." This response validates the student's feelings while offering them a constructive way to self-regulate (Dods, 2015). Techniques like these reinforce the teacher's role as a supportive figure, creating an atmosphere of mutual respect that is essential in trauma-sensitive education.

Restorative practices provide another effective strategy for addressing behaviours without retraumatising students. Unlike traditional disciplinary approaches, restorative practices focus on repairing relationships and fostering accountability through dialogue. When a student's behaviour disrupts the classroom, restorative practices invite them to reflect on their actions, consider their impact on others, and identify steps for moving forward. For example, rather than imposing a consequence, a teacher might facilitate a restorative conversation, asking the student, "How do you think your actions affected your classmates? What could we do differently next time?" This method encourages self-reflection and accountability, emphasising growth and connection rather than punishment (Bullard, 2021; Perry & Szalavitz, 2017). By addressing behaviour in a compassionate, non-punitive way, restorative practices support trauma-impacted students in developing positive coping strategies that foster long-term resilience.

> ## Case Study and Practical Application
>
> ### Case Study: Implementing Trauma-Informed Interventions for a Student Exhibiting Trauma-Related Behaviours
> To illustrate the application of trauma-informed strategies in a classroom, consider the case of James, a Year 5 student exhibiting frequent disruptive outbursts and patterns of withdrawal. James had recently experienced family upheaval, and his behaviours reflected the impact of trauma on his emotional regulation and social engagement. He would often react with aggression when asked to complete tasks and withdraw entirely during group activities. His teacher, Ms. Ellis, noticed these behaviours early in the term and recognised that James might be responding to unaddressed trauma.
>
> Drawing on the trauma-informed strategies outlined in previous chapters, Ms. Ellis approached James's behaviours with a non-punitive mindset, understanding that they were likely survival mechanisms rather than deliberate defiance. She started by implementing predictable routines in her classroom, aiming to create a structured environment that would reduce James's anxiety. Ms. Ellis established a consistent daily schedule and used visual cues to signal upcoming transitions, ensuring that James and his peers had clear expectations, which helped foster a sense of control and stability for James.
>
> When James exhibited outbursts, Ms. Ellis employed de-escalation techniques, maintaining a calm tone and offering him choices to help him feel more in control. For instance, if he became frustrated with a

particular task, she would quietly ask, "Would you like to take a few minutes in the calm corner, or would you like to try a different activity for now?" Providing these options helped James regain agency over his responses and reinforced the classroom's environment of emotional safety. Over time, James began to use the calm corner independently when he felt overwhelmed, showing progress in his ability to self-regulate.

Ms. Ellis also used restorative practices to address conflicts arising from James's reactions with peers. After a particularly tense incident in which he lashed out verbally, she facilitated a restorative conversation between James and the affected students, asking open-ended questions like, "How did that make you feel?" and "What can we do differently next time?" This approach allowed James to reflect on his actions without feeling judged, reinforcing the importance of empathy and self-awareness. Through these restorative practices, James gradually improved his peer relationships and became more comfortable participating in group activities.

In managing these situations, Ms. Ellis prioritised her own self-care, an essential component of sustaining empathy and compassion in trauma-informed teaching. Recognising the emotional demands of working with trauma-affected students, she engaged in regular reflection, journaling her experiences and discussing strategies with colleagues. These self-care practices allowed Ms. Ellis to maintain her patience and resilience, ensuring she could support James and her other students effectively without risking burnout.

Chapter Summary

In this chapter, we have explored essential strategies for recognising and addressing trauma in students, highlighting the educator's role in building a safe, compassionate environment that promotes both academic engagement and emotional healing. By recognising the signs of trauma early and implementing non-punitive interventions, educators create classrooms that support all students, particularly those impacted by adverse experiences.

The Importance of Early Recognition

Identifying trauma indicators early is a crucial step in supporting students' long-term well-being and success. When educators are attuned to behaviours such as irritability, withdrawal, or physical complaints, they are better positioned to offer targeted support before behaviours escalate into more disruptive or self-protective patterns. Early recognition allows for timely, supportive interventions that address students' needs and reinforce a sense of safety and belonging within the classroom. By being observant and responsive, educators lay the groundwork for a trauma-informed environment, building trust and stability for students who may lack these foundations in other areas of their lives.

In addition to supporting individual students, early recognition of trauma signals fosters an inclusive classroom culture where all students feel seen and valued. Educators who actively monitor for these indicators can better understand the underlying challenges their students face, adapting their teaching strategies and expectations to create a nurturing environment conducive to learning. Through their daily interactions, educators not only support trauma-affected students but also model empathy, resilience, and understanding for the entire class, cultivating an environment that promotes healing and growth.

The Non-Punitive, Compassionate Approach

A key principle of trauma-informed education is the shift from punitive responses to empathy-driven interventions. Rather than viewing challenging behaviours as defiance or disobedience, educators who adopt a trauma-informed approach recognise these behaviours as expressions of unmet needs or protective mechanisms. By responding with compassion and understanding, teachers help students feel secure and respected, fostering a sense of trust that is essential for their emotional and academic growth.

Empathy-driven responses benefit the entire classroom, enhancing peer relationships and creating a more supportive learning environment. When students witness their teacher handling difficult situations with patience and care, they learn the value of empathy and respect, reinforcing positive behaviours among peers. This non-punitive approach also reduces the likelihood of re-traumatising students who may already be sensitive to authority and discipline, contributing to a school culture rooted in trust, safety, and mutual respect. Ultimately, trauma-informed interventions not only support individual well-being but also enrich the classroom dynamics, enabling all students to thrive in an environment where compassion is valued over punishment.

Guiding Questions for Reflection

1. **What are the common signs of trauma in students?**
   Reflect on the behaviours you observe in your classroom. Are there students displaying signs of trauma such as mood swings, withdrawal, or heightened sensitivity? Identifying these signs is the first step in offering meaningful support.

2. **How can teachers respond effectively to challenging behaviours linked to trauma?**
   Consider your responses to challenging behaviours. Are there areas where you could incorporate more trauma-sensitive practices, such as providing choices or using empathetic language? Identifying opportunities to adjust your approach can strengthen your role in supporting trauma-impacted students.

3. **How does a non-punitive approach impact classroom dynamics?**
   Reflect on the effects of empathy-driven responses in your classroom. How does a compassionate approach to behaviour management influence students' relationships and engagement? Understanding this impact can reinforce your commitment to trauma-informed practices.

4. **What strategies can be implemented to create a supportive, trauma-informed classroom environment?**
   Evaluate the strategies you currently use to support emotional safety, such as calm spaces or predictable routines. Are there additional methods you could integrate to build a more trauma-sensitive classroom? Identifying these steps can help you enhance your role in fostering an environment that promotes healing and learning for all students.

Teachers Toolbox

Teachers' Toolbox for Chapter 6

STRATEGY	DESCRIPTION
TRAUMA OBSERVATION CHECKLIST	Use this checklist to identify potential signs of trauma in students. Track emotional (e.g., mood swings, sensitivity), behavioural (e.g., aggression, withdrawal), and physical indicators (e.g., somatic complaints like headaches). Document patterns weekly and seek input from support staff when needed. This helps in early recognition and intervention before behaviours escalate
STRUCTURED, PREDICTABLE ROUTINES	Establish a clear daily schedule with visual aids for younger students or those with reading difficulties. Display the schedule in a visible location, and give students a few minutes' warning before transitions to reduce anxiety. Stability through routines is critical for trauma-impacted students, helping them feel more in control of their environment
CALM SPACES FOR SELF-REGULATION	Designate a calm area within the classroom with sensory tools such as stress balls, weighted blankets, or noise-cancelling headphones. Encourage students to use this space when they feel overwhelmed. This approach offers a non-punitive option for self-regulation and aligns with creating emotionally safe environments
NON-PUNITIVE BEHAVIOUR RESPONSES	Respond to challenging behaviours using de-escalation techniques rather than punitive measures. Speak calmly, validate the student's feelings, and offer choices to empower them. For example, ask, "Would you like a break, or do you want to try another activity?" This approach supports students in regaining control and reduces the likelihood of further escalation
RESTORATIVE CONVERSATIONS	Use restorative conversations to address conflicts and help students reflect on their actions without judgement. For instance, ask questions like, "How do you feel about what happened?" or "What can we do to make things right?" This strategy fosters accountability and relationship repair, supporting a trauma-informed, non-punitive approach.

(Continued)

(Continued)

STRATEGY	DESCRIPTION
EMPATHY-BASED COMMUNICATION	Engage with students using phrases that acknowledge their emotions. For example, say, "I can see you're feeling upset. Let's work together to find a solution." Use active listening, reflective responses, and maintain a calm tone to demonstrate empathy. Empathetic communication reinforces emotional safety and promotes trust between teacher and student
TEACHER SELF-CARE ROUTINE	Incorporate regular self-care practices to maintain resilience. This could include daily mindfulness exercises, setting boundaries around work hours, or connecting with a peer support network for shared experiences and encouragement. Practising self-care not only benefits teachers but also enables them to approach trauma-impacted students with greater patience and empathy
STUDENT COPING SKILLS TOOLBOX	Teach students basic coping techniques like deep breathing, counting to ten, or guided visualisation for managing stress. Integrate these practices into the classroom routine, and model their use during times of transition or when students appear anxious. Regular use of coping strategies can help trauma-affected students develop self-regulation skills over time

References

Bartlett, J. D., Smith, S., & Bringewatt, E. (2017). Helping young children who have experienced trauma: Policies and strategies for early care and education. https://doi.org/10.7916/d8-f1gn-7n98

Blair, C., & Raver, C. C. (2015). School readiness and self-regulation: A developmental psychobiological approach. *Annual Review of Psychology, 66*(1), 711–731.

Bowlby, J. (1988) Developmental psychiatry comes of age. *The American Journal of Psychiatry, 145,* 1–10.

Brunzell, T., Stokes, H., & Waters, L. (2016). Trauma-informed positive education: Using positive psychology to strengthen vulnerable students. *Contemporary School Psychology, 20,* 63–83. https://doi.org/10.1007/s40688-015-0070-x

Bullard, M. (2021). Strengthening the impact of using a trauma-informed lens in the classroom. *Kairaranga, 22*(1), 50–65. https://doi.org/10.54322/kairaranga.v22i1.357

Cavanaugh, B. (2016). Trauma-informed classrooms and schools. *Beyond Behavior, 25*(2), 41–46. https://doi.org/10.1177/107429561602500206

Copeland, W. E., Keeler, G., Angold, A., & Costello, E. J. (2007). Traumatic events and posttraumatic stress in childhood. *Archives of General Psychiatry, 64*(5), 577–584. https://doi.org/10.1001/archpsyc.64.5.577

Costello, J., Erkanli, A., Fairbank, J., & Angold, A. (2002). The prevalence of potentially traumatic events in childhood and adolescence. *Journal of Traumatic Stress, 15*(2), 99–112. https://doi.org/10.1023/a:1014851823163

Dods, J. (2015). Bringing trauma to school: Sharing the educational experience of three youths. *Exceptionality Education International, 25*(1), 112–135. https://doi.org/10.5206/eei.v25i1.7719

Finkelhor, D., Ormrod, R. K., & Turner, H. A. (2007). Poly-victimization: A neglected component in child victimization. *Child Abuse & Neglect, 31*(1), 7–26. https://doi.org/10.1016/j.chiabu.2006.06.008

McEwen, B. S. (2012). Brain on stress: How the social environment gets under the skin. *Proceedings of the National Academy of Sciences, 109*(Supplement_2), 17180–17185.

McNeeley, C. (2005). Connection to school. In K. A. Moore & L. H. Lippman (Eds.), *What do children need to flourish: Conceptualizing and measuring indicators of positive development* (pp. 289–303). Springer.

Minahan, J. (2019). Trauma-informed teaching strategies. *Educational Leadership, 77*(2), 30–35.

Perry, B. D. (2006). Applying principles of neurodevelopment to clinical work with maltreated and traumatized children: The neurosequential model of therapeutics. In N. Boyd Webb (Ed.), *Working with traumatized youth in child welfare* (pp. 27–52). Guilford Press.

Perry, B. D., & Szalavitz, M. (2017). *The boy who was raised as a dog and other stories from a child psychiatrist's notebook: What traumatized children can teach us about loss, love, and healing*. Basic Books.

Spence, R., Kagan, L., Kljakovic, M., & Bifulco, A. (2021). Understanding trauma in children and young people in the school setting. *Educational and Child Psychology, 38*(1), 87–98. https://shop.bps.org.uk/educational-child-psychology-vol-38-no-1-march-2021-trauma

Van der Kolk, B. A. (2005). Developmental. *Psychiatric Annals, 35*(5), 401.

7 Trauma-Informed Communication and Crisis Intervention

Introduction to Trauma-Informed Communication and Crisis Management

In trauma-informed classrooms, every interaction – both verbal and non-verbal – has the potential to support or destabilise students. For trauma-affected students, who may experience heightened emotional responses to everyday challenges, the way teachers communicate can make a profound difference. Understanding how to recognise and respond to signs of distress is critical to maintaining a safe and supportive learning environment.

This chapter builds on foundational trauma-informed principles, offering educators practical strategies for managing and de-escalating crisis situations. By focusing on both the immediate and long-term needs of students, teachers can help them navigate moments of heightened emotion while maintaining the stability of the broader classroom community. The tools and techniques presented here highlight the importance of empathy, calmness, and collaboration, ensuring that every student feels valued, respected, and supported during challenging moments.

Through reflective case studies, step-by-step strategies, and opportunities for skill-building, this chapter equips educators with the confidence to respond to crises effectively. By integrating these approaches into daily practice, teachers contribute to a trauma-informed culture that fosters trust, emotional resilience, and learning for all students.

DOI: 10.4324/9781003535386-8

Trauma-Sensitive Communication

Trauma-sensitive communication is fundamental to effective intervention. Using language that acknowledges and validates students' emotions fosters a sense of empathy and security, encouraging students to feel understood and respected. Simple, compassionate phrases can make a substantial difference in how students experience interactions with authority figures. For example, instead of reacting sternly to a student's outburst, a teacher might say, "I can see that you're really upset. Let's take a moment to figure out what you need." Such statements convey empathy, validating the student's feelings without judgement and offering them a collaborative path to resolution (Spence et al., 2021).

This approach to communication is closely aligned with the empathy and compassion strategies discussed in Chapter 4. Educators who communicate in a trauma-sensitive manner not only support students' immediate emotional needs but also model positive interpersonal skills that students can apply in their own interactions. For trauma-impacted students, feeling seen and acknowledged is crucial for building trust, which can significantly impact their willingness to engage in the classroom. As Bullard (2021) emphasises, consistent, empathetic communication reinforces a supportive environment where students feel valued and understood, laying the groundwork for effective learning and emotional development.

In addition, trauma-sensitive communication includes active listening, where teachers give students space to express their feelings without interruption or correction. When students are given the opportunity to articulate their emotions, they develop greater self-awareness and emotional regulation skills. Educators can support this process by using open-ended questions and reflective listening, such as responding with, "It sounds like you're feeling overwhelmed. Would you like to talk about what's bothering you?" This approach not only validates students' experiences but also encourages them to develop language skills for identifying and expressing emotions constructively.

Trauma-informed intervention strategies, when implemented thoughtfully, transform the classroom into a space of safety, empathy, and resilience. By integrating structured routines, calm spaces, individualised support, and compassionate communication, educators create an environment where trauma-impacted students feel empowered and capable. Such interventions allow students to build trust, develop self-regulation skills, and engage positively with their peers and learning experiences, reinforcing the foundational principles of trauma-informed education discussed in earlier chapters. Through these strategies, teachers foster a classroom culture that respects each student's unique needs and experiences, promoting healing and growth for all.

Core Techniques for Trauma-Informed Communication

Active Listening

Active listening is at the heart of trauma-informed communication. It involves giving students your full attention, withholding judgement, and resisting the urge to interrupt. For students who may feel dismissed or invalidated in other areas of their lives, being genuinely heard by an adult can be profoundly affirming (Adams et al., 2022). Active listening communicates that their experiences and emotions matter, which is a powerful way to build trust and safety.

Practically, this means leaning into the conversation with open body language, reflecting back what the student shares, and validating their feelings. A simple response like, "It sounds like you're feeling overwhelmed," can help students feel acknowledged and understood, which is often enough to ease their anxiety and encourage further communication.

Non-Verbal Communication

Non-verbal cues often speak louder than words, particularly for trauma-affected students who may be acutely attuned to perceived threats. A calm tone of voice, relaxed posture, and gentle gestures can convey safety and approachability, whereas crossed arms, a raised voice, or sudden movements might trigger fear or defensive reactions (Gebb, 2023).

Maintaining consistent eye contact – without being overly intense – and using gestures that invite rather than command interaction can help students feel at ease. These subtle forms of communication play a critical role in reducing stress and creating a classroom atmosphere where students feel safe to share and engage.

Empathy and Validation

Empathy and validation are vital tools in trauma-informed communication. Empathy allows teachers to step into the emotional world of their students, understanding their feelings and struggles from a place of genuine care. Validation takes this a step further by explicitly acknowledging those emotions. For example, saying, "I can see this has been a tough day for you," reassures students that their experiences are seen and respected (Sandoval, 2013).

Validation is particularly effective in de-escalating challenging behaviours. When students feel that their emotions are recognised rather than dismissed, they are less likely to become defensive or shut down. Over time, this builds a classroom culture where students feel secure in expressing themselves and trusting their teachers.

The Importance of Positive Teacher-Student Relationships

Trauma-informed communication underpins the development of strong, positive teacher-student relationships. Research shows that when students trust their teachers, they are more likely to engage, take risks in their learning, and seek help when needed (Brock et al., 2013). These relationships are particularly important for trauma-affected students, who often face difficulties in forming connections due to past experiences of betrayal or neglect.

By combining active listening, mindful non-verbal communication, and empathetic validation, teachers can build the kind of trust that supports both emotional well-being and academic success. These strategies align with trauma-informed principles, which prioritise safety, trust, and collaboration in creating a classroom environment where all students can thrive.

Crisis Intervention in a Trauma-Informed Classroom

Understanding Crisis Situations

Crisis situations in a classroom setting are unpredictable events that can disrupt the learning environment and significantly impact students' emotional and psychological well-being. For trauma-affected students, even minor incidents – such as a sudden loud noise or unexpected changes in routine – can feel overwhelming and may trigger a fight, flight, or freeze response. As highlighted by Brock et al. (2013), these heightened reactions often stem from past experiences that have left students in a state of hypervigilance, making it difficult for them to differentiate between safe and unsafe situations in real time.

In the classroom, a crisis might manifest as a behavioural outburst, a student withdrawing entirely, or an escalation in anxiety-driven behaviours such as pacing, rapid speech, or defiance. For trauma-sensitive educators, recognising these signs early is critical to intervening effectively. Indicators of escalating behaviour can include clenched fists, rapid breathing, raised voices, or sudden physical withdrawal (Sandoval, 2013). By remaining attuned to these signals, teachers can act proactively to de-escalate the situation before it worsens.

As already covered in Chapter 4, empathy and self-awareness are key tools for educators when navigating such moments. Teachers must not only interpret the student's behaviour through a trauma-informed lens but also manage their own emotional responses. Reacting calmly and compassionately, rather than with frustration or urgency, sets the tone for a resolution that prioritises the student's safety and dignity.

Immediate Response Strategies

When a crisis arises, the immediate goal is to stabilise the situation while minimising harm to the student, their peers, and the teacher. Trauma-informed approaches emphasise responses that are calm, non-punitive, and focused on meeting the student's emotional needs in the moment. Punitive measures, such as removing the student abruptly or raising one's voice, often escalate the crisis, leaving the student feeling further alienated and misunderstood (Gebb, 2023).

Key immediate response strategies include:

1. **Creating a Calm and Predictable Presence:** The teacher's tone, body language, and words must convey calmness and control. Speaking slowly and softly can help de-escalate the situation, while abrupt or loud responses may heighten the student's anxiety. Positioning oneself at the student's eye level rather than standing over them reduces the perception of threat and creates a sense of connection.
2. **Offering Choices and Control:** Trauma-affected students often feel powerless during crises. Providing them with simple choices – such as stepping outside for a moment or moving to a quieter part of the room – can restore a sense of agency and prevent the situation from escalating further (Brunzell et al., 2019)

3. **Grounding Techniques:** Grounding exercises are particularly effective in helping students regain control of their emotions. Simple techniques like deep breathing, counting objects in the room, or naming things they can see, hear, or touch can interrupt the cycle of panic and reorient the student to the present moment (Horner et al., 2010). Teachers can model these techniques or guide students through them gently, ensuring that the approach feels supportive rather than instructional.
4. **Minimising Stimulation:** For students who are easily overwhelmed, reducing external stimuli – such as dimming lights, lowering noise levels, or moving other students to a different area – can help create a more soothing environment. These adjustments not only support the student in crisis but also prevent their peers from becoming overly distressed by the situation.

As Chapter 6 outlined, the educator's response during a crisis must balance empathy with structure, ensuring that the student feels supported while maintaining the overall safety of the classroom. A trauma-informed response focuses on immediate regulation rather than assigning blame, recognising that the behaviour is a symptom of the student's internal struggle rather than an intentional act of disruption (Figure 7.1).

De-escalation Steps

Recognise Early Signs

Notice changes in behavior, body language, or engagement.

Maintain Calm Presence

Regulate your own emotions and responses.

Reduce Demands

Simplify instructions and minimize stimulation.

Offer Choices

Provide options to restore sense of control.

Support Regulation

Guide through breathing or grounding techniques.

Figure 7.1 Steps for Responding to Student Escalation Using a Calm and Regulated Approach

Post-Crisis Support

After a crisis has subsided, the focus shifts to recovery and repair. This phase is critical for helping the affected student process their emotions, rebuild their sense of safety, and reintegrate into the classroom community. Post-crisis support also reinforces the trauma-informed principles of trust and collaboration, as highlighted in Chapter 5.

1. **Debriefing with the Student:** Providing the student with a safe and private space to reflect on what occurred can help them make sense of the event and their emotional response. During this debriefing, it is important for the teacher to approach the conversation without judgement. Questions like, "How were you feeling when that happened?" or "What can I do to help you if this happens again?" invite the student to share their perspective and feel validated.

    Teachers can also use this time to reinforce grounding techniques, discussing what worked during the crisis and exploring other strategies that the student might find helpful in the future. This collaborative approach empowers the student and strengthens their trust in the teacher.

2. **Rebuilding Trust and Safety:** A crisis can leave trauma-affected students feeling vulnerable and embarrassed, particularly if their peers witnessed the event. Reassuring the student that they are not defined by the incident is vital for restoring their confidence and sense of belonging. Simple affirmations, such as "I know today was hard, but I'm proud of how you're trying," can go a long way in rebuilding trust.

    Re-establishing safety also involves ensuring that the broader class understands what occurred without breaching the student's privacy. Teachers can frame the incident as an opportunity to model empathy and support, emphasising that everyone has challenging moments and that the classroom is a space where mistakes and emotions are okay.

3. **Restorative Practices:** If the crisis impacted the class dynamics – for example, by causing fear or disruption – restorative practices can help repair relationships and rebuild a sense of community. This might involve a class discussion about managing stress, sharing coping strategies, or engaging in a collective activity that fosters collaboration and positive engagement.

Linking Back to Trauma-Informed Principles

Trauma-informed crisis intervention is not a standalone practice but an extension of the principles outlined throughout this book. As Chapter 5 explored, creating a supportive school culture requires systemic approaches that prioritise emotional safety and inclusivity. Crisis intervention provides an opportunity to embody these principles in action, demonstrating to students that their well-being is a priority.

By responding to crises with calmness, empathy, and a focus on repair, teachers reinforce the values of trust, collaboration, and empowerment that underpin trauma-informed education. Over time, these consistent responses contribute to a classroom environment where students feel secure, respected, and capable of overcoming challenges.

Through these strategies, educators not only manage the immediate effects of a crisis but also lay the groundwork for resilience and growth, supporting students in becoming active participants in their learning and their community.

De-escalation Techniques

Verbal De-escalation Techniques

Verbal de-escalation is a vital skill for educators working with trauma-affected students. When tensions rise in the classroom, a teacher's ability to respond calmly and empathetically can prevent a challenging situation from escalating into a crisis. The strategies outlined here focus on creating a supportive environment where students feel heard, respected, and safe.

Step 1: Speak Slowly and Softly

The first step in verbal de-escalation is to adopt a tone that conveys calmness and reassurance. Speaking slowly and softly not only prevents overwhelming the student but also signals that the teacher is in control of their emotions. Research shows that a calm tone can help reduce the student's perception of threat and encourage a more measured response (van der Kolk, 2014). This approach aligns with trauma-informed principles, which emphasise the importance of reducing anxiety through predictable and soothing interactions (SAMHSA, 2014).

Step 2: Use Reflective Language

Reflective language is a powerful tool for de-escalation because it validates the student's feelings and demonstrates empathy. By paraphrasing the student's words or emotions – such as saying, "It sounds like you're really frustrated right now" – the teacher acknowledges the student's experience without judgement. This technique not only helps the student feel understood but also encourages them to articulate their emotions more clearly, reducing the likelihood of further escalation (Sandoval, 2013).

Reflective language also shifts the focus from behaviour to emotions, reinforcing the trauma-informed perspective that challenging behaviours often stem from unmet needs or internal distress. As Gebb (2023) highlights, responding to students with empathy and validation fosters trust and supports emotional regulation, key components of a trauma-sensitive classroom.

Step 3: Offer Choices

Trauma-affected students often struggle with feelings of powerlessness, which can intensify during moments of stress. Offering simple choices – such as asking if the student would prefer to step outside or move to a quieter space – restores a sense of control and agency. This strategy not only de-escalates tension but also empowers the student to take ownership of their response, aligning with the trauma-informed principle of collaboration (Walkley & Cox, 2013).

Providing choices also helps to redirect the student's focus from the source of their distress to actionable steps they can take to regain calm. For instance, a teacher might say, "Would you like to take a break for a few minutes, or would it help if I sat with you quietly?" Such options reassure the student that their needs are being prioritised and reduce the pressure to conform to the classroom's demands immediately.

The Importance of Neutral, Non-Threatening Language

In all interactions, it is crucial to use language that is neutral and non-threatening. Avoiding statements that might be perceived as commands – such as "You need to calm down now" – prevents the student from feeling cornered or defensive. Instead, phrasing that conveys support, such as "Let's figure this out together," encourages cooperation and reinforces the teacher-student relationship (Brock et al., 2013).

Neutral language also helps to maintain the overall emotional safety of the classroom, ensuring that other students do not become anxious or reactive in response to the interaction. By modelling calm and respectful communication, teachers set the tone for a supportive learning environment that benefits all students.

Non-Verbal De-escalation Techniques

Non-verbal communication often speaks louder than words, particularly in high-stress situations where students may be hyper-attuned to perceived threats. Trauma-affected students, in particular, are likely to interpret body language, tone, and facial expressions as cues about their safety and worth. For this reason, non-verbal de-escalation strategies are as important as verbal ones in maintaining a calm and supportive classroom environment.

Relaxed Posture and Avoiding Sudden Movements

Maintaining a relaxed posture is one of the simplest yet most effective ways to signal safety. Standing or sitting with an open stance – arms uncrossed, shoulders relaxed, and movements deliberate – helps to convey that the teacher is approachable and not a threat. Sudden or abrupt movements, on the other hand, can escalate the student's anxiety, particularly if they have a history of trauma that has heightened their sensitivity to physical cues (Van der Kolk, 2003).

Taking slow, intentional steps and remaining mindful of the student's personal space further reduces the likelihood of triggering a defensive reaction. These small adjustments demonstrate respect for the student's boundaries while maintaining the teacher's authority and composure.

Positioning at Eye Level

Standing over a seated or crouching student can be perceived as intimidating, particularly for those who have experienced power imbalances in past relationships. Positioning oneself at the student's eye level reduces the perception of threat and fosters a sense of equality and mutual respect (Sandoval, 2013). This technique also makes it easier for the teacher to establish eye contact without appearing confrontational, creating an opportunity for connection and reassurance.

Avoiding Confrontational Body Language

Crossed arms, a furrowed brow, or a tense jaw are all examples of body language that may inadvertently communicate frustration or disapproval. For students who are already feeling vulnerable, such cues can exacerbate their distress and lead to further escalation. Instead, teachers should strive to maintain an open and neutral expression, using gentle gestures to reinforce their verbal communication.

In moments of heightened tension, even subtle changes in posture or facial expression can make a significant difference. For instance, leaning slightly forward while maintaining a relaxed stance signals engagement and attentiveness, whereas leaning back with crossed arms may appear dismissive or aloof. By being intentional about their non-verbal cues, teachers can create an environment that feels both physically and emotionally safe.

Connecting Non-Verbal Strategies to Classroom Safety

The non-verbal de-escalation techniques described here align closely with the principles of trauma-informed education, as outlined in earlier chapters. As Chapter 3 emphasised, emotional safety is foundational to a positive teacher-student relationship. Non-verbal communication plays a critical role in establishing this safety, particularly for students who rely on visual and physical cues to assess their environment.

Similarly, Chapter 5 highlighted the importance of creating a supportive school culture that prioritises inclusivity and trust. Non-verbal strategies such as relaxed posture, open gestures, and mindful positioning contribute to this culture by ensuring that all students feel respected and valued, regardless of their behavioural challenges.

By integrating these techniques into their daily practice, teachers can not only prevent escalation but also model the calm and respectful interactions they wish to see in their students. Over time, these consistent responses help to build a classroom environment where trust, empathy, and collaboration are the norm, rather than the exception.

Addressing Violent or Unsafe Crises in the Classroom

While most classroom crises can be managed with trauma-informed communication and de-escalation techniques, there are situations where safety becomes the immediate priority. When a student's behaviour poses a danger to themselves, their peers, or the teacher, the primary focus must shift to ensuring the well-being of all involved. In these cases, the initial steps often require securing the safety of the group before addressing the underlying causes of the crisis.

Prioritising Safety Over Resolution

In violent or unsafe situations, the teacher's first responsibility is to protect all students in the classroom. If a student's actions threaten the safety of others, calmly instructing the class to exit the room or move to a pre-designated safe area is the appropriate first step. Phrases such as "Everyone, please leave the room quickly and wait in the hallway" help maintain order while de-escalating panic. Teachers should position themselves to monitor the student in crisis while ensuring the rest of the class is safely evacuated.

In some cases, such as when a student is actively self-harming, the teacher may need to remain with the student while simultaneously calling for immediate assistance. Ensuring that additional staff or external support, such as school leadership or emergency services, is contacted promptly is critical to managing such situations effectively.

Involving Support Systems

When safety is at risk, teachers should not hesitate to involve additional staff, school leadership, or external agencies. Most schools have crisis protocols in place for these situations, and teachers should be familiar with their specific roles and responsibilities. For example, in schools with crisis response teams, teachers may alert designated staff who are trained to handle physical or violent disruptions. For extreme situations involving imminent harm, emergency services should be contacted immediately.

Trauma-Informed Safety Responses

Even in cases of imminent danger, trauma-informed principles remain relevant. While safety must take precedence, maintaining calm and avoiding escalation are key. For example, using a firm but steady tone, rather than shouting or appearing panicked, can prevent further agitation. Avoiding confrontational language and maintaining open body language where possible can also reduce perceived threats.

Additionally, recognising that such behaviours often stem from overwhelming emotions or past trauma allows educators to approach these situations with a mindset of care, even when intervention is necessary. This perspective can guide restorative actions after the immediate danger has passed, ensuring that the student receives support rather than solely punitive responses.

Balancing Safety and Compassion

Ensuring safety does not mean abandoning compassion. After a violent or unsafe crisis, follow-up actions should include a debrief with both the class and the individual student to restore trust and address any emotional or psychological impacts. Restorative approaches, such as facilitating conversations about how to repair relationships or providing the student with access to counselling, can help rebuild the classroom community and reduce the likelihood of future incidents.

By prioritising safety, seeking appropriate support, and maintaining a trauma-informed perspective, teachers can navigate even the most challenging crises with professionalism and care, protecting all students while setting the stage for recovery and growth.

Creating Trauma-Informed Classrooms

Case Study and Practical Strategies

Scenario: A Heated Outburst Escalates

The classroom is busy with group discussions during a social studies lesson. Liam, a student who often struggles with anxiety, sits at his desk with a tense expression. His group is brainstorming, but Liam has withdrawn, tapping his pencil aggressively against the desk. One of his peers says, "Come on, Liam, just say something!" Frustration builds, and suddenly, Liam throws his pencil across the room and shouts, "Leave me alone! You don't even care!" He pushes his chair back forcefully, knocking it over, and storms towards the door, his face flushed and breathing heavy.

The rest of the class freezes. Some students whisper, while others look visibly scared. A few giggle nervously, but the teacher recognises the seriousness of the situation. Rather than reacting with immediate authority or raising their voice, the teacher focuses on de-escalating the crisis with trauma-informed strategies.

Step 1: Stay Calm and Validate

The teacher takes a deep breath, steadies their posture, and keeps their voice low and controlled. They step towards Liam slowly, staying at a respectful distance, and say, "Liam, I can see that you're really upset right now. It's okay to feel that way. Let's take a moment."

This use of calm, validating language acknowledges Liam's emotions without assigning blame or judgement. The teacher avoids demanding that Liam sit down or stop shouting, recognising that such directives might escalate his distress further.

Step 2: Defuse the Immediate Threat

Recognising that the situation is distressing for the rest of the class, the teacher gestures to the other students and says quietly but firmly, "Let's all focus on our own work for now. I'll take care of this." This reassures the class while keeping the focus on de-escalating Liam's outburst.

The teacher then offers Liam a choice, saying, "Would you like to step outside with me, or would you feel better taking a few breaths here?" By presenting Liam with options, the teacher restores a sense of agency, which is critical for trauma-affected students who may feel powerless during moments of distress.

Liam hesitates, still visibly upset, but eventually nods towards the door. The teacher maintains a calm and steady presence, ensuring the other students feel secure as they guide Liam out of the classroom.

Step 3: Regulate and Reflect
Outside the classroom, the teacher uses grounding techniques to help Liam regain control of his emotions. "Let's take a few slow breaths together. Breathe in through your nose … and out through your mouth." They guide Liam through the exercise until his breathing slows and his shoulders relax.

Once Liam appears calmer, the teacher engages in a reflective conversation. "What happened in there? Can you tell me what was going on?"

Initially, Liam shrugs, but with gentle prompting, he shares, "They weren't listening to me. They always ignore my ideas."

The teacher validates Liam's perspective: "I understand how that would feel really frustrating. It's hard when it seems like no one's hearing you."

However, the teacher also introduces a restorative element, helping Liam reflect on his actions. "You know, it's okay to feel upset, but throwing things and shouting made it harder for us to solve the problem. What do you think we could do differently next time?"

This approach helps Liam process his emotions and acknowledges the impact of his behaviour on the group. The teacher reinforces that emotions are valid, but there are better ways to express them. "Maybe next time, you could raise your hand and let me know how you're feeling so we can fix it before it gets too big. Does that sound like a plan?"

Through this balanced conversation, the teacher not only supports Liam's emotional recovery but also guides him towards more constructive responses in the future. They conclude with reassurance: "Let's head back inside. I'll talk to your group about making sure everyone gets a chance to share their ideas."

Chapter Summary

This chapter has explored the critical role of trauma-informed communication, de-escalation techniques, and practical strategies in supporting students during moments of heightened emotional distress. By integrating theoretical frameworks with actionable tools, educators can create a classroom environment that prioritises safety, trust, and emotional regulation.

The Crisis Intervention in a Trauma-Informed Classroom section emphasised the importance of recognising early signs of distress and responding with non-punitive, calm interventions. Strategies such as offering choices and using grounding techniques allow teachers to support students in regaining control over their emotions while maintaining the stability of the broader classroom. Post-crisis support, including reflective conversations and restorative practices, ensures that trust and safety are rebuilt after challenging incidents.

In the De-escalation Techniques section, both verbal and non-verbal methods were detailed to help educators manage tense situations effectively. Verbal strategies such as reflective language and empathetic validation demonstrate to students that their emotions are understood, while non-verbal techniques like maintaining a relaxed posture and positioning oneself at eye level reinforce a sense of safety. Together, these approaches not only de-escalate immediate tensions but also model respectful and constructive communication.

Finally, the Case Study and Practical Strategies section illustrated the application of trauma-informed principles through a realistic classroom scenario. The case study demonstrated how educators can employ calm language, non-verbal reassurance, and reflective conversations to navigate a crisis and support emotional recovery. The accompanying toolkit and role-play scenarios provide teachers with practical tools to refine their responses and build confidence in managing similar situations.

This chapter reinforces the idea that trauma-informed practices are not isolated interventions but part of a holistic approach to creating supportive and inclusive learning environments. By responding to crises with empathy, structure, and a focus on growth, educators can empower students to navigate their challenges and foster a resilient classroom culture.

Guiding Questions

1. **Understanding Crisis and Communication:**
   - How can recognising the early signs of distress in a student help prevent a situation from escalating into a crisis?
   - Why is it important to validate a student's emotions during moments of tension, and how can this impact the overall classroom environment?

2. **Applying De-escalation Techniques:**
   - What are the key verbal strategies that can be used to de-escalate a student's heightened emotions?
   - How does body language, such as maintaining a relaxed posture or positioning at eye level, contribute to creating a sense of safety during a crisis?

3. **Reflecting on Trauma-Informed Practices:**
   - Why is offering choices during a crisis an effective way to empower students and reduce tension?
   - How can teachers use grounding techniques, such as deep breathing or sensory exercises, to help students regain control during a crisis?

4. **Post-Crisis Reflection and Growth:**
   - What role do restorative conversations play in helping students learn constructive ways to express their emotions?
   - How can a teacher balance validating a student's feelings with encouraging accountability for their actions?

Teachers Toolbox

Teachers' Toolbox for Chapter 7

STRATEGY	DESCRIPTION
EMPATHY LOOP	Use a reflective cycle of listening, validating, and rephrasing the student's concerns (e.g., "You're feeling [emotion] because [reason]. Did I get that right?").

(Continued)

(Continued)

STRATEGY	DESCRIPTION
ENVIRONMENTAL SOFTENING	Adjust the physical environment during crises, such as dimming lights, lowering noise levels, or clearing the immediate area to reduce external stressors.
SILENT PRESENCE	Sit near the student quietly without engaging verbally to provide calm, non-threatening support when they are unable to communicate or process verbal interaction.
COLLABORATIVE RESET	Involve the student in co-developing a quick, restorative plan for re-engaging after a disruption (e.g., "How do you think we can move forward from here?").
TIMED INTERVENTIONS	Offer the student a fixed amount of time to collect themselves before re-engaging with the class, framed as support rather than consequence.
CONNECTION CUES	Use non-verbal gestures like an open hand or a slight nod to signal availability for support without interrupting their process.
EMOTION NAMING	Help students identify and label their emotions during heightened states to reduce confusion and foster self-awareness.
SCHEDULED REGULATION ACTIVITIES	Build regular, calming activities into the daily schedule (e.g., morning mindfulness or post-recess breathing exercises) to pre-emptively manage tension.
RAPID CHECK-INS	Conduct brief, one-on-one check-ins with students during transitions to assess emotional states and provide reassurance as needed.
DECODING BEHAVIOURS	Frame observed behaviours as signals of underlying needs and verbalise possible explanations with the student to foster insight and reduce defensive reactions.

References

Adams, C. R., Blueford, J. M., & Diambra, J. F. (2022). Trauma-informed crisis intervention. *Journal of Professional Counseling: Practice, Theory & Research*. https://doi.org/10.1080/15566382.2022.2148810

Brock, S. E., Ballard, J. M., & Saad, L. E. (2013). The PREPaRE model: Crisis prevention and intervention in schools. *School Psychology Review, 42*(2), 258–274.

Brunzell, T., Stokes, H., & Waters, L. (2019). Shifting teacher practice in trauma-affected classrooms: Practice pedagogy strategies within a trauma-informed positive education model. *School Mental Health, 11*(3), 600–614. https://doi.org/10.1007/s12310-018-09308-8

Bullard, M. (2021). Strengthening the impact of using a trauma-informed lens in the classroom. *Kairaranga, 22*(1), 50–65. https://doi.org/10.54322/kairaranga.v22i1.357

Gebb, A. (2023). Improving crisis communication through a trauma-informed lens: A guide for institutions of higher education. (Unpublished Master's thesis). California State University, Chico.

Horner, R. H., Sugai, G., & Anderson, C. M. (2010). Examining the evidence base for school-wide positive behavior support. *Focus on Exceptional Children, 42*(8), 1–14.

Substance Abuse and Mental Health Services Administration. (2014). *SAMHSA's Concept of Trauma and Guidance for a Trauma-Informed Approach*. HHS Publication No. (SMA) 14-4884. Rockville, MD: Substance Abuse and Mental Health Services Administration.

Sandoval, J. (2013). *Crisis counseling, intervention, and prevention in the schools*. Routledge.

Spence, R., Kagan, L., Kljakovic, M., & Bifulco, A. (2021). Understanding trauma in children and young people in the school setting. *Educational and Child Psychology, 38*(1), 87–98.

Van der Kolk, B. A. (2003). The neurobiology of childhood trauma and abuse. *Child and Adolescent Psychiatric Clinics, 12*(2), 293–317. https://doi.org/10.1016/S1056-4993(03)00003-8

Van der Kolk, B. (2014). The body keeps the score: Brain, mind, and body in the healing of trauma. *New York, 3*, 14–211.

Walkley, M., & Cox, T. L. (2013). Building trauma-informed schools and communities. *Children & Schools, 35*(2), 123–128. https://doi.org/10.1093/cs/cdt007

Adapting the Curriculum and Instruction for Trauma Sensitivity

Introduction to Trauma-Sensitive Curriculum Design

Trauma-sensitive curriculum design is a cornerstone of creating equitable and supportive learning environments where all students, particularly those affected by trauma, can thrive. This chapter builds on the principles and strategies outlined earlier, focusing on practical approaches to designing curricula that foster emotional safety, inclusivity, and academic engagement.

For students who have experienced trauma, traditional curriculum structures can often present barriers to learning, exacerbating feelings of stress and disengagement. Trauma-sensitive curriculum design seeks to address these challenges by embedding flexibility, relevance, and choice into the teaching process. By considering the diverse needs of students, educators can create lessons that empower learners, promote resilience, and support well-being.

This chapter introduces key frameworks, such as Universal Design for Learning (UDL) and differentiated instruction (DI), to provide a foundation for trauma-informed curriculum design. It outlines how these approaches can help educators deliver content in ways that align with students' unique needs and strengths, fostering an inclusive environment where all learners feel valued and capable.

This chapter also explores a range of practical strategies, including project-based learning (PBL), scaffolded support, and reflective activities, demonstrating how educators can create flexible pathways for engagement and achievement. Real-world case studies and a comprehensive teacher's toolbox provide actionable insights, helping educators integrate trauma-sensitive practices into their daily teaching.

Ultimately, this chapter emphasises the transformative potential of a well-designed curriculum in shaping a classroom environment that nurtures both academic success and emotional growth. By embedding trauma-sensitive practices into curriculum design, educators can create spaces where learning becomes a tool for healing, resilience, and empowerment.

Principles of Trauma-Sensitive Curriculum Design

Trauma-sensitive curriculum design ensures that teaching practices and classroom environments actively support students who have experienced trauma. By embedding flexibility, relevance, and inclusivity into the curriculum, educators can help students feel safe, valued, and ready to learn. These principles are informed by research on trauma's impact on brain development and learning capacities, as well as strategies that promote emotional and academic resilience.

Flexibility

Flexibility is a cornerstone of trauma-sensitive curriculum design. Trauma often disrupts cognitive processes such as attention, memory, and executive functioning, which makes rigid expectations and deadlines challenging for some students (Brunzell et al., 2015). Offering students choices in assignments, alternative formats for assessments, or extended deadlines reduces stress and empowers them to engage meaningfully in learning.

Structured routines that allow for adjustments are particularly important for trauma-affected students, who may feel overwhelmed by unpredictability (Australian Childhood Foundation, 2010). For example, establishing predictable schedules while allowing students to take sensory breaks or access quiet areas supports their ability to self-regulate. These strategies align with the evidence that safe, predictable environments enhance the capacity for learning by reducing stress and promoting emotional stability (Perry, 2006).

Relevance

Relevance in curriculum design helps trauma-affected students connect with their learning. Incorporating real-world topics, culturally responsive content, and themes of resilience allows students to see themselves in the curriculum and understand the importance of education in their lives. Trauma can often lead to feelings of disconnection or hopelessness, making it vital to design content that reflects students' lived experiences and fosters a sense of purpose (Brunzell et al., 2015).

For example, incorporating stories of overcoming adversity into literature or history lessons can inspire students while teaching essential skills. Similarly, PBL that addresses community issues enables students to see the real-world impact of their work, further enhancing engagement and motivation. Research suggests that trauma-informed positive education, which combines trauma-awareness with strengths-based approaches, is particularly effective in fostering resilience and optimism among trauma-affected students (Owens & Waters, 2020).

Inclusivity

Inclusivity is fundamental to creating trauma-sensitive classrooms. Students who have experienced trauma often come from diverse cultural and socio-economic backgrounds. Ensuring that classroom materials reflect a wide range of perspectives helps all students feel respected and valued. This involves selecting texts, visuals, and examples that represent various identities and experiences, promoting a sense of belonging (Department of Education Tasmania, 2020).

Inclusive teaching also means recognising that students learn in different ways. UDL principles encourage providing multiple pathways for students to access content and demonstrate their knowledge. For example, offering options such as written assignments, oral presentations, or art-based projects ensures that all students can participate in ways that align with their strengths and preferences (CAST, 2018). By embedding inclusivity into every aspect of the curriculum, educators create an environment where diversity is celebrated, and all students can thrive.

Connecting Principles to Empathy and Inclusivity

The principles of flexibility, relevance, and inclusivity directly connect to the empathy and supportive school culture discussed in previous chapters. Empathy enables educators to understand and respond to the challenges faced by trauma-affected students, while inclusivity ensures that no student feels marginalised. Together, these principles create a framework for trauma-sensitive curriculum design that supports students academically and emotionally.

Trauma-sensitive curriculum design is not simply about meeting the minimum standards of support; it is about fostering an environment where all students can grow, learn, and succeed. By prioritising these principles, educators help trauma-affected students navigate their challenges and build a foundation for lifelong resilience and well-being.

Differentiated Instruction and Universal Design for Learning

Differentiated Instruction

DI is an approach that recognises the diversity of learners within a classroom and seeks to provide flexible strategies to support their varying needs. It acknowledges that students differ in their readiness to learn, interests, and preferred ways of engaging with content. By tailoring lessons to accommodate these differences, educators can foster more equitable and inclusive learning environments (Tomlinson, 2014).

At its core, DI involves modifying the key elements of teaching: content (what students learn), process (how students engage with material), and product (how students demonstrate their learning). For example, a lesson on ecosystems might include resources at multiple reading levels, interactive experiments, and a choice between creating a visual model or writing a report. Such flexibility ensures that all students, including those affected by trauma, can engage in ways that align with their strengths and needs (Tomlinson, 2001).

Trauma-affected students, in particular, benefit from differentiated approaches that account for their emotional readiness and cognitive capabilities. Research indicates that trauma can impact memory, concentration, and self-regulation, making traditional one-size-fits-all methods less effective (Brunzell et al., 2015). For instance, offering students the option of quiet, independent work alongside collaborative group tasks allows them to choose a mode of engagement that feels safe and manageable. Similarly, building opportunities for self-regulation, such as mindfulness activities or movement breaks, helps create a classroom environment that reduces stress and promotes engagement (Perry, 2006).

Practical strategies for implementing DI include:

- **Ongoing assessment**: Regularly monitoring student progress enables teachers to adapt instruction to meet evolving needs.
- **Flexible grouping**: Organising students into different groups for specific tasks encourages collaboration and accommodates varying skill levels.
- **Personalised assignments**: Providing choices in topics or formats supports student autonomy and motivation while catering to individual preferences.

By embedding differentiation into daily teaching practices, educators can ensure that all students, particularly those impacted by trauma, have access to meaningful and supportive learning experiences.

UDL Principles in Trauma-Informed Education

UDL is a framework that aims to reduce barriers to learning by designing flexible and inclusive curricula from the outset. Inspired by the architectural concept of universal design, UDL anticipates the diverse needs of students and embeds accessibility into the learning environment, benefiting all learners, including those affected by trauma (Rose & Meyer, 2002).

UDL operates on three key principles, which align closely with trauma-informed teaching practices:

1. **Multiple Means of Engagement**

    Engagement is the foundation of effective learning, and UDL emphasises the importance of providing a variety of ways to capture students' interest. Trauma-affected students often face challenges with focus and motivation, making it essential to offer options that cater to their preferences and emotional states (CAST, 2018). For example, incorporating PBL, self-paced activities, or peer collaboration allows students to engage in ways that feel comfortable and relevant.

Creating a connection to real-world issues can also foster a sense of purpose and engagement. For instance, linking a maths lesson to practical budgeting scenarios or a community project can make learning more meaningful. These strategies, coupled with consistent routines and emotional check-ins, build a supportive environment that prioritises trust and belonging (Australian Childhood Foundation, 2010).

2. **Multiple Means of Representation**

   Trauma can affect how students process and retain information, necessitating diverse ways of presenting content. UDL encourages teachers to use multiple formats, such as videos, diagrams, audio recordings, and interactive tools, to ensure accessibility for all learners (Rose et al., 2005).

For example, a science lesson on weather patterns could include visual models, hands-on experiments, and digital simulations. These varied approaches not only accommodate different learning preferences but also enhance comprehension and engagement. By reducing reliance on a single mode of instruction, educators can create a more inclusive classroom environment where all students can succeed.

3. **Multiple Means of Action and Expression**

   UDL supports flexibility in how students demonstrate their learning, recognising that traditional assessments may not suit everyone. For trauma-affected students, offering alternative methods of expression – such as oral presentations, art projects, or digital storytelling – can reduce anxiety and build confidence (CAST, 2018).

For instance, in a unit on Australian history, students might choose to create a timeline, write a reflective essay, or produce a short film. These options allow students to showcase their understanding in ways that align with their strengths and interests, fostering a sense of autonomy and accomplishment.

Linking UDL Principles to Trauma-Informed Practices

The principles of UDL align naturally with the trauma-informed strategies discussed in earlier chapters. By prioritising flexibility, engagement, and inclusivity, UDL helps to create classrooms that are both supportive and empowering for all learners. These principles echo the emphasis on empathy and inclusivity in Chapters 3 and 5, reinforcing the importance of meeting students where they are and valuing their unique contributions.

Moreover, UDL complements DI by embedding flexibility and accessibility into curriculum design from the beginning. While DI focuses on adapting teaching to individual needs, UDL aims to remove systemic barriers to learning, creating a foundation for equity and inclusion. Together, these approaches provide a powerful framework for addressing the complex needs of trauma-affected students while fostering resilience and growth.

Instructional Strategies for Trauma-Responsive Teaching

Trauma-responsive teaching requires intentional strategies that create safe, inclusive, and supportive learning environments. By addressing the emotional and cognitive needs of students impacted by trauma, these approaches promote resilience, engagement, and academic success. This section explores four key instructional strategies: PBL, cooperative learning, scaffolded support, and grounding and self-regulation breaks.

Project-Based Learning

PBL is an instructional approach that empowers students to explore real-world topics through sustained inquiry. For trauma-affected students, PBL offers unique benefits by fostering autonomy and relevance in learning. Trauma often impacts a student's ability to concentrate, regulate emotions, and feel a sense of control. PBL addresses these challenges by allowing students to work at their own pace, pursue topics that interest them, and take ownership of their learning journey (Brunzell et al., 2015).

One of the key advantages of PBL is its emphasis on student agency. When students are given the opportunity to choose the focus of their projects, they feel a sense of ownership and pride, which can rebuild confidence often eroded by trauma. For example, a class studying environmental sustainability might allow students to design community-based projects, such as organising a recycling programme or creating an awareness campaign. These tasks not only provide meaningful connections to the real world but also encourage students to see themselves as capable contributors to their communities (Rose & Meyer, 2002).

PBL also provides flexibility, accommodating the varying needs of trauma-affected students. Tasks can be divided into smaller, manageable components, enabling students to engage without feeling overwhelmed. Moreover, the collaborative and inquiry-based nature of PBL aligns with trauma-informed principles by reducing pressure and offering multiple entry points for participation (Australian Childhood Foundation, 2010).

Cooperative Learning

Cooperative learning emphasises collaboration and positive peer interactions, which are especially beneficial for trauma-affected students who may struggle with social skills or trust. Trauma can disrupt relationships and create feelings of isolation, making supportive peer interactions a powerful tool for healing and growth. By working together in structured teams, students can build connections, develop empathy, and enhance their communication skills (Perry, 2006).

To ensure cooperative learning is trauma-responsive, teachers must create a safe and inclusive space for group work. Clear roles and expectations should be established, helping students understand their responsibilities and feel secure within their teams. For example, assigning specific roles – such as recorder, presenter, or timekeeper – can provide structure and reduce the anxiety that may arise from unstructured tasks (Brunzell et al., 2015).

Small, carefully selected groups are also essential. Teachers should consider each student's emotional readiness and interpersonal dynamics when forming teams. Pairing trauma-affected students with empathetic and supportive peers can foster trust and minimise potential conflicts. Additionally, monitoring group interactions and providing regular feedback ensures that all students feel valued and respected.

Cooperative learning activities, such as peer mentoring or group projects, also build social-emotional skills that extend beyond the classroom. These experiences reinforce a sense of belonging and community, which are critical for trauma recovery and academic engagement (Tomlinson, 2001).

Scaffolded Support

Scaffolding is a foundational strategy in trauma-responsive teaching, providing students with the support they need to tackle challenging tasks while gradually fostering independence. Trauma-affected students often experience difficulty with executive functioning, making it essential to break down complex tasks into smaller, more manageable steps (CAST, 2018).

Effective scaffolding involves clear instructions, guided practice, and ongoing feedback. For example, a writing assignment might begin with brainstorming ideas as a class, followed by individual outlines, drafts, and peer reviews. By providing targeted support at each stage, teachers can help students build confidence and develop the skills needed to complete the task successfully.

Check-ins are another critical element of scaffolding. Regularly monitoring progress and addressing concerns ensures that students feel supported and can stay on track. For trauma-affected students, these interactions also provide opportunities for emotional regulation and reassurance. Gradually reducing support as students gain confidence and competence encourages resilience and self-efficacy, key components of long-term academic and personal success (Tomlinson, 2014).

Scaffolding not only enhances learning outcomes but also helps students develop the resilience needed to face future challenges. By guiding students through the process of overcoming obstacles, teachers foster a growth mindset and the belief that effort and perseverance lead to success.

Use of Grounding and Self-Regulation Breaks

Grounding and self-regulation breaks are vital tools in trauma-responsive classrooms, helping students manage emotional triggers and maintain focus. Trauma often heightens stress responses, making it difficult for students to stay present and engaged. Incorporating grounding techniques, such as mindfulness exercises, deep breathing, or sensory activities, can help students regain control and feel more centred (Australian Childhood Foundation, 2010).

Mindfulness breaks, for instance, might involve guided breathing exercises or visualisation activities at the start of a lesson. These practices not only reduce anxiety but also prepare students for learning by activating the prefrontal cortex, the area of the brain responsible for focus and decision-making (Perry, 2006). Similarly, sensory breaks – such as squeezing a stress ball or engaging in light physical activity – can provide an outlet for excess energy and promote self-regulation.

Grounding activities are particularly effective before challenging tasks or transitions, which can be triggering for trauma-affected students. For example, a short stretching exercise or a moment of reflective journaling before a test can help students approach the task with a calmer and more focused mindset.

These practices align with the strategies outlined in Chapter 4 on fostering resilience and Chapter 6's emphasis on emotional regulation. By integrating grounding techniques into daily routines, teachers create a supportive environment where students feel empowered to manage their emotions and participate fully in their education.

Connecting Strategies to Trauma-Responsive Teaching

Each of these strategies – PBL, cooperative learning, scaffolding, and grounding breaks – contributes to a trauma-responsive approach that prioritises safety, connection, and engagement. By addressing the unique needs of trauma-affected students, these practices not only enhance academic outcomes but also support emotional healing and personal growth.

The integration of these strategies also aligns with the broader principles of trauma-informed education discussed in previous chapters. By fostering a sense of agency, belonging, and competence, teachers can help students build resilience and thrive in the face of adversity.

Trauma-responsive teaching is not simply a set of techniques; it is a commitment to creating classrooms that honour the individuality and potential of every student. Through thoughtful implementation of these strategies, educators can transform learning into a powerful tool for healing and empowerment.

Case Study and Practical Application

Case Study on Adapting Curriculum for a Trauma-Impacted Student
Case Overview
Ella, a Year 9 student, has a history of trauma stemming from family instability and exposure to domestic violence. Recently, she has exhibited difficulty concentrating in class, avoiding participation in group activities, and struggling to complete assignments. Her teacher, Ms. Carter, recognises that Ella's academic struggles are likely connected to her emotional and cognitive challenges. In response, Ms. Carter develops a trauma-sensitive approach to teaching a unit on Australian history.

Application of UDL Principles
To support Ella, Ms. Carter applies the principles of UDL, embedding flexibility and choice into the unit. She begins by offering Ella multiple options for engaging with the content. For example, instead of assigning a single textbook chapter, Ms. Carter provides alternative resources, such as videos, interactive websites, and short articles at varied reading levels. This ensures that Ella can access the material in a format that feels manageable and less overwhelming.

When it comes to assessments, Ms. Carter allows Ella to choose how she demonstrates her understanding of key concepts. Options include writing an essay, creating a digital presentation, or producing a timeline with visual elements. By offering these choices, Ms. Carter empowers Ella to select a format that aligns with her strengths and minimises stress.

Flexible Deadlines and Personalised Feedback
Ms. Carter recognises that Ella often becomes overwhelmed by rigid timelines. For this unit, she implements flexible deadlines, breaking the assessment into smaller milestones with extended timeframes.

Each milestone is accompanied by personalised feedback, allowing Ella to build confidence and adjust her work incrementally. This approach not only reduces Ella's anxiety but also fosters a sense of accomplishment.

Safe Opportunities for Participation
Group discussions are a key part of the history unit, but Ella's discomfort with speaking in front of her peers is evident. To address this, Ms. Carter introduces smaller, low-pressure groups and offers Ella the option to contribute her ideas through written reflections instead of verbal participation. This adjustment ensures that Ella's voice is heard while honouring her emotional boundaries.

Outcomes
Over the course of the unit, Ella begins to engage more consistently. She expresses an increased sense of control and pride in her work, and her confidence in her academic abilities grows. Ms. Carter's trauma-sensitive adaptations not only help Ella access the curriculum but also support her overall well-being.

Practical Strategies for Implementing Trauma-Sensitive Curriculum Adaptations

Creating a trauma-sensitive classroom requires intentional strategies that address the diverse needs of students while promoting inclusivity and flexibility. The following practical strategies provide a roadmap for educators seeking to embed trauma-informed practices into their teaching.

1. **Providing Alternative Reading Materials**
   Certain texts can be triggering for trauma-affected students. Offering alternative reading options that convey the same concepts or themes allows students to engage with the material in a way that feels safe. For example, substituting a violent historical account with a broader, non-graphic overview ensures inclusivity while maintaining educational integrity.

2. **Incorporating Reflective Activities**

   Reflective activities, such as journaling or drawing, provide students with opportunities to process their emotions in a private and controlled way. These activities can serve as powerful tools for self-expression and emotional regulation, particularly before or after engaging with challenging content.

3. **Structuring Assignments with Multiple Completion Paths**

   Assignments should offer students flexibility and choice. For instance, a science project might allow students to create a poster, write a report, or design a model. Providing options not only caters to diverse learning styles but also fosters a sense of agency and control.

4. **Embedding Grounding Techniques into Lessons**

   Simple grounding activities, such as deep breathing exercises or mindfulness moments, can help students reset and focus. Incorporating these techniques at the start of lessons or during transitions supports emotional regulation and reduces anxiety.

5. **Offering Flexible Deadlines and Checkpoints**

   Trauma-affected students may struggle with meeting strict deadlines due to difficulty managing stress or maintaining focus. Flexible deadlines, paired with clearly defined checkpoints, allow students to pace themselves and receive feedback throughout the process.

Checklist for Trauma-Sensitive Curriculum Adaptations

The following checklist provides educators with practical steps to ensure their lessons are trauma-sensitive:

- Offer multiple options for content engagement (e.g., videos, readings, interactive activities).
- Provide alternative texts for materials that may be triggering.
- Design assignments with flexible formats to accommodate diverse learning preferences.
- Break tasks into smaller, manageable steps with clear timelines.
- Incorporate reflective activities to support emotional processing.
- Include grounding techniques, such as mindfulness breaks, in daily routines.

- Monitor group dynamics to ensure safe and inclusive participation.
- Offer personalised feedback to guide student progress and build confidence.

Chapter Summary

This chapter explores how educators can adapt curriculum and instructional strategies to support trauma-affected students, fostering a safe and inclusive learning environment. Emphasis is placed on understanding and implementing trauma-sensitive principles, including flexibility, relevance, and inclusivity. These principles empower teachers to design lessons that reduce stress, promote engagement, and accommodate the diverse needs of their students.

This chapter highlights the critical role of UDL in trauma-informed education. By providing multiple means of engagement, representation, and expression, UDL ensures that all students, including those impacted by trauma, can access and succeed in their learning. Strategies such as offering varied instructional materials, allowing choice in assessments, and creating predictable routines demonstrate how UDL principles can be embedded in daily teaching practices to support equity and inclusion.

DI is presented as another essential tool for addressing the unique needs of students. By tailoring lessons to account for individual strengths, interests, and readiness, educators can create meaningful and supportive learning experiences. Practical examples, such as flexible grouping, personalised assignments, and ongoing assessment, showcase how differentiation can help trauma-affected students thrive.

Instructional strategies such as PBL, cooperative learning, scaffolding, and grounding techniques are also examined. These approaches encourage student agency, foster positive peer interactions, and provide the structure and support needed to build resilience and confidence. The importance of integrating reflective activities, sensory breaks, and other self-regulation tools into lessons is underscored as a way to help students manage emotional triggers and stay engaged.

Ultimately, this chapter provides a comprehensive guide for educators to design and implement trauma-sensitive curriculum and instruction. By adopting these strategies, teachers can create classrooms where all students feel valued, supported, and empowered to succeed.

Creating Trauma-Informed Classrooms

Guiding Questions

1. How can curriculum and instruction be designed to address the diverse needs of trauma-affected students?
2. What are the key principles of trauma-sensitive curriculum design, and how can they be implemented in daily teaching practices?
3. How do UDL principles support equitable access to learning for trauma-affected students?
4. In what ways can DI and flexible teaching methods promote inclusivity and engagement?
5. What practical strategies can teachers use to create a safe and supportive classroom environment for all students?

Teachers Toolbox

Teacher's Toolbox for Chapter 8: Designing Trauma-Sensitive Curricula

FOCUS AREA	STRATEGY	PRACTICAL APPLICATION
BUILDING RESILIENCE THROUGH CURRICULUM	Embed resilience narratives into subject content.	Use stories, case studies, or historical examples highlighting perseverance and recovery to inspire and empower students.
	Integrate opportunities for student reflection and connection to personal experiences.	Assign reflective writing tasks or creative projects that allow students to explore and express their resilience and growth.
ESTABLISHING PREDICTABLE ROUTINES	Create consistent lesson structures to reduce anxiety and increase engagement.	Start each class with a routine activity such as a grounding exercise, brief discussion, or a clear overview of the lesson objectives.
	Develop structured yet flexible timelines for assignments to accommodate individual needs.	Use visual timelines or flexible task deadlines, ensuring students understand the structure and expectations while having room for adjustments.

(Continued)

Adapting the Curriculum and Instruction for Trauma Sensitivity

(Continued)

FOCUS AREA	STRATEGY	PRACTICAL APPLICATION
SUPPORTING EMOTIONAL REGULATION	Provide sensory tools and designated calm areas within the classroom.	Offer items like fidget tools or weighted lap pads, and create a "calm corner" where students can go when they feel overwhelmed.
	Teach and practice grounding techniques.	Incorporate breathing exercises, mindfulness activities, or short movement breaks during transitions or challenging tasks.
PROMOTING INCLUSIVITY AND CHOICE	Offer culturally relevant materials that reflect diverse experiences and backgrounds.	Include literature, media, or examples from a variety of cultures and perspectives to ensure all students feel represented.
	Allow students to choose how they engage with and demonstrate learning.	Provide multiple options for assignments, such as creating a video, writing an essay, or presenting a visual project.
ENCOURAGING STUDENT AUTONOMY	Use co-created goals and contracts to give students a voice in their learning journey.	Develop learning contracts where students outline their goals, preferred support strategies, and timelines, building ownership and agency.
	Foster peer mentorship or collaborative learning opportunities.	Pair students with peers for mutual support and guidance, especially in project-based tasks or group discussions.
ENHANCING TEACHER-STUDENT RELATIONSHIPS	Use trauma-sensitive communication techniques.	Regularly validate students' emotions, such as saying, "It seems like this task is challenging – how can we make it more manageable for you?"
	Schedule regular, brief one-on-one check-ins to build trust.	Dedicate a few minutes per week to talk privately with each student about their progress, challenges, and successes.

References

Australian Childhood Foundation. (2010). *Making space for learning: Trauma-informed practice in schools*. Australian Childhood Foundation. Retrieved from https://professionals.childhood.org.au/course/making-space-for-learning

Brunzell, T., Waters, L., & Stokes, H. (2015). Trauma-informed positive education: Using positive psychology to strengthen vulnerable students. *Contemporary School Psychology, 20*(1), 63–83. https://doi.org/10.1007/s40688-015-0070-x

CAST. (2018). *Universal design for learning guidelines version 2.2*. Retrieved from https://udlguidelines.cast.org

Department of Education Tasmania. (2020). *Good teaching: Trauma-informed practice*. State of Tasmania (Department of Education). Retrieved from https://publicdocumentcentre.education.tas.gov.au/library/Shared%20Documents/Good-Teaching-Trauma-Informed-Practice.pdf

Owens, R. L., & Waters, L. (2020). What does positive psychology tell us about early intervention and prevention with children and adolescents? A review of positive psychological interventions with young people. *The Journal of Positive Psychology, 15*(5), 588–597.

Perry, B. D. (2006). Applying principles of neurodevelopment to clinical work with maltreated and traumatized children: The neurosequential model of therapeutics. In N. Boyd Webb (Ed.), *Working with traumatized youth in child welfare* (pp. 27–52). The Guildford Press.

Rose, D. H., & Meyer, A. (2002). *Teaching every student in the digital age: Universal design for learning*. Association for Supervision and Curriculum Development.

Rose, D. H., Hasselbring, T. S., Stahl, S., & Zabala, J. (2005). Assistive technology and universal design for learning: Two sides of the same coin. *Handbook of special education technology research and practice*, 507–518.

Tomlinson, C. A. (2001). *How to differentiate instruction in mixed-ability classrooms* (2nd ed.). Association for Supervision and Curriculum Development.

Tomlinson, C. A. (2014). *The differentiated classroom: Responding to the needs of all learners* (2nd ed.). Association for Supervision and Curriculum Development.

Fostering Emotional Regulation and Resilience in Students

Chapter Overview

This chapter explores how trauma-informed classrooms can become spaces where emotional regulation and resilience are actively nurtured. Recognising that trauma often disrupts students' ability to manage their emotions and navigate challenges, this chapter presents practical strategies that equip students with tools to understand, express, and regulate their emotional responses.

Through the cultivation of self-awareness, proactive coping techniques, and supportive routines, educators can help students develop the confidence to manage stress, persist through setbacks, and experience themselves as capable learners. This chapter also emphasises the importance of modelling and embedding self-care practices into daily classroom life – supporting not only emotional recovery but long-term well-being.

Grounded in evidence and classroom realities, this chapter positions emotional regulation and resilience not as "extras" but as fundamental skills for all students, particularly those shaped by trauma.

Section 1: The Importance of Emotional Regulation

Overview of Emotional Regulation Skills

Emotional regulation – the ability to recognise, understand, and manage emotional responses – is a foundational skill in trauma-sensitive education. For students affected by trauma, the capacity to regulate emotions can be significantly

DOI: 10.4324/9781003535386-10

compromised due to disruptions in neurodevelopment caused by chronic stress or adverse experiences. These disruptions can manifest as heightened emotional reactivity, impulsivity, or withdrawal, often leading to behavioural challenges that are misinterpreted as defiance or disinterest rather than expressions of emotional dysregulation (Cavanaugh, 2016; van der Kolk, 2005).

Trauma-affected students frequently operate in a state of hyperarousal. Their nervous systems are primed for survival rather than learning, which means even minor classroom disruptions – a sudden noise, an unexpected transition, or a perceived slight – can trigger intense emotional responses. These students may become tearful, agitated, or withdrawn without apparent provocation. Others may externalise their distress through aggression, shouting, or disengagement. Importantly, such behaviours are often the result of impaired emotional regulation capacities rooted in early and ongoing exposure to trauma (Blair & Raver, 2015; Perry, 2006).

Helping students build skills in emotional regulation is not simply a behavioural intervention – it is an act of healing. When educators teach and model emotional regulation, they support students in developing neural pathways that promote calmness, self-awareness, and flexibility in response to stress. These are the very capacities that trauma disrupts, and they are essential for both learning and long-term well-being (Brunzell et al., 2015).

As introduced in Chapter 3, the establishment of emotionally safe classroom environments provides the critical foundation upon which emotional regulation skills can be practised and refined. Emotional safety allows students to take interpersonal and academic risks without fear of ridicule or re-traumatisation. When students feel safe – physically, emotionally, and relationally – their brains are more able to access higher-order cognitive functions required for reflection and self-regulation (Karris, 2022). Predictable routines, positive teacher-student relationships, and non-punitive responses to behaviour all contribute to a sense of emotional safety that makes regulation possible.

The link between emotional regulation and academic engagement is well-established. Students who are unable to manage their emotions often struggle to focus, cooperate with peers, or complete tasks. Conversely, those with stronger regulation skills are more likely to persist through challenges, resolve conflicts constructively, and recover quickly from setbacks. For trauma-affected students, this means that emotional regulation is not just a tool for managing behaviour – it is a prerequisite for learning (Pickens & Tschopp, 2017).

Educators can take deliberate steps to foster these skills through both explicit teaching and the modelling of calm, regulated responses to stress. Just as academic skills are scaffolded, emotional regulation can be nurtured gradually, with support, encouragement, and repeated practice. When students are given the tools to identify and manage their emotions within a safe and compassionate environment, they begin to reclaim a sense of agency over their internal world – a powerful antidote to the powerlessness that often characterises traumatic experience.

Key Emotional Regulation Skills for Students

Helping students cultivate emotional regulation skills is essential in trauma-informed education. For trauma-affected students, who often struggle with self-regulation due to chronic stress or early adverse experiences, these skills provide a critical foundation for learning and interpersonal success (Figure 9.1).

Zones of Regulation

Blue Zone

Sad, tired, bored, sick. Strategies: movement breaks, energy boosters, connection.

Green Zone

Calm, happy, focused, ready to learn. Strategies: maintain through routines.

Yellow Zone

Frustrated, anxious, silly, excited. Strategies: breathing, counting, self-talk.

Red Zone

Angry, terrified, out of control. Strategies: space, time, sensory tools.

Figure 9.1 The Zones of Regulation Model

Mindfulness

Mindfulness practices – paying deliberate attention to the present moment – are increasingly recognised as effective tools for supporting emotional regulation. In trauma-informed classrooms, mindfulness can serve as a calming anchor, helping students develop awareness of their thoughts and emotions without judgement. Techniques such as focusing on the breath, guided visualisations, and mindful listening can support a return to emotional balance, especially when introduced consistently and with student buy-in.

Brunzell et al. (2015) describe how mindfulness practices, including brief "brain breaks," visualisations, and focused attention activities, have been adapted effectively in flexible learning environments to support students with severe regulatory challenges. These interventions are most effective when they are part of classroom routines and connected to clear expectations around mutual respect and safety. Mindfulness not only helps manage immediate stress responses but also supports long-term development of executive functioning and emotional resilience.

Breathing Techniques

Intentional breathing is another foundational regulation strategy that supports the calming of the nervous system. Simple techniques such as box breathing or "smell the flower, blow out the candle" provide trauma-affected students with accessible tools to manage intense emotions and prevent escalation. Alexander (2019) emphasises the importance of equipping students with breathing techniques and movement-based strategies to help them regain control during emotionally charged moments.

When practised regularly, these techniques build neural pathways associated with the parasympathetic nervous system, reducing the prevalence and intensity of fight, flight, or freeze responses. Teachers can reinforce these practices by modelling them in non-crisis situations, embedding them into transitions, or using them to begin and end lessons.

Self-Awareness and Emotional Literacy

Before students can regulate emotions, they must first learn to recognise and name them. This process – often called emotional literacy – is particularly critical for trauma-affected students, many of whom have learned to suppress or mistrust their feelings due to experiences of neglect, abandonment, or threat. Developing a vocabulary for emotional expression enables students to better articulate their needs and seek support when needed.

Batte (2021) describe this process as the "name it to tame it" approach, where students learn to connect bodily cues (such as heart rate or nausea) to emotional states, improving their self-regulatory capacity. Tools such as feelings charts, emotional thermometers, or daily check-ins can scaffold this learning. Classrooms that normalise emotional expression – where students hear their feelings reflected back to them accurately and without judgement – create an environment that fosters emotional growth and psychological safety.

Additionally, research highlights the value of social-emotional learning (SEL) programmes in reinforcing emotional literacy and self-awareness. When embedded into school culture, SEL teaches students how to identify triggers, apply regulation strategies, and engage in respectful peer interactions – building both intrapersonal and interpersonal competence.

Integration Across the Day

These emotional regulation strategies – mindfulness, breathing, and emotional literacy – are most effective when woven into the rhythm of the school day. As Brunzell et al. (2015) found, when teachers embed regulation practices into predictable routines, students begin to self-initiate these strategies, using them as tools for returning to a calm, ready-to-learn state. Importantly, these strategies are not one-off lessons but ongoing skills that require regular practice, scaffolding, and encouragement.

By equipping students with a regulation toolkit, educators not only address behaviour at the surface level but also empower students to navigate complex emotional landscapes. This is particularly transformative for trauma-affected learners, who may never have had access to environments where emotional expression and self-soothing were taught, encouraged, or safe.

Integrating Emotional Regulation into the Classroom

For emotional regulation strategies to be effective, they must be embedded into the daily rhythms, routines, and relationships that define classroom life. Trauma-affected students do not simply benefit from one-off lessons on emotions; rather, they need ongoing opportunities to practise, observe, and refine self-regulation in the context of a safe and responsive learning environment. Integration is key – it is through consistent modelling, structured practice, and responsive teaching that regulation skills take root.

Embedding Regulation into Routines

Daily classroom routines provide a natural and powerful structure for supporting emotional regulation. Beginning the day with predictable rituals – such as morning check-ins, guided breathing, or circle time – signals safety and helps students transition into a calm, focused state. Brunzell et al. (2015) highlight the effectiveness of "rhythm and repetition" in trauma-informed classrooms, noting that structured transitions and routines allow students to shift out of reactive survival states and into readiness for learning.

These routines might include mindful starts to lessons, movement breaks between tasks, or closing reflections at the end of the day. When routines are consistent yet flexible enough to accommodate student needs, they offer both structure and a sense of control – two essential components for traumatised learners (Alexander, 2019).

Co-Regulation: The Educator as a Regulatory Anchor

Before students can self-regulate, they often need co-regulation – support from a calm, emotionally attuned adult who helps them navigate distress. Educators, in this sense, act as regulatory anchors. By remaining grounded and emotionally available during moments of student dysregulation, teachers create a bridge towards calm. This involves more than reacting calmly; it requires active empathy, validation, and relational consistency.

Wolpow et al. (2016) stress the importance of relational teaching – where the teacher's emotional state, tone of voice, and non-verbal cues become a model for students' own regulation efforts. In these moments, a teacher's presence can shift a student from chaos to safety. Phrases like "I'm here with you," or "Let's take a moment together," are more than kind words – they are regulatory cues that rewire how students respond to stress.

Over time, repeated experiences of co-regulation lead to internalised regulation: students begin to adopt the calming strategies modelled by trusted adults and build confidence in their own emotional resilience.

Classroom Spaces That Support Regulation

The physical and sensory layout of the classroom also influences students' capacity to regulate. Trauma-informed classrooms are designed with intentionality: they minimise unnecessary stimulation and offer quiet areas where students can retreat without stigma. Calm corners, sensory kits, noise-cancelling headphones, and low-stimulation visuals can support students who are overwhelmed or overstimulated. As Spence et al. (2020) describe, these spaces function as proactive regulation tools, not punitive isolation zones.

Providing students with choice in when and how they access these tools is also key. When students are trusted to make use of regulation spaces as needed – and when those choices are respected – it communicates empowerment and builds agency.

Curriculum Connections

Integrating emotional regulation also involves connecting it to learning content. SEL frameworks offer formal structures for this integration, but even outside of SEL programmes, teachers can embed regulation themes into discussions, stories, and classroom dialogue. For example, literature lessons might include analysis of how characters manage emotions; health units might cover stress responses and coping strategies.

Alexander (2019) notes that educators can help students draw direct connections between physiological signals (e.g., tight chest, racing heart) and the strategies that help them reset – further strengthening the brain-body awareness needed for self-regulation. This type of integration normalises the emotional experience and positions regulation as a learned, valued skill – not something reserved for times of crisis.

Section 2: Building Resilience in Students

Understanding Resilience and Its Role in Trauma Recovery

As students begin to develop emotional regulation skills – learning to pause, name, and manage their emotions – the next step in their healing and growth involves the cultivation of resilience. Where regulation supports the moment-to-moment experience of calm and safety, resilience is the broader capacity to recover, adapt, and thrive over time. For students who have experienced trauma, resilience does not emerge spontaneously. It must be intentionally nurtured through relationships, environments, and pedagogical approaches that foster hope, agency, and confidence.

Resilience in trauma-informed education is best understood not as an innate personality trait but as a process – a set of skills, attitudes, and experiences that allow students to navigate adversity without being overwhelmed by it. These skills include problem-solving, help-seeking, emotional literacy, and the ability to view setbacks as part of the learning journey. In the context of trauma, where students may have learned to expect unpredictability, powerlessness, or failure, resilience represents a powerful shift: from surviving to growing.

Research shows that trauma can significantly disrupt students' capacity for executive functioning, impulse control, and sustained effort – all of which are essential to resilient behaviours (Brunzell et al., 2015). Without intervention, students may internalise their difficulties as fixed deficiencies, leading to chronic disengagement or self-sabotage. In this context, building resilience becomes a core function of trauma-informed practice. It is not enough to remove stressors or create calm; educators must also equip students with the internal resources and relational support to persist and succeed.

One effective entry point to this work is the concept of growth mindset. Developed by Carol Dweck, growth mindset describes the belief that intelligence and ability can improve through effort, strategy, and support. For students who have experienced trauma – many of whom may carry deep-seated beliefs that they are "not good enough," "too damaged," or "incapable" – growth mindset offers a counter-narrative rooted in possibility. When students are encouraged to see challenges as part of the learning process, rather than as proof of inadequacy, they begin to reframe their identity as capable, evolving learners.

This mindset shift requires more than posters on classroom walls; it must be modelled, reinforced, and integrated into daily interactions. Teachers can support this shift by praising process over product ("You worked really hard to solve that problem"), framing mistakes as learning opportunities, and highlighting individual growth. Alexander (2019) found that students exposed to consistent growth-oriented feedback developed a stronger sense of personal agency and were more likely to persist in the face of difficulty.

Importantly, resilience should never be confused with toughness. In trauma-informed education, it is not about telling students to "push through" or "get over" adversity. Rather, it involves recognising the weight of their

Resilience Building Pyramid

Self-efficacy
"I can handle challenges"

Hope
Positive future orientation

Skills
Coping strategies, problem-solving

Relationships
Supportive connections

Safety
Physical and emotional security

Figure 9.2 Resilience-Building Pyramid

lived experiences while offering them the tools, relationships, and learning environments that allow for recovery and growth. As Wolpow et al. (2016) argue, resilience is fostered when students experience themselves as competent, connected, and in control of their choices.

Through deliberate, relational teaching, educators can help trauma-affected students rediscover their strengths, reshape their narratives, and build the capacity not only to regulate emotions but to rebuild confidence, purpose, and hope (Figure 9.2).

Strategies for Building Resilience

Once educators understand the significance of resilience in the context of trauma recovery, the next step is to embed it intentionally into daily classroom practices. This is not achieved through occasional "character education" lessons but through consistent, embedded strategies that promote coping, problem-solving, and goal-setting within a safe, strengths-based environment. These practical tools offer students tangible ways to navigate emotional stress and academic challenges while reinforcing the message that their experiences do not define their potential.

Coping Skills

Coping strategies give students immediate tools for managing anxiety, frustration, and stress – common emotional states for those who have experienced trauma. While emotional regulation lays the groundwork for recognising these states, coping skills support students in responding constructively.

Educators can teach simple, practical techniques such as positive self-talk ("I can try again," "I've done hard things before"), grounding exercises (naming five things they can see, four they can touch, etc.), or visualising a "safe place" – a mental image of calm that students can retreat to in overwhelming moments. These tools should be introduced during calm periods, practised regularly, and normalised within classroom routines so that students feel empowered to use them when needed.

As Brunzell et al. (2015) note, coping skills are most effective when embedded in environments that communicate psychological safety and relational consistency. When these practices are paired with co-regulation and emotional validation from trusted adults, students begin to internalise them as reliable responses to stress.

Problem-Solving Skills

Teaching students how to approach challenges systematically is a core component of resilience-building. Trauma-affected students may perceive problems as insurmountable, either because of previous failures or because their stress responses override executive function. For these students, breaking problems into manageable steps can reframe difficulties as solvable and foster a growing sense of competence.

Explicit instruction in problem-solving – such as identifying the issue, brainstorming solutions, weighing consequences, and choosing a plan – helps students navigate not only academic challenges but also interpersonal and emotional conflicts. Role-playing, think-aloud modelling, and collaborative problem-solving exercises offer practical opportunities to build these skills in supportive environments.

This aligns with the strengths-based approaches discussed in Chapter 4, where educators are encouraged to respond to students' challenges with empathy and to frame behavioural or academic difficulties as opportunities for growth. Teachers who maintain high expectations alongside scaffolded support help students experience struggle not as a threat, but as a path to resilience (Brunzell et al., 2015; Foreman & Bates, 2021).

Goal-Setting

Small, achievable goals provide students with clear markers of progress and success. For students who have internalised a fixed or negative self-concept, even modest wins – completing an assignment, participating in class, staying calm during a challenge – can significantly impact their confidence and motivation.

Goal-setting becomes a resilience-building tool when it is student-led, realistic, and celebrated. Educators can guide students in identifying meaningful personal or academic goals, breaking them down into steps, and reflecting on progress regularly. Visual goal trackers, classroom celebrations, or one-on-one check-ins can reinforce the message that effort and improvement are valued.

This connects directly with the culture of empowerment described in Chapter 5, where schools foster resilience through practices that emphasise student agency, inclusion, and consistent support. When students experience themselves as capable of setting and achieving goals, they are more likely to approach future challenges with persistence and optimism (Brunzell et al., 2015; Cavanaugh, 2016).

Growth Mindset and Positive Reinforcement

Trauma can leave students with deep-seated beliefs about their inadequacy. They may interpret difficulties in learning or relationships not as challenges to overcome, but as confirmation that they are incapable, broken, or destined to fail. In trauma-informed classrooms, adopting a *growth mindset* is a powerful antidote to these internalised narratives. It helps students reconceptualise mistakes, persist through difficulty, and begin to view themselves as learners with potential.

A growth mindset, as defined by Carol Dweck, is the belief that intelligence and ability are not fixed traits, but can be developed through effort, feedback, and perseverance. For trauma-affected students – many of whom have experienced repeated failure, inconsistent feedback, or emotional invalidation – this approach provides a new framework for understanding their own capacity. Instead of seeing mistakes as evidence that they are "not good enough," students are encouraged to see them as part of the process of learning.

Embedding growth mindset language in everyday teaching reinforces this shift. Phrases like "You haven't got it yet, but you're improving" or "Let's think about what we can learn from this" help reframe struggle as natural and productive. As highlighted by Howard (2019), affirming the process of learning rather than just the end result fosters both motivation and self-worth.

Moreover, a trauma-informed growth mindset avoids the trap of toxic positivity. It does not ignore the weight of adversity; rather, it acknowledges the difficulty while still affirming the student's capacity to move forward. This aligns with research by Barton and Garvis (2019), who emphasise that combining growth mindset principles with emotional validation is more effective than applying motivational slogans in isolation.

Alongside growth mindset, positive reinforcement plays a critical role in building students' resilience and shaping self-perception. For students impacted by trauma, behavioural responses are often shaped by a history of criticism or punishment. Shifting the narrative towards strengths, effort, and improvement helps students internalise a sense of competence.

Effective positive reinforcement focuses on specific, observable behaviours and connects them to growth or values. For example:

- "I noticed how you kept trying even when that task was hard – great persistence."
- "You asked for help when you were stuck. That's a really strong choice."
- "You stayed calm and used your breathing technique. That shows growth in managing your emotions."

Praise that highlights effort, strategy, and resilience is far more effective than generic praise ("Good job") or praise solely for outcomes ("You're so smart"). As Blair and Raver (2015) explain, when praise reinforces self-regulatory skills and cognitive effort, it builds both academic motivation and emotional regulation over time.

These practices also support classroom equity. When effort and growth are valued across all ability levels, students who may be academically behind due to trauma or disrupted schooling are still recognised and affirmed. This connects to the inclusive ethos discussed in Chapter 5, where resilience is cultivated not by lowering expectations, but by celebrating progress and personal achievement (Brunzell et al., 2015)

By consistently reinforcing growth and acknowledging progress, educators help students rewrite their internal scripts. Over time, students come to see themselves as capable of learning, adapting, and succeeding – not in spite of their trauma, but through the very process of moving beyond it.

Section 3: Teaching Self-Care Practices for Emotional Well-Being

Importance of Self-Care for Students

Just as self-care is essential for teachers working in emotionally demanding environments, it is equally vital for students – especially those who have experienced trauma. While the term "self-care" is often associated with adult wellness, in trauma-informed education, it takes on a deeper role: self-care becomes a strategy for empowerment, regulation, and long-term emotional health.

Defining Self-Care in the Classroom Context

Self-care for students refers to the intentional development of habits and strategies that support emotional, mental, and physical well-being. These may include mindfulness, seeking help when overwhelmed, identifying personal boundaries, using grounding strategies, or engaging in activities that restore calm and focus. For trauma-affected students, who may be accustomed to instability or emotional suppression, learning that they have both the right and the capacity to care for themselves is a radical and reparative message.

Importantly, self-care in this context is not indulgence – it is survival. Students who have lived through adversity often struggle with dysregulation, anxiety, exhaustion, or shame. Teaching them to recognise their internal states and take steps to restore balance fosters agency and self-efficacy. As Jennings et al. (2011) highlight, explicitly teaching students to engage in restorative practices can help interrupt cycles of hyperarousal and support the development of resilience.

Self-Care as a Form of Self-Advocacy

When students understand and practise self-care, they also begin to develop the language and skills of self-advocacy. Instead of acting out or withdrawing in response to stress, students can learn to articulate their needs: "I need a break," "I'm feeling overwhelmed," or "Can I use a calming strategy?" These behaviours are not signs of weakness – they are signs of growth.

Brunzell et al. (2015) describe the value of teaching students to "exit the red zone" – to recognise when they are dysregulated and use personalised strategies to return to a state of calm. Embedding these practices into classroom routines reinforces the idea that self-care is not only acceptable but expected and supported.

Modelling Self-Care as Educators

The classroom is not only a place where students learn content but also a space where they learn by example. As discussed in Chapter 4, teacher self-care is not just a personal matter – it is pedagogical. When educators model boundary-setting, reflective pauses, breathing exercises, or debriefing after difficult moments, they demonstrate to students what it looks like to care for oneself in healthy and respectful ways (Miller & Flint-Stipp, 2019).

This modelling sends a powerful, implicit message: emotional needs are valid, and there are constructive ways to address them. It also helps dismantle stigma around help-seeking – particularly important for students who may have been raised in environments where emotional expression was discouraged or punished.

Creating a Self-Care Culture

Building a classroom culture of self-care requires more than occasional lessons on "wellness." It involves creating rituals, spaces, and norms that consistently reinforce the value of emotional health. Morning check-ins, breathing breaks, movement opportunities, reflective journaling, and access to calming spaces can all be part of a trauma-informed self-care culture.

As highlighted by Foreman and Bates (2021), when classrooms normalise care – both giving and receiving – it nurtures a deeper sense of safety and trust. Over time, students internalise these messages, gradually learning to take responsibility for their well-being in ways that are proactive, compassionate, and sustainable.

Practical Self-Care Techniques for Students

While the concept of self-care may be abstract for some students – particularly those who have experienced instability or neglect – its effectiveness lies in the routine, accessible practices that can be taught, modelled, and reinforced within the school environment. Trauma-informed educators play a vital role in equipping students with strategies that support emotional balance, promote self-reflection, and build resilience. These practices should not be reserved for moments of crisis but woven into the fabric of the school day, helping students internalise them as proactive tools for everyday well-being.

Mindfulness and Relaxation Techniques

Mindfulness is one of the most widely researched and effective self-care strategies for students. When practised regularly, it helps calm the nervous system, reduce anxiety, and increase students' capacity to stay present and engaged. Trauma-affected students, whose stress responses are often hyperactive, benefit particularly from grounding exercises that bring their attention to the here and now.

Simple mindfulness activities might include breath awareness, body scans, visualisation (such as imagining a calm, safe place), or using sensory prompts to refocus attention. As highlighted by Jennings et al. (2011), mindfulness not only improves self-regulation but also contributes to improved attention and academic outcomes, particularly when integrated into classroom routines rather than delivered as isolated interventions.

Brunzell et al. (2015) further note that regular, low-stakes mindfulness practices – such as "brain breaks" or short guided moments of stillness – help students develop resilience to daily stressors, while also enhancing their sense of classroom safety and control.

Journaling

Reflective journaling offers students a quiet, individualised way to process emotions, identify patterns, and express thoughts that might otherwise remain internalised. For trauma-affected students, journaling can serve as a form of emotional release and narrative-building – an opportunity to make sense of their experiences and track moments of growth.

When introduced as a flexible, non-evaluative practice, journaling supports self-awareness and emotional literacy. Prompts such as "What helped me feel calm today?" or "What am I proud of this week?" can help students begin to notice their own strengths and resilience over time. According to Barton and Garvis (2019), reflective practices such as journaling are essential tools in trauma-informed learning environments, fostering both autonomy and insight.

In addition, journaling aligns with strategies from Chapter 6 on recognising signs of distress: it provides students with a private, structured way to monitor their emotional state, which may also give educators helpful insights when shared voluntarily.

Physical Activity

There is a well-documented connection between movement and emotional regulation. Physical activity supports the release of stress hormones, enhances mood, and helps students reconnect with their bodies – something particularly important for those whose trauma experiences have involved dissociation or chronic tension.

Movement-based strategies do not have to be elaborate or structured. Short bursts of stretching, walking, dancing, or play-based activity can be highly effective. As Spence et al. (2020) explain, physical activity can serve as a self-regulation strategy in and of itself, particularly when students are encouraged to notice how their body feels before and after movement.

Incorporating movement into classroom transitions, offering active options during breaks, and encouraging participation in physical education with an emphasis on well-being rather than competition all support this goal.

Healthy Routines

Many trauma-affected students arrive at school without consistent routines around sleep, nutrition, and hydration – yet these physiological foundations have a significant impact on learning, behaviour, and mood. While schools cannot control what happens in the home, educators can promote awareness and provide guidance that empowers students to make healthier choices.

Classroom discussions around the role of sleep, balanced nutrition, and hydration in helping the brain and body function can be embedded in health lessons or morning meetings. Visual reminders about drinking water, simple tips on healthy snacks, and encouragement to get regular rest help students begin to take ownership of their physical wellness.

Moreover, by embedding predictability and rhythm into the school day – such as structured breaks, consistent transitions, and designated calming periods – teachers model the importance of routine, which can help students begin to replicate similar habits in other parts of their lives (Rodaughan et al., 2024).

Incorporating Self-Care into Classroom Activities

To be effective, self-care practices must move beyond the margins of the school day and into its core routines. For trauma-affected students in particular, healing and resilience are supported not just by what is taught, but by how the classroom feels, flows, and functions. When self-care strategies are embedded into everyday classroom life, they become normalised – expected, accessible, and owned by students as legitimate tools for regulation and well-being.

Short Self-Care Breaks

Small moments can have a powerful impact. Short, structured self-care breaks throughout the day can help students regulate their energy levels, manage emotions, and re-engage with learning tasks. These "micro-practices" also help prevent the build-up of stress, supporting students who might otherwise reach emotional overload.

One popular approach is the "mindful minute": a brief pause where the class focuses on deep breathing, sensory awareness, or quiet reflection. These can be used during transitions between lessons, after recess, or before assessments. Teachers might also guide students through simple stretching routines, a few rounds of chair yoga, or quiet grounding activities such as "5-4-3-2-1" (noticing five things you see, four you can touch, and so on).

Alexander (2019) advocates for proactive, embedded regulation practices that allow students to recalibrate before their stress becomes overwhelming. When these breaks are built into the structure of the day, students begin to internalise them as helpful habits rather than as interventions reserved for behavioural crises.

Importantly, these breaks benefit all students – not just those with a trauma background – and contribute to a calmer, more focused classroom environment.

Normalising Self-Regulation through Routine

Beyond occasional breaks, educators can foster self-care by integrating regulation strategies into the daily rhythm of classroom life. Regular morning check-ins, options for quiet spaces, breathing cues before transitions, or closing reflections can become reliable anchors for students. These routines reinforce the message that managing emotions is part of learning – not something separate or shameful.

This echoes the findings of Brunzell et al. (2015), who describe how the predictable application of regulation routines across the school day helps build students' confidence in their own ability to return to calm. For trauma-affected students, the regularity of these practices creates a sense of safety and agency, even in the face of dysregulation.

Teachers can also promote self-regulation by offering choices when students are struggling – inviting them to use calming strategies, take a sensory break, or journal their emotions. These options empower students to identify what works for them and take responsibility for their emotional state in a supported way.

As with all trauma-informed strategies, success lies not in novelty but in consistency. When students know that taking care of their well-being is encouraged, supported, and modelled in the classroom, they are more likely to engage in these practices independently. Over time, what begins as externally supported regulation evolves into lifelong self-awareness and resilience.

Section 4: Case Study and Practical Strategies

Case Study: A Student Learning Emotional Regulation and Resilience

In order to bring the concepts of emotional regulation and resilience to life, we turn to a practical classroom example that illustrates how trauma-informed strategies can support meaningful student growth. While this case study draws on real-world teaching experiences, the student and context have been fictionalised to maintain confidentiality.

Case Study: "Amira" – Finding Calm and Confidence Through Consistency

When Amira joined her Year 6 class mid-year, she presented as withdrawn and easily overwhelmed. Small conflicts led to tears or abrupt exits from the classroom, and she often avoided group activities. Her teacher, Ms. Lee, learned from the school counsellor that Amira had experienced multiple disruptions in care, including periods of homelessness and family violence. It was clear that Amira carried both emotional and relational trauma, and that traditional behaviour management approaches would be ineffective – and potentially retraumatising.

Ms. Lee began by focusing on emotional safety and predictability. She introduced daily emotional check-ins using a feelings chart, which allowed Amira to indicate her mood privately each morning. Ms. Lee also introduced simple regulation strategies to the whole class, such as deep breathing and grounding exercises after transitions. These strategies were practised regularly and framed as tools for everyone – not just for when someone was "in trouble."

In one instance, after Amira became dysregulated following a loud disagreement between two classmates, Ms. Lee gently guided her to the classroom calm corner and offered a sensory object and breathing cue: "Let's try the five-finger breathing we practised this morning – one breath for each finger." Amira responded, and over time, began using the space and tools proactively.

As the weeks progressed, Ms. Lee introduced structured problem-solving lessons using role-play, where students acted out common social challenges and practised coping and communication strategies. Amira was hesitant at first but eventually volunteered to participate. Her confidence began to grow – not just socially, but academically. She started raising her hand in class discussions and took pride in completing tasks she once avoided.

Crucially, Ms. Lee consistently used positive reinforcement to acknowledge Amira's effort and growth. Rather than offering vague praise, she highlighted specific behaviours:

- "I noticed you took a breath and used your words when you felt upset. That shows real strength."
- "You stayed with the group during that task, even though it was tricky. That's persistence."

Creating Trauma-Informed Classrooms

Amira's self-perception slowly shifted. By term's end, she had written a reflection in her journal: "I feel proud of myself. I know how to calm down now. I don't run away – I stay and try."

This case illustrates the transformative impact of trauma-informed teaching when it is grounded in safety, consistency, co-regulation, and encouragement. Amira's growth was not linear, but with personalised support and relational trust, she developed key self-regulation skills and began to experience herself as capable and resilient.

Practical Strategies for Teaching Emotional Regulation and Resilience

To support all students – not just those with known trauma backgrounds – teachers can implement everyday practices that foster emotional awareness, self-regulation, and resilience. Below is a practical toolkit of strategies that can be easily integrated into the classroom.

Toolkit for Classroom Integration

- **Daily Mindfulness and Emotional Check-Ins**
  Begin the day with a simple 2–3 minute mindfulness practice, such as deep breathing, body scans, or guided visualisation. Pair this with an emotional check-in using a visual chart or "mood meter" that allows students to reflect on how they're arriving emotionally.
- **Interactive Role-Play Scenarios**
  Use short, age-appropriate scenarios to explore common emotional or social challenges (e.g., someone skipping your turn, receiving feedback, or feeling left out). Have students practise "what could I do or say?" and reflect on the impact of different choices. These role-plays not only build coping skills but also reinforce empathy.
- **Self-Assessment and Reflection Tools**
  Provide students with simple self-assessment forms where they can rate their ability to manage emotions, respond to challenges, or use calming strategies. Prompts might include:

  - "One time I used a strategy that helped me was…"
  - "When I feel upset, something that helps me is…"
  - "One thing I'm proud of today is…"

Sample Scripts and Prompts for Teachers

To make self-regulation tools accessible and consistent, teachers can use brief, supportive scripts during key moments:

- **To guide breathing or grounding:**
  "Let's take a mindful breath together – breathe in slowly through your nose … and out through your mouth. Let's do that again, this time counting to four."
- **To acknowledge effort in regulation:**
  "I saw how you paused and took a breath before speaking – that's a really powerful choice."
- **To support a dysregulated student:**
  "You're safe here. It looks like your body needs a moment – would you like to use a calm card or your journal?"
- **To invite reflection:**
  "What helped you stay calm during that task? Can you use that again tomorrow?"

These verbal cues help build a shared language of regulation in the classroom and reinforce the idea that emotional skills are just as teachable – and valuable – as academic ones.

Chapter Summary

Recap: The Importance of Emotional Regulation and Resilience

Throughout this chapter, we have explored how emotional regulation and resilience are essential life skills for all students, and particularly crucial for those impacted by trauma. Teaching these skills does more than reduce disruptive behaviours – it empowers students to navigate stress, engage in learning, and build meaningful relationships. When students learn how to recognise and manage their emotional responses, they are better equipped to stay present in the classroom, persist through academic challenges, and respond constructively to social conflict.

Creating Trauma-Informed Classrooms

For trauma-affected students, emotional regulation is not a "nice-to-have" – it is foundational to safety and engagement. And resilience is not about simply "bouncing back," but about building the inner resources and relational support systems that allow students to recover, grow, and redefine their sense of identity and capacity. Together, these skills support a shift from survival to thriving.

Educators are key to this process. By embedding trauma-sensitive practices into classroom routines, modelling regulation strategies, and reinforcing growth and progress, teachers create an environment in which emotional development is as valued as academic achievement.

Highlight: Key Strategies for Emotional Well-Being

This chapter has outlined a number of practical approaches for supporting students' emotional development. From breathing techniques and mindfulness activities to goal-setting and role-play, these strategies offer students concrete tools for managing their internal worlds.

We have also emphasised the importance of self-care – not only for teachers (as explored in Chapter 4), but for students themselves. Helping students develop healthy routines, reflective practices, and ways to calm their nervous systems lays the groundwork for long-term well-being.

Problem-solving, coping strategies, and positive reinforcement form the core of a classroom culture that is not only safe but empowering. These approaches teach students that they are not passive recipients of life's challenges – they are active participants in their own regulation, growth, and healing.

By cultivating these capacities consistently and compassionately, educators help all students – and especially those carrying the burden of trauma – develop the confidence, agency, and resilience they need to move forward with strength.

Guiding Questions for Reflection

- **In what moments do students show you who they are beneath the behaviour?**

    Consider how emotional regulation strategies might help you respond to these moments – not with correction, but with curiosity and care. What helps your students return to calm, and how might you support that process more intentionally?

- **What tells you a student is starting to believe in their own capacity?**
  Reflect on how your feedback, expectations, and routines contribute to the stories students begin to tell about themselves. How do you notice resilience taking shape, even in small and quiet ways?

Teachers Toolbox

Supporting Emotional Regulation and Resilience

STRATEGY	DESCRIPTION
EMOTION THERMOMETER CHECK-IN	Use visual tools such as an emotion thermometer or mood meter to help students self-identify how they're feeling. This builds emotional literacy and normalises emotional awareness.
RESILIENCE JOURNALS	Encourage students to keep a resilience journal where they track moments of effort, coping, or small wins. Promotes self-reflection and confidence.
"RESET" CHOICE CARDS	Provide a menu of co-created "reset" activities (e.g., colouring, stretching, deep breathing) that students can choose from when they feel dysregulated. Offers autonomy in moments of distress.
CELEBRATION OF EFFORT WALL	Create a classroom space to acknowledge student persistence, regulation wins, or peer support moments. Shifts focus from outcomes to personal growth.
GUIDED VISUALISATION SCRIPTS	Use short, calming visualisations (e.g., "safe place" imagery) during transitions or after lunch breaks to ground students and promote relaxation.
PROBLEM-SOLVING PARTNERS	Pair students to rehearse real-life dilemmas using role-play. Practising collaborative language builds resilience, empathy, and interpersonal regulation.
ROUTINE "MICRO-PAUSES"	Introduce 60-second pauses during transitions for mindful stretching, breathing, or grounding. Builds tolerance for quiet and emotional reset.
"WHAT HELPED ME TODAY" EXIT TICKETS	Invite students to reflect briefly at the end of the day on strategies that supported them. Encourages metacognition and reinforces self-regulation habits.

References

Alexander, K. (2019). Relationship over reproach: Fostering resilience by embracing a trauma-informed approach to elementary education. *Journal of Aggression, Maltreatment & Trauma, 30*(1). https://doi.org/10.1080/10926771.2020.1737292

Batte, S. (2021). *Name and Tame Your Anxiety: A Kid's Guide*. Free Spirit Publishing.

Barton, G., & Garvis, S. (2019). Theorizing compassion and empathy in educational contexts: what are compassion and empathy and why are they important? In *Compassion and empathy in educational contexts* (pp. 3–14). Cham: Springer International Publishing.

Blair, C., & Raver, C. C. (2015). School readiness and self-regulation: A developmental psychobiological approach. *Annual Review of Psychology, 66*(1), 711–731. https://doi.org/10.1146/annurev-psych-010814-015221

Brunzell, T., Stokes, H., & Waters, L. (2015). Trauma-informed flexible learning: Classrooms that strengthen regulatory abilities. *International Journal of Child, Youth and Family Studies, 7*(2), 218–239. https://doi.org/10.18357/ijcyfs72201615719

Cavanaugh, B. (2016). Trauma-informed classrooms and schools. *Beyond Behavior, 25*(2), 41–46. https://doi.org/10.1177/107429561602500206

Foreman, T., & Bates, P. (2021). Equipping preservice teachers with trauma informed care for the classroom. *Northwest Journal of Teacher Education, 16*(1), 2. https://doi.org/10.15760/nwjte.2021.16.1.2

Howard, J. A. (2019). A systemic framework for trauma-informed schooling: Complex but necessary! *Journal of Aggression, Maltreatment & Trauma, 28*(5), 545–565. https://doi.org/10.1080/10926771.2018.1479323

Jennings, P. A., Snowberg, K. E., Coccia, M. A., & Greenberg, M. T. (2011). Improving Classroom Learning Environments by Cultivating Awareness and Resilience in Education (CARE): Results of Two Pilot Studies. *The Journal of Classroom Interaction, 46*(1), 37–48. http://www.jstor.org/stable/23870550

Karris, S. W. (2022). *The Impact of Trauma on Learning and Behaviors in the Classroom and how a Trauma-Informed Classroom Helps* [Master's thesis, Bethel University]. Spark Repository. https://spark.bethel.edu/etd/778

Miller, K., & Flint-Stipp, K. (2019). Preservice teacher burnout: Secondary trauma and self-care issues in teacher education. *Issues in Teacher Education, 28*(2), 28–45. https://eric.ed.gov/?id=EJ1239631

Perry, B. D. (2006). Applying Principles of Neurodevelopment to Clinical Work with Maltreated and Traumatized Children: The Neurosequential Model of Therapeutics. In N. B. Webb (Ed.), *Working with traumatized youth in child welfare* (pp. 27–52). The Guilford Press.

Pickens, I. B., & Tschopp, N. (2017). *Trauma-informed classrooms*. National Counciil of Juvenile and Family Court Judges.

Rodaughan, J., Murrup-Stewart, C., & Berger, E. (2024). Aboriginal practitioners' perspectives on culturally informed practice for trauma healing in Australia. *The Counseling Psychologist, 52*(7), 1113–1141. https://doi.org/10.1177/00110000241268798

Spence, C. (2020). Using ambient scent to enhance well-being in the multisensory built environment. *Frontiers in Psychology, 11*, 598859. https://doi.org/10.3389/fpsyg.2020.598859

Van der Kolk, B. A. (2005). Developmental trauma disorder. *Psychiatric Annals, 35*(5), 401–408. https://hartfocus.nl/wp-content/uploads/2021/10/Developmental-Trauma.pdf

 Mindfulness and Relaxation Techniques in the Classroom

Chapter Overview

This chapter introduces mindfulness and relaxation techniques as essential components of trauma-informed practice, offering students accessible ways to regulate their emotions, manage stress, and reconnect with learning. For students affected by trauma, the ability to return to calm is often compromised by chronic stress responses. Mindfulness provides structured, repeatable strategies to interrupt these patterns and re-establish a sense of internal safety.

This chapter explores how techniques such as breathing exercises, guided visualisation, and progressive muscle relaxation can be embedded into daily classroom routines to support focus, emotional regulation, and resilience. Practical guidance is offered for setting up mindful routines, creating regulation-friendly environments, and responding to the varied needs of students as they build comfort with these strategies.

By incorporating mindfulness gradually and consistently, educators foster a learning environment that is both calming and empowering – where emotional regulation is taught, modelled, and supported as a shared responsibility. The result is not just a quieter classroom, but a stronger foundation for learning, connection, and long-term well-being.

DOI: 10.4324/9781003535386-11

Section 1: Introduction to Mindfulness Practices and Their Benefits

What Is Mindfulness?

Mindfulness, at its core, is the practice of paying focused attention to the present moment, intentionally and without judgement. It is both a state of awareness and a set of strategies that support individuals in tuning in to their thoughts, emotions, and bodily sensations. In educational contexts, mindfulness is increasingly recognised as a valuable tool for supporting student well-being, enhancing concentration, and improving emotional regulation.

For trauma-affected students, the benefits of mindfulness are particularly relevant. Many of these students live in a state of persistent hypervigilance, with their nervous systems primed for threat. This often results in emotional reactivity, difficulty concentrating, and a limited ability to regulate stress. Mindfulness practices offer an accessible and non-invasive means to calm the body, focus the mind, and increase students' sense of safety and self-control.

Mindfulness and Self-Regulation

Within trauma-informed education, mindfulness is not simply about relaxation – it is a foundational strategy for mind-body regulation. When students practise focusing attention (on the breath, a sound, or a visual image), they engage the parasympathetic nervous system, which helps counteract stress responses and restore calm. As Brunzell et al. (2016) explain, mindfulness activates neural pathways that promote self-regulation and executive functioning – skills that trauma-affected students may not have had the opportunity to fully develop.

In their study of trauma-informed pedagogical environments (TIPE), Brunzell and colleagues noted that teachers introduced mindfulness through brief, low-stakes classroom adaptations. These included "brain breaks," breath awareness activities, and short visualisations of safe or familiar places (like the beach or a bedroom). These mindful "mini-breaks" were used to ground students, reduce anxiety, and build a sense of control over their internal state.

Additionally, mindfulness was found to support attuned communication, helping students become more aware of how they feel and better able to communicate those feelings to others. This contributes not only to individual well-being, but to improved classroom climate and peer relationships.

Establishing Buy-In and Routine

As with any trauma-informed intervention, mindfulness must be introduced carefully and with consistency. Students benefit when mindfulness practices are woven into daily routines and supported by clear expectations. Teachers in Brunzell et al.'s study emphasised the importance of creating safe and respectful spaces for these practices to occur, noting that buy-in increased when students understood the purpose and could personalise their experience.

While the evidence base for mindfulness in mainstream education is well established – demonstrating improvements in attention, behaviour, and academic outcomes (Waters et al., 2014) – there is growing recognition of its value for trauma-affected learners as well. When embedded into classroom life with intention and care, mindfulness offers students more than just a moment of calm: it offers a pathway to reclaiming control over their bodies, their minds, and their learning.

Benefits of Mindfulness for Trauma-Affected Students

In trauma-informed classrooms, mindfulness is not just a calming activity – it is a foundational tool that supports students in developing self-awareness, emotional balance, and the ability to engage meaningfully with learning. For students whose experiences of trauma have shaped their nervous systems to expect danger or disruption, mindfulness offers a way to gently reintroduce a sense of internal safety and control.

Emotional Regulation

Mindfulness helps students recognise and respond to their emotional states with greater intention. Through practices like focused breathing, body scans, or quiet observation, students begin to notice how emotions show up in their bodies – tight shoulders, a racing heart, clenched fists – and are then guided in how to respond with gentleness rather than reactivity. Over time, this builds capacity for emotional regulation, reducing impulsive behaviours and helping students return to calm more quickly after being triggered.

Chase-Cantarini, S., & Christiaens (2019) found that school-based mindfulness practices led to significant improvements in emotional control and reduced aggression, particularly in students who had previously exhibited heightened reactivity. These findings echo classroom observations where students, given regular mindfulness practice, became better at pausing, breathing, and using self-talk to manage overwhelming emotions – practices that directly support the regulation strategies discussed in Chapter 2.

Stress Reduction

For trauma-affected students, stress is not just a passing experience – it is often a persistent state. Mindfulness interrupts that cycle. Even brief practices can signal to the body that it is safe, reducing the physiological intensity of the stress response and allowing students to re-engage with the present moment.

Lopez-Gonzales (2018) describe how regular mindfulness practice lowers cortisol levels and supports nervous system recovery, particularly for children who have experienced chronic adversity. In educational settings, this means fewer meltdowns, a decrease in avoidance behaviours, and an overall shift towards greater emotional stability. Teachers report that embedding calming practices throughout the day – rather than reserving them for "problem moments" – helped all students, but especially those with trauma histories, remain better regulated and more emotionally available for learning.

Improved Focus and Concentration

Mindfulness also strengthens attention. In classrooms where students struggle to maintain focus – often due to the mental fog or distractibility associated with trauma – mindfulness offers a way to return to the task at hand. Practices that emphasise noticing thoughts and gently returning to a point of focus help students build both awareness and persistence.

Waters et al. (2014) found improvements in working memory and sustained attention among students participating in mindfulness programmes. This is particularly relevant when considering the executive functioning challenges discussed in Chapter 3. When students practise mindfulness regularly, they are better able to follow instructions, shift between tasks, and stay engaged in lessons, even when external or internal distractions arise.

The benefits of mindfulness are not immediate, nor are they one-size-fits-all. But over time, these practices offer trauma-affected students something essential: the experience of feeling calm in their own bodies and capable in their learning. Paired with the emotional regulation strategies explored in earlier chapters, mindfulness deepens students' capacity for resilience – supporting not just recovery from trauma, but growth beyond it.

Section 2: Relaxation Techniques and Their Role in Trauma-Sensitive Education

Deep Breathing Exercises

In classrooms shaped by trauma-informed practice, the emphasis is not just on content delivery but on the regulation of the body and mind. Deep breathing exercises are among the simplest and most effective tools teachers can use to help students access calm and readiness for learning. When guided appropriately, these exercises help regulate the nervous system, improve focus, and reduce the intensity of emotional responses.

Understanding the Practice

Breathing is both automatic and intentional. Trauma-affected students often live in a state of shallow, rapid breathing that reflects ongoing hyperarousal. Teaching these students how to slow their breath, through deliberate and patterned techniques, can help shift them out of fight-or-flight mode and into a state of greater calm and control.

Common techniques include:

- **Box Breathing**: Inhale for four counts, hold for four, exhale for four, and hold again for four. This creates a rhythmic pattern that is easy to remember and promotes parasympathetic nervous system activation.
- **4–7–8 Breathing**: Inhale for four, hold for seven, and exhale for eight counts. This technique has been linked to reductions in anxiety and improved emotional control.

These patterns work by giving the mind a focus and helping students become aware of the connection between their breath and their emotional state (Figure 10.1).

Mindfulness and Relaxation Techniques

 5-5-5 Breathing

Inhale for 5 counts, hold for 5 counts, exhale for 5 counts.

 5-4-3-2-1 Grounding

Notice 5 things you see, 4 things you feel, 3 things you hear, 2 things you smell, 1 thing you taste.

 Body Scan

Progressively relax each body part from toes to head.

 Guided Imagery

Visualize a safe, peaceful place using all senses.

Figure 10.1 Mindfulness and Relaxation Techniques

Introducing Breathing in the Classroom

Breathing strategies are most effective when taught proactively – before students are in crisis. By embedding brief breathing moments into everyday classroom transitions (e.g., after lunch, before assessments), students become more comfortable using them independently in times of need. For example, teachers might begin each day with a short breathing exercise, paired with soft visuals or calming music, to centre the class and support a settled start.

Nicholls (2014) highlights the role of simple, embodied regulation strategies – such as breathing and stretching – in helping students regain control during emotionally charged moments. These tools are not framed as discipline but as care – offered to students with trust and consistency.

Brunzell et al. (2016) describe how teachers incorporated "exit the red zone" language alongside breathwork, helping students identify dysregulation and apply grounding strategies before escalation occurred.

Breathing thus becomes both a prevention and a response – teaching students to attend to early signs of distress and respond with agency.

From Practice to Pattern

When used regularly, deep breathing exercises do more than calm the moment. They begin to reshape students' relationships with their own bodies – offering reassurance that calm is possible, even in the face of distress. Over time, this contributes to stronger emotional regulation, improved attention, and greater resilience to daily stressors.

The goal is not perfection, but practice. Students may fidget, giggle, or resist at first. But with patience, repetition, and modelling, breathing becomes another tool in their regulation toolkit – quietly reinforcing the message that emotions are manageable, and support is always within reach.

Progressive Muscle Relaxation (PMR)

PMR is a simple yet effective technique that supports students in releasing physical tension and calming the nervous system. For trauma-affected students, who may carry chronic muscular tension as a result of hypervigilance, PMR offers a safe and structured way to reconnect with their bodies and access calm.

Understanding PMR

PMR involves intentionally tensing and then releasing different muscle groups in a sequential order – often starting from the feet and moving upward through the body. This contrast between tightness and relaxation helps students become more attuned to physical sensations and learn what relaxation actually feels like. In trauma-sensitive settings, where many students experience a disconnect from their bodies, PMR provides a gentle, accessible tool for building body awareness.

Wolpow et al. (2016) recommend PMR as a core strategy in trauma-informed education, especially for students who benefit from predictable, sensory-based regulation techniques. The physical nature of PMR makes it particularly effective for students who may struggle with more cognitive or language-heavy approaches to regulation.

How to Guide a PMR Session

PMR can be practised as a whole-class activity, in small groups, or even individually. It requires only a quiet space and a few minutes of focused attention. Teachers may guide students through the following steps, using a calm and steady voice:

1. **Start at the feet**: Ask students to press their toes down into the floor, holding the tension for five seconds, then releasing and noticing the difference.
2. **Move up through the body**: Continue with calves, thighs, stomach, fists, shoulders, and finally the face – tensing each muscle group, holding, and releasing.
3. **Breathe with the rhythm**: Encourage students to inhale as they tense and exhale as they release.
4. **End with stillness**: Invite students to sit or lie quietly for a moment, noticing how their body feels and what has changed.

Sessions can be adapted to suit the developmental level and comfort of the group. For younger students, it may be helpful to use imaginative language (e.g., "squeeze your fists like you're holding lemons") to make the practice more engaging.

PMR as a Routine and Responsive Strategy

Like all regulation techniques, PMR is most effective when used both proactively and responsively. Some classrooms schedule short PMR sessions during high-stress periods of the day (such as after recess or before assessments). Others offer it as a tool students can choose when they feel overwhelmed or disconnected.

When PMR becomes part of the classroom culture, students begin to internalise it as a self-care strategy. They learn that their body can be a resource for calm rather than a source of stress. As noted in the trauma-informed framework presented by Alexander (2019), structured, movement-based techniques such as PMR help students rebuild trust in their bodily sensations and foster a greater sense of control.

Visualisation and Guided Imagery

For trauma-affected students, imagination can be more than a creative tool – it can be a pathway to regulation and calm. Visualisation and guided imagery allow students to mentally step away from a stressful moment and enter a space that feels safe, soothing, and in their control. In trauma-informed classrooms, these practices help create new emotional scripts – ones that reinforce a sense of agency, rest, and internal safety.

Reclaiming Calm Through Imagination

Guided imagery involves leading students through a mental scenario that promotes a sense of peace, often by inviting them to imagine a place where they feel calm and secure. This might be a beach, a forest, their bedroom, or even an imagined landscape filled with comforting colours, sounds, and smells. The goal is not to escape reality, but to offer students a practice that allows them to reset emotionally and return to the present with more clarity and calm.

As highlighted by Brunzell et al. (2015), regular visualisation practices – especially those tied to rhythm, repetition, and sensory cues – enhance students' regulatory capacity, especially when embedded into classroom routines. These strategies support the restoration of calm and help reduce the frequency and intensity of stress responses that can interfere with learning.

Introducing Visualisation Practices

For these practices to be effective, they must be introduced with care. Students may initially find the process unfamiliar or even uncomfortable, especially if past trauma has affected their sense of safety when closing their eyes or relaxing their bodies. For this reason, it's helpful to begin with short, accessible scripts and allow students the option to participate with eyes open, sitting upright, or simply listening without visualising.

A simple script might sound like this:

> Let's take a moment to imagine a place that feels peaceful to you. Maybe it's real, maybe it's something you create. Picture what you see there—what colours, shapes, or light. Notice what sounds you hear, what the air feels like, what you might smell. Let your body begin to relax as you spend time in this place.

Some teachers pair visualisation with quiet music, soft lighting, or sensory objects to help deepen the experience. Sessions can be kept brief – two to five minutes – and gradually lengthened as students become more familiar with the practice.

Why It Works for Trauma-Affected Students

For students who have experienced adversity, the body can often feel like a place of tension or alertness. Guided imagery offers a gentle way to counter this, helping students access calm through sensory memory and imagination. Jennings et al. (2011) observed that such practices support neurological regulation by engaging the prefrontal cortex and reducing activity in the amygdala – helping students shift from survival mode into a more receptive state for learning.

Moreover, because the imagery is self-directed, students regain a sense of control – choosing where they go in their minds, how they experience it, and how they return. This process, when repeated regularly, can gradually reshape internal experiences and improve emotional flexibility.

Benefits of Relaxation Techniques for Emotional and Physical Well-Being

In trauma-sensitive classrooms, relaxation techniques are more than wellness activities – they are essential tools for restoring balance and creating the conditions for learning. Whether through breathwork, progressive muscle relaxation, or guided imagery, these practices support students in managing their internal states and responding to external stressors with increased calm and control.

Relaxation techniques directly impact the body's stress response. By engaging the parasympathetic nervous system, they slow the heart rate, reduce muscular tension, and shift the body out of the heightened alertness that many trauma-affected students experience as a baseline. This physical shift allows for a greater sense of safety and presence – both of which are necessary for engagement in learning tasks.

Emotionally, these strategies help students build self-awareness. By regularly pausing to notice how their bodies feel, what they are thinking, or how their breath is moving, students begin to develop the capacity to identify early signs of stress or dysregulation. Over time, this supports the development of emotional literacy – an essential skill discussed in earlier chapters – and gives students greater choice in how they respond to challenges.

In practical terms, students who use relaxation techniques report feeling calmer, more in control, and better able to focus. Teachers often observe improvements in classroom tone: quieter transitions, reduced reactivity, and increased cooperation. As noted in Chapters 2 and 3, emotional safety and self-regulation are foundational to learning. Relaxation practices reinforce these foundations, not by eliminating stress entirely, but by equipping students with ways to navigate it.

Importantly, these strategies are not one-size-fits-all. What works for one student may not work for another. But by offering a range of options – and embedding them into daily classroom routines – teachers help students discover the practices that support their own well-being. Over time, these practices become more than just classroom tools; they become habits that students carry into their lives beyond school, contributing to resilience, confidence, and a deeper sense of calm.

Section 3: Implementing Mindfulness and Relaxation Techniques in the Classroom

Setting Up a Routine for Mindfulness and Relaxation

For trauma-affected students, unpredictability can feel threatening. Creating consistent, predictable rhythms in the classroom helps students feel safe and grounded. Mindfulness and relaxation techniques are most effective not when used reactively in moments of crisis, but when embedded gently and regularly into the school day. When students come to expect these moments of pause, their nervous systems begin to anticipate calm – and with practice, they start to seek it out for themselves.

A simple yet powerful starting point is to anchor mindfulness at key transition points in the day. This might include beginning the morning with a mindful minute, using breathwork after recess to support re-entry, or ending each lesson with a short body scan or quiet reflection. These micro-practices do not require significant instructional time, but their cumulative impact can be profound – offering students repeated opportunities to regulate, reset, and re-centre.

Teachers who implement these practices often describe a noticeable shift in classroom tone. The act of pausing – even briefly – can signal to students that their inner world matters, and that the classroom is a space where regulation is supported, not punished. Over time, this daily rhythm of calm becomes something students rely on, particularly those who may not experience such consistency elsewhere.

As introduced in Chapters 2 and 3, trauma-sensitive environments depend on relational safety and emotional predictability. Embedding mindfulness into classroom routines strengthens both. It reinforces a culture where students learn that emotions are welcome, manageable, and supported – not just in moments of difficulty, but as a natural part of the learning journey.

Dedicating just five to ten minutes a day to mindfulness or relaxation is not about adding something new to an already full day – it's about approaching the day differently. When the pace is punctuated with calm, students are more likely to be emotionally available, intellectually engaged, and physically at ease. In this way, mindfulness becomes a rhythm, not a disruption – and regulation becomes a shared classroom habit.

Creating a Mindfulness-Friendly Environment

Establishing a classroom culture that supports mindfulness and emotional regulation involves more than implementing individual strategies – it requires the physical and emotional environment to reinforce calm, predictability, and self-awareness. One highly effective approach is the inclusion of a dedicated "calm corner" or "mindfulness space" within the classroom: a designated area where students can go to decompress, breathe, or practise a familiar regulation strategy when they need a break.

These spaces are not punitive "time-outs" but proactive, empowering options. They signal to students that emotional needs are valid and that self-regulation is supported. When students learn that they can step away safely and return when ready, they are more likely to self-monitor and advocate for their own well-being.

In their trauma-informed classroom frameworks, Brunzell et al. (2015) noted that such spaces were particularly beneficial when paired with routines and expectations. Teachers in their study described calm areas that included comfortable seating, soft lighting, visual prompts for breathing or grounding exercises, and sensory objects that supported tactile regulation.

Designing a Calm, Supportive Space

A mindfulness-friendly space does not need to be elaborate or large. What matters most is that it feels welcoming, predictable, and free of judgement. Educators might consider including:

- **Soft furnishings** like cushions, a rug, or beanbags.
- **Sensory tools** such as fidget toys, stress balls, weighted lap pads, or textured fabrics.
- **Visual supports** like calm-down cue cards, emotion charts, or nature imagery.
- **Quiet prompts** like a laminated breathing script or "5-4-3-2-1" grounding poster.

Chapter 6 also emphasised the value of these sensory-based strategies in creating a culture of co-regulation and safety. Tools such as weighted blankets, noise-cancelling headphones, or visual schedules help students orient themselves and manage stimulation without needing to verbalise distress.

Importantly, students should be introduced to the space before they need it. Practice sessions, class discussions about its purpose, and co-created guidelines for respectful use help reduce stigma and normalise emotional care. Some educators offer students the chance to personalise the space or suggest new items to include – deepening the sense of ownership and comfort.

Embedding Regulation into the Environment

Beyond a specific corner, mindfulness can be woven into the classroom's physical design. Teachers might use calming colour palettes, reduce visual clutter, or play ambient music during transitions. These subtle environmental cues reinforce a tone of calm and intentionality.

A trauma-informed classroom communicates safety not only through words and actions, but through the sensory landscape it creates. When students see their environment consistently supporting regulation, it reinforces the idea that their well-being is valued and that they are not alone in learning how to manage it.

Creating a Mindfulness-Friendly Environment

A trauma-informed classroom is more than a philosophy – it is a space that signals safety and regulation in every detail. One of the most practical and powerful ways to support mindfulness in the classroom is by establishing a designated "calm corner" or "mindfulness space." This is not a place students are sent to, but one they choose to use – an environment that offers physical and emotional refuge when the demands of the day feel overwhelming.

For many trauma-affected students, self-regulation does not come naturally. They may experience heightened physiological arousal or emotional shutdowns in response to even mild stressors. Having a clearly defined space where they can pause, breathe, and regroup empowers them to take ownership of their regulation without fear of judgement or punishment. It also communicates a powerful message: emotions are not disruptions – they are signals, and they are welcome here.

Designing the Space

A mindfulness corner does not require extensive resources or space. What matters most is intentionality. A small, thoughtfully arranged area can have a significant impact on how students feel and function. Teachers have successfully included:

- **Soft furnishings** like floor cushions, beanbags, or a small rug to encourage physical comfort and grounding.
- **Sensory tools** such as stress balls, textured objects, fidget tools, weighted lap blankets, or calming jars. These tools can help students discharge nervous energy or reconnect with their bodies.
- **Visual supports**, including calming images (like nature scenes), breathing posters, emotion check-in charts, or visual scripts for grounding and self-regulation.
- **Noise-dampening elements** like curtains, soft dividers, or headphones to reduce sensory overstimulation.

As Brunzell et al. (2015) observed, mindfulness spaces were most effective when accompanied by supportive routines and clear, respectful expectations. Students were more likely to use these spaces meaningfully when they were introduced proactively and modelled by trusted adults.

Normalising Use and Building Trust

The most effective calm corners are those that are integrated into the rhythm of classroom life. Teachers can introduce the space through class discussions, gentle modelling, or role-play. It helps to describe the space not as a retreat from the classroom, but as part of it – a tool for staying present and safe.

As noted in Chapter 6, trauma-informed classrooms rely on co-regulation and sensory scaffolding. Weighted items, grounding visuals, and quiet rituals provide non-verbal cues that support students in returning to balance without requiring them to explain or justify their emotions.

Some teachers invite students to co-create the space by selecting images, naming the area, or suggesting tools that help them reset. This builds ownership and increases the likelihood that students will use it purposefully.

Ultimately, a mindfulness-friendly environment reinforces the larger message of trauma-informed practice: that regulation is teachable, emotions are manageable, and students are not alone in learning how to care for themselves.

Introducing Techniques Gradually

Successfully embedding mindfulness into classroom life requires patience, flexibility, and responsiveness to student needs. For some students – particularly those affected by trauma – slowing down and turning inward may initially feel unfamiliar or even uncomfortable. Introducing these techniques gradually allows students to build trust in the process, develop comfort with the practices, and discover which strategies support their regulation.

Start Small, Stay Consistent

Rather than launching into long mindfulness sessions, many educators find success by starting with micro-practices – one minute of breathing, a single moment of silent observation, or a brief body scan. These small windows of calm help students ease into the routine and reduce the pressure to "do it right." As familiarity grows, practices can be extended in duration or layered into transitions throughout the day.

Teachers in trauma-informed classrooms often begin with whole-class sessions, then gradually encourage individual use of techniques – such as students choosing to go to the calm corner or independently engaging with breathing strategies. This scaffolding supports student agency while keeping the learning environment emotionally safe.

Tailor to Developmental Needs

Mindfulness practices should be responsive to developmental levels. Younger students often benefit from movement-based strategies or visual prompts, such as blowing out imaginary candles or following a "breathing star" with their finger. Older students may prefer quiet reflection, journaling, or guided visualisation. Inviting students to reflect on which strategies work best for them fosters ownership and normalises help-seeking.

Collecting feedback – formally or informally – helps educators fine-tune their approach. Questions like "What helped you feel calm today?" or "Would you like to try something different tomorrow?" give students a voice in shaping their regulation toolkit and reinforce that their experiences matter (Figure 10.2).

Incorporating Mindfulness into Academic Activities

Mindfulness doesn't need to live in isolation from academic instruction. In fact, its benefits can be amplified when integrated directly into learning.

Mindful Moments in the School Day

- **Morning Meeting** — Centering activity to start day
- **Transitions** — Brief breathing before switching subjects
- **Post-Recess** — Body scan to refocus energy
- **Before Tests** — Calming visualization
- **Dismissal** — Reflection on day's learning

Figure 10.2 Examples of Embedding Mindfulness throughout the School Day

This not only strengthens students' regulation and focus but also helps shift the classroom culture towards one that values reflection, presence, and intentional engagement.

Mindful Moments in the Lesson Flow

Teachers can introduce small rituals that link mindfulness to academic tasks. For example:

- Taking one deep breath before answering a question aloud.
- Pausing for three seconds of silence after a student shares, to create space for reflection.
- Beginning writing tasks with a short moment of quiet to "clear the mind."
- Using mindful observation in science ("What do you notice?") or art ("What colours stand out to you?") as a way to build attention and detail awareness.

These embedded practices reinforce the message that thinking and feeling are interconnected – and that calm enhances learning.

Linking to Trauma-Sensitive Curriculum Design

As discussed in Chapter 4, trauma-sensitive education involves more than behaviour management – it requires an intentional shift in how we design and deliver learning. Integrating mindfulness into academic routines reflects that shift. It slows the pace, invites students to be present, and acknowledges the emotional landscape of the classroom.

In Chapter 5, we explored the role of relational teaching and student-centred management. Mindfulness supports this by reducing reactive behaviour, increasing reflective pause, and encouraging self-regulation over compliance. Rather than controlling students' attention, it cultivates their ability to direct it.

Section 4: Case Study and Practical Strategies

Case Study: Mindfulness in Practice

In a Year 5 classroom in suburban Melbourne, Ms. Langley, a teacher with over a decade of experience, began integrating mindfulness into her daily teaching practice. Her class included several students with known trauma histories – children who had experienced foster care placement, exposure to domestic violence, or the death of a parent. Many exhibited difficulty with attention, impulsivity, and emotional outbursts, particularly during unstructured times of the day.

At the outset, Ms. Langley introduced mindfulness with short, one-minute breathing exercises each morning. Her initial observations were mixed: a few students giggled or fidgeted, others resisted closing their eyes, and some refused to participate. But she remained consistent, framing the practice as a shared tool – not a requirement. Within weeks, several students began to initiate the breathing practice themselves, requesting it before tests or after playground conflicts.

One student, Leo, had a pattern of escalating quickly during conflict, often shouting or storming out of the classroom. After Ms. Langley introduced a "mindful moment" practice during transitions, Leo began using a stress ball and quietly moving to the calm corner before reacting. Over time, he was able to articulate when he felt overwhelmed and even led a breathing practice for the class during a peer-led activity.

Ms. Langley credits this shift to two key strategies: embedding mindfulness into predictable routines and maintaining a non-judgemental, flexible approach. She also adapted the practice to suit different comfort levels – offering options such as eyes-open breathing, quiet drawing, or using grounding objects. Rather than framing mindfulness as discipline, she positioned it as self-care. As discussed in earlier chapters, this alignment with student agency and emotional safety contributed to both behavioural improvements and stronger peer relationships (see Chapters 3 and 5).

Resistance did not disappear entirely – some students continued to opt out, and others used the calm space to avoid work. But instead of removing the option, Ms. Langley engaged these students in conversations about what helped them reset and what didn't. This dialogue strengthened student trust and built a shared language of regulation and reflection across the class.

Practical Strategies for Effective Implementation

Bringing mindfulness and relaxation into the classroom does not require a specialist background or expensive resources – what it does require is intention, consistency, and a willingness to adapt practices to meet the needs of diverse learners. For educators seeking to introduce these techniques in a sustainable and meaningful way, a few well-chosen tools and routines can have a powerful and lasting impact.

One of the most accessible entry points is the use of scripts and short guided practices. These can be read aloud by the teacher, played through audio recordings, or even co-created with students over time. A simple mindfulness script – such as focusing attention on the breath for one minute or guiding students to notice the sounds around them – can serve as a reliable anchor point at the beginning or end of the day. Consistency is more important than complexity. Students benefit from repetition and predictability, particularly those who may initially find it difficult to focus or trust the process.

Brief activities can also be woven into academic transitions. A "mindful pause" before assessments, a two-minute body scan after lunch, or a breathing exercise before group work helps students reset and re-engage. These short interventions don't disrupt instruction – they support it. Over time, these practices help establish a rhythm of regulation that becomes part of the classroom's identity, not just an add-on.

For educators unsure where to start, there is a growing library of age-appropriate mindfulness resources. Apps like *Smiling Mind*, *Insight Timer*, and *Headspace* offer guided sessions tailored to school-aged children. These can be used to supplement teacher-led activities or offer variety in tone and style. Books such as *Sitting Still Like a Frog* or *Breathe Like a Bear* provide scripts and stories that make mindfulness relatable and engaging for younger learners.

In classrooms with access to technology, a rotating "mindfulness station" might include noise-cancelling headphones and a tablet with audio-guided practices. For others, a simple basket of mindfulness cards, calming visuals, or regulation tools can serve the same function. The goal is not to replicate a clinical setting, but to offer students accessible, low-stakes opportunities to practise being still, noticing their emotions, and returning to calm.

Finally, implementation is most effective when it grows out of observation and dialogue. Teachers who check in with students – asking what they found helpful, which practices they liked, or when they wished they'd had a calming strategy – build student agency and shape practices around real needs. This responsiveness reinforces the classroom's emotional safety and signals to students that regulation is a shared journey, not an imposed routine.

As with all trauma-informed practices, the goal is not perfection but presence. Mindfulness and relaxation techniques work best when they are embedded with care, offered without pressure, and supported by the broader classroom culture explored throughout this book.

Chapter Summary

This chapter explored the role of mindfulness and relaxation techniques as core components of trauma-informed practice. Far from being optional add-ons, these strategies offer students accessible ways to regulate their emotions, manage stress, and reconnect with learning. When implemented consistently, they support not only individual well-being but also help to shape a classroom culture that prioritises calm, compassion, and emotional literacy.

For trauma-affected students – many of whom experience chronic hyper-arousal or emotional disconnection – mindfulness practices provide a structured way to experience safety within their own bodies. Whether through deep breathing, progressive muscle relaxation, or guided imagery, these techniques can serve as anchors in the midst of dysregulation and stress. Over time, students begin to internalise these tools, building confidence in their ability to return to calm and re-engage with learning.

Equally important is the environment in which these practices occur. As discussed in previous chapters, emotional safety grows from consistency and predictability. Establishing a rhythm of regulation and designing spaces that support it – such as calm corners or sensory-friendly environments – helps make mindfulness accessible, inclusive, and sustainable. With care and creativity, teachers can make these practices a natural part of daily classroom life.

Guiding Questions for Reflection

- **Where in your day do students seem to need a moment of pause – and what might it change if they had one?**
    Consider the natural rhythms and stress points in your classroom. What routines or transitions might become opportunities for mindfulness?

- **What does it mean for a classroom to feel emotionally available – not just for students, but for teachers too?**
    Reflect on how your current environment supports or challenges emotional regulation. How might a mindfulness-friendly culture reshape how students (and educators) show up to learn?

Teachers Toolbox

Mindfulness and Relaxation Strategies

STRATEGY	DESCRIPTION
MINDFUL SOUND SEARCH	Invite students to close their eyes and notice all the sounds they can hear for one minute – both near and far. This builds present-moment awareness and supports sensory grounding.
EMOTION MAPPING	After a mindfulness exercise, students colour or annotate a simple body outline to show where they felt tension or calm. Helps build emotional literacy and body awareness.
CLASSROOM BREATHING RITUALS	Establish a consistent breathing pattern (e.g., "Two breaths in, one long breath out") to begin or end transitions. Repeating the same pattern builds routine and reliability.
VISUAL BREATHING PROMPTS	Post calm visuals (e.g., "breathing star" or "figure-eight breathing" diagrams) around the room to cue independent practice. Offers a visual reminder for self-regulation.
SENSORY PATHWAYS	Create simple taped paths on the floor with embedded movements (e.g., stomp, stretch, pause) that students can follow to reset. Offers movement-based regulation without requiring verbal direction.
GUIDED IMAGERY BOOK BASKET	Curate a small collection of books with calming themes or guided visualisation stories. Allow students to quietly choose one when using the calm corner.
REGULATION CHOICE MENU	Provide a laminated menu of four to five brief mindfulness or relaxation strategies students can choose from when they feel dysregulated. Builds agency and scaffolds self-awareness.
SILENT START ROUTINE	Begin the day with one to two minutes of silent focus – students may sit quietly, breathe, draw, or simply notice their thoughts. Normalises calm as the foundation for learning.

References

Brunzell, T., Stokes, H., & Waters, L. (2015). Trauma-informed flexible learning: Classrooms that strengthen regulatory abilities. *International Journal of Child, Youth and Family Studies, 7*(2), 218–239. https://doi.org/10.18357/ijcyfs72201615719

Brunzell, T., Stokes, H., & Waters, L. (2016). Trauma-informed positive education: Using positive psychology to strengthen vulnerable students. *Contemporary School Psychology, 20*(1), 63–83. https://doi.org/10.1007/s40688-015-0070-x

Chase-Cantarini, S., & Christiaens, G. (2019). Introducing mindfulness moments in the classroom. *Journal of Professional Nursing, 35*(5), 389–392. https://doi.org/10.1016/j.profnurs.2019.04.002

Jennings, P. A., Snowberg, K. E., Coccia, M. A., & Greenberg, M. T. (2011). Improving Classroom Learning Environments by Cultivating Awareness and Resilience in Education (CARE): Results of Two Pilot Studies. *The Journal of Classroom Interaction, 46*(1), 37–48. http://www.jstor.org/stable/23870550

López-González, L., Amutio, A., & Herrero-Fernández, D. (2018). The relaxation-mindfulness competence of secondary and high school students and its influence on classroom climate and academic performance. *European Journal of Education and Psychology, 11*(1), 5–17. https://doi.org/10.30552/ejep.v11i1.182

Nicholls, C. (2014). *Body, Breath and Being: A new approach to the Alexander Technique*. D&b Publishing.

Waters, L., Barsky, A., Ridd, A., & Allen, K. (2014). Contemplative education: A systematic, evidence-based review of the effect of meditation interventions in schools. *Educational Psychology Review, 27*(1), 103–134. https://doi.org/10.1007/s10648-014-9258-2

Wolpow, R., Johnson, M. M., Hertel, R., & Kincaid, S. O. (2016). *The heart of learning and teaching: Compassion, resiliency, and academic success*. Washington State Office of Superintendent of Public Instruction.

Peer Support, Social Connections, and Restorative Practices

Chapter Overview

In trauma-informed classrooms, relationships are not peripheral – they are central to healing, learning, and growth. This chapter explores how peer support, social connections, and restorative practices serve as foundational pillars in creating safe and inclusive learning environments. When students experience consistent, authentic relationships with their peers and teachers, they begin to rebuild trust, develop empathy, and navigate conflict with greater resilience.

Rather than viewing peer relationships as incidental or secondary to learning, this chapter positions them as essential elements of trauma recovery. It outlines how structured peer support systems, intentional social bonding activities, and restorative practices help students reconnect with others, regulate their emotions, and engage more fully in classroom life.

Throughout the chapter, the role of the teacher emerges as both facilitator and model of relational safety. By guiding restorative conversations, fostering shared responsibility, and creating opportunities for students to support one another, educators shape a classroom culture rooted in mutual respect and emotional accountability. In doing so, they move beyond behaviour management and into the realm of relational repair – where connection becomes both the method and the outcome.

DOI: 10.4324/9781003535386-12

Section 1: The Importance of Peer Support in Trauma-Informed Classrooms

Understanding Peer Support

Peer support is more than a strategy – it is a philosophy rooted in mutual care, empathy, and shared experience. In trauma-informed classrooms, peer support refers to a system in which students offer one another emotional and social support. This helps build a sense of safety and belonging, both of which are foundational for learning and recovery. Importantly, peer support affirms that students are not alone in their experiences and that meaningful relationships can emerge even in the aftermath of trauma.

For students impacted by trauma, relationships with peers are often fraught. Some may carry deep mistrust; others may struggle to read social cues or feel chronically unsafe in group settings. These relational difficulties can lead to social isolation, withdrawal, or behaviours misinterpreted as defiance or disengagement. Peer support, when implemented intentionally, can help bridge these divides. It creates opportunities for students to build trust in safe, reciprocal ways and offers pathways for social healing that cannot be replicated solely through adult-child interactions.

Trauma-informed peer support is grounded in core values of mutuality, respect, and empowerment. Unlike traditional helping models, which often emphasise top-down support, peer support aims to eliminate power differentials and validate each student's lived experience. This horizontal approach fosters a sense of agency and shared understanding, allowing students to give and receive support in a way that feels authentic and affirming.

The benefits of peer support are well-documented. Students who feel connected to their peers report higher levels of school engagement, lower rates of emotional distress, and greater resilience in the face of adversity (Mead & MacNeil, 2005; Phillips, 2017). Moreover, positive peer relationships have been linked to stronger social-emotional development and improved academic outcomes, particularly in environments where trauma is prevalent.

It is also important to acknowledge that peer support does not emerge spontaneously. It must be modelled, scaffolded, and nurtured within a classroom culture of emotional safety. As Brunzell et al. (2016) highlight, peer relationships play a critical role in restoring disrupted attachment patterns. When students experience repeated moments of relational repair and empathy from peers, they begin to internalise new narratives about themselves and their worthiness of connection.

In this way, peer support becomes a healing modality – one that empowers students to see themselves not just as recipients of care, but as capable of offering it. Within trauma-informed classrooms, these small yet powerful acts of support reshape the social landscape of the school and create spaces where all students can feel seen, valued, and connected.

Benefits of Peer Support for Trauma-Impacted Students

In trauma-informed classrooms, the social landscape is just as critical as the instructional one. While teacher-student relationships provide foundational safety, peer support adds a layer of relational resilience that is uniquely potent. Students often look to their peers for cues about belonging, trust, and identity. For trauma-impacted students – who may carry deep feelings of isolation or shame – peer support offers something essential: emotional resonance without hierarchy.

One of the most immediate benefits of peer support is the sense of emotional safety it provides. When students are accepted by their peers, they are less likely to feel judged, and more likely to take risks – both socially and academically. Positive peer interactions serve as micro-moments of repair, counteracting internalised beliefs of unworthiness or rejection. Research indicates that trauma-informed peer relationships promote healing by offering reciprocal validation, empathy, and shared understanding, all of which help reduce stress and anxiety.

Peer support also correlates with increased classroom engagement. Students who feel connected to their peers are more likely to participate in discussions, collaborate in group work, and take initiative in their learning. A sense of social belonging is closely tied to academic motivation and behavioural regulation, both of which are often disrupted by trauma. As peer bonds strengthen, so too does a student's investment in the school environment.

Beyond emotional support and engagement, peer relationships also serve as a fertile ground for developing essential social skills. Through structured interactions, students practise empathy, active listening, boundary-setting, and conflict resolution. These are not only protective factors for mental health but also life skills that foster resilience. Research in social-emotional learning confirms that peer-centred interventions lead to improvements in cooperation, communication, and emotional awareness (Jones & Bouffard, 2012; Zins et al., 2004).

Importantly, peer support doesn't need to be complex to be effective. Opportunities for cooperative learning, paired activities, and reflective dialogue circles can all contribute to a relationally rich environment. When students are invited to be both vulnerable and supportive, the classroom becomes a site of shared humanity rather than individual performance. In this way, peer support becomes more than a strategy – it becomes part of the ethos of a trauma-informed school.

Creating Structured Peer Support Systems

Peer support thrives in environments that prioritise intentionality and inclusion. While informal peer relationships can certainly be valuable, structured systems offer consistent opportunities for students to experience connection, empathy, and collaboration. These frameworks provide trauma-affected students with predictable, emotionally safe contexts in which to practise and receive social support – essential ingredients for healing and growth.

One effective approach is implementing peer mentoring programmes. These systems pair older or more socially confident students with younger or more vulnerable peers. With appropriate training and oversight, peer mentors can model empathy, provide encouragement, and act as relational bridges for students who might otherwise struggle with connection. This structure works particularly well when mentors are taught to listen without judgement and to respond with curiosity and compassion – qualities that help foster mutual respect and psychological safety.

Similarly, buddy systems can be introduced at any age level to promote belonging. By assigning students a designated peer for transitions, group activities, or play-based learning, teachers create opportunities for consistent relational practice. For trauma-affected students, the presence of a reliable peer – even in small moments – can help reduce anxiety and increase willingness to participate. These partnerships should be revisited regularly to ensure they remain equitable and mutually beneficial.

Group-based activities that emphasise collaboration over competition also reinforce prosocial behaviours. Restorative circles, cooperative learning tasks, and structured class jobs allow students to experience their role as a contributing member of the group. When built into the rhythm of the classroom, these practices foster a culture of interdependence – one in which students learn not only to support others but to accept support themselves.

The success of these systems relies on a strong foundation of emotional safety. As outlined in Chapter 3, classrooms that are predictable, inclusive, and relationship-driven are more likely to sustain authentic peer support. Without that groundwork, even well-designed programmes can falter. Teachers play a key role in establishing the tone – modelling vulnerability, responding to conflict with curiosity, and reinforcing the value of kindness and mutual respect.

Structured peer support is not about placing the emotional burden on students to fix one another. Rather, it is about creating the conditions for healthy, empowering relationships to flourish. In doing so, educators not only support trauma-impacted students – they cultivate a classroom culture where everyone learns that connection is both possible and powerful.

Section 2: Building Strong Social Connections in the Classroom

The Role of Social Connections in a Supportive Classroom Community

Social connections are a foundational element of any classroom, but in trauma-informed settings, their importance is magnified. Positive relationships help create a learning environment where students feel seen, valued, and respected. When students experience the classroom as a place of belonging, they are more likely to take academic risks, engage with their peers, and navigate challenges with resilience.

For many trauma-impacted students, forming connections with others can be a difficult process. Early experiences of neglect, instability, or harm may have shaped their understanding of relationships in ways that lead to mistrust, withdrawal, or conflict. These students may approach the social world with caution or defensiveness, interpreting neutral interactions as threatening or unpredictable. Without support, they can become socially isolated or misperceived as disinterested, when in fact they are longing for connection.

Teachers play a critical role in guiding students towards healthier social engagement. Through consistent modelling, emotional coaching, and inclusive practices, educators help students relearn what it means to be in a community. This includes establishing clear expectations for respectful interaction, celebrating diverse perspectives, and creating routines that invite collaboration and peer affirmation. Social-emotional learning programmes can also enhance students' relational capacity, equipping them with language, strategies, and self-awareness to build and sustain positive relationships.

These efforts are not incidental to learning – they are the soil in which learning grows. When students feel safe and connected, their cognitive and emotional resources are freed up for academic engagement. Classrooms become more cohesive, behaviour challenges decrease, and the overall climate becomes one of mutual respect and support. As Brunzell et al. (2015) note, trauma-informed practice emphasises repairing disrupted attachment capacities, and this includes fostering healthy peer bonds within a nurturing learning environment.

In many ways, the work of building social connections is not about teaching something new – it's about restoring what trauma may have interrupted. By creating classroom communities that are emotionally responsive and relationally rich, educators offer students a new blueprint for connection – one rooted in empathy, safety, and mutual care.

Strategies for Building Social Connections

Building positive peer relationships in trauma-informed classrooms requires more than encouragement – it requires structure, repetition, and intentional design. For students who have experienced trauma, relational confidence may have been disrupted by past experiences of loss, instability, or betrayal. These students may need gentle, repeated opportunities to practise connection in low-stakes ways, supported by teachers who understand the relational challenges trauma can create.

One of the most effective ways to support connection is through collaborative learning activities. When students are encouraged to work together towards a shared goal, they begin to develop mutual respect, accountability, and a sense of belonging. In trauma-informed classrooms, these activities promote interdependence and reinforce the idea that learning is a shared journey. According to Phillips (2017), collaborative structures can play a central role in peer support, especially when students are guided in how to listen, compromise, and reflect together.

Classroom meetings – also referred to as community circles or morning meetings – offer another structured space for relational practice.

These sessions allow students to speak, listen, and reflect in a guided setting, helping them build empathy and emotional literacy. Schumacher (2014) found that restorative circle practices gave students the opportunity to feel heard, especially those whose voices were often overlooked in traditional classroom dynamics. By offering a routine space for sharing and connection, classroom meetings help establish a community built on openness, mutual respect, and the shared regulation of behaviour.

Team-building exercises, such as cooperative games or short problem-solving tasks, can also provide low-pressure ways for students to connect. These activities are especially valuable at the beginning of a term or after class transitions, when relationships are still forming or have been disrupted. When facilitated with care, they give students a chance to participate socially without fear of being judged or excluded. Research suggests that these structured, playful interactions can strengthen group cohesion and support the development of social confidence in trauma-affected youth (Kaveney & Drewery, 2011).

These practices are most impactful when grounded in a broader culture of safety and predictability – as explored in Chapter 3. When students know that their interactions will be facilitated with care, and that connection is expected and supported, they are more likely to take the relational risks that lead to meaningful peer bonds. In time, these everyday routines become the scaffolding for a strong classroom community – one where students learn not only how to collaborate, but how to care.

Creating Inclusive Classroom Norms

Strong peer relationships don't emerge in isolation – they are supported by a classroom culture that explicitly values respect, kindness, and shared responsibility. Establishing clear, inclusive classroom norms is one of the most effective ways to communicate these values. When expectations around behaviour, language, and relationships are co-created and consistently reinforced, students begin to internalise them as part of the way things are done here.

These norms serve as a foundation for social connection, especially for students impacted by trauma. For those who may be hypervigilant, mistrustful, or uncertain about their place in the group, clearly articulated behavioural expectations offer structure and predictability. When students know that kindness will be upheld, that conflict will be addressed respectfully, and that difference is welcomed, they are more likely to participate authentically and take relational risks.

Rather than simply posting a list of rules, many trauma-informed educators work with students to co-construct a shared agreement about how they want to treat one another. This collaborative process not only gives students voice but also strengthens their investment in maintaining a safe and inclusive environment. As explored in Chapter 3, classrooms that feel emotionally safe are those in which students feel both heard and held – where their well-being is part of the collective responsibility.

Of course, norms are most powerful when modelled. Teachers set the tone by how they respond to conflict, handle mistakes, and speak to students and colleagues. Consistently demonstrating empathy, listening with curiosity, and using relational repair after missteps reinforces the culture far more effectively than punitive discipline. As Schumacher (2014) notes, modelling relational accountability helps students understand that repairing harm is part of community life – not a failure, but a process of re-connection.

These inclusive norms also help shift the social burden from individual students to the classroom as a whole. In a trauma-informed setting, all students learn that they have a role in maintaining a supportive environment – not through policing one another, but through practising compassion and speaking up for shared values. Over time, this creates a culture where peer support is no longer an isolated intervention but an expectation embedded into the fabric of classroom life.

Section 3: Introduction to Restorative Practices

What are Restorative Practices?

In trauma-informed education, relational safety is not only foundational – it is also reparative. Restorative practices are structured approaches that uphold this principle by focusing on relationship-building and repairing harm rather than assigning punishment. Rooted in Indigenous traditions and adapted for contemporary education settings, restorative practices shift the focus from control and exclusion to accountability, empathy, and communal healing.

At their core, restorative practices provide students and educators with tools to navigate conflict, address harm, and strengthen community ties. Rather than responding to misbehaviour with exclusionary practices such as suspension or detention, restorative approaches invite those involved to engage in dialogue, understand the impact of their actions, and take steps to repair relationships. This approach recognises that behaviour is a form of communication, particularly for students affected by trauma, and that punitive discipline often exacerbates harm rather than resolving it.

As outlined by Darling-Hammond (2023), restorative practices in schools can be categorised into two main types: repair practices and community-building practices. Repair practices include restorative conversations, circles, and conferences designed to address and resolve specific incidents of harm. Community-building practices, on the other hand, are proactive measures that foster trust, emotional connection, and a positive classroom climate, reducing the likelihood of conflict in the first place.

Importantly, restorative practices are not isolated interventions. When implemented as part of a whole-school approach, they serve as a cultural shift – transforming how schools understand misbehaviour, relationships, and discipline. This shift aligns closely with trauma-informed principles: rather than seeing the student as the problem, educators are invited to ask, "What happened?" and "What does this student need to heal and grow?".

Research also supports the alignment between restorative practices and trauma-informed goals. Schools that replace zero-tolerance policies with restorative frameworks report improved school climate, reduced behavioural incidents, and enhanced student well-being (González, 2012; Reimer, 2011). These outcomes are particularly significant for trauma-impacted students, for whom traditional punitive measures often re-trigger feelings of rejection or powerlessness.

In essence, restorative practices provide a pathway for healing within schools – not just for individual students, but for the entire community. By centring relationships and honouring each student's dignity, they embody the belief that accountability and compassion can coexist, and that growth is possible for all.

Key Components of Restorative Practices

Restorative practices offer a powerful alternative to traditional discipline approaches, especially in trauma-informed classrooms where punitive measures can reinforce shame and exclusion. Grounded in principles of empathy, accountability, and community, restorative practices centre human relationships – prioritising healing over punishment and connection over control. For students impacted by trauma, these practices offer consistent opportunities for relational repair, emotional safety, and the rebuilding of trust. The following section explores three core components of restorative practice: restorative circles, conflict resolution, and relationship repair.

Restorative Circles

Restorative circles provide a structured yet flexible way for students to come together, share experiences, and co-create a sense of belonging. Often guided by a teacher or peer facilitator, these circles invite students to speak and listen in turn, fostering mutual respect and emotional visibility. The very format – students sitting in a circle, facing one another – communicates equality and connection. In trauma-informed classrooms, restorative circles serve as gentle, repeated rituals where students can practise vulnerability, empathy, and trust in a safe, supportive space.

Circles are not only used reactively, after harm has occurred, but also proactively to strengthen community and prevent conflict. They provide space for students to express feelings, raise concerns, and engage in collective problem-solving. For students who have experienced relational trauma or struggle with trust, this consistent format helps develop a sense of predictability and emotional safety. As Schumacher (2014) notes in her study of adolescent girls in urban schools, talking circles created meaningful opportunities for students to explore their identities, challenge harmful narratives, and experience being heard – often for the first time.

Circles are also sites of co-regulation. Students learn to slow down, attune to one another's emotional cues, and witness perspectives different from their own. These micro-moments of connection foster both individual growth and collective resilience, forming a foundation for classroom culture grounded in care.

Conflict Resolution

Restorative approaches to conflict resolution are fundamentally different from punitive models. Rather than asking "Who broke the rule?" and "What is the punishment?", restorative questions focus on harm, impact, and repair. Students are invited to explore what happened, how others were affected, and what needs to happen next to make things right. This process aligns with trauma-informed values by offering voice, choice, and dignity to all involved.

Importantly, restorative conflict resolution does not excuse harmful behaviour – it addresses it in ways that are both compassionate and accountable. When students are supported to reflect on the impact of their actions, they begin to understand their role in the community and develop the empathy needed for repair. For many trauma-impacted students, who may have learned to defend themselves through defiance or withdrawal, this model offers a new relational script: one where they are not defined by their worst moments, but supported in moving beyond them.

Research confirms that restorative approaches reduce suspension rates, improve peer relationships, and enhance overall school climate (Lodi et al., 2022). In classrooms shaped by these values, students come to see conflict not as a rupture to be punished, but as an opportunity for growth, reconnection, and healing (Figure 11.1).

Relationship Repair

At the heart of restorative practices is the belief that when harm occurs, the most important outcome is not punishment but relational repair. This principle is especially powerful in trauma-informed contexts, where students may carry deep wounds around trust, betrayal, and abandonment. In these classrooms, the goal is not to enforce compliance but to support healing – both for the individual and the community.

Relationship repair involves recognising the emotional impact of actions, offering sincere apologies, and taking meaningful steps towards making amends. This process helps students build emotional literacy, understand the ripple effects of their behaviour, and experience what it means to be

Restorative Practices

What Happened?
Explore perspectives without blame

Who Was Affected?
Consider impact on all parties

How Can We Prevent?
Build skills for future situations

How Can We Repair?
Develop meaningful solutions together

Figure 11.1 Key Questions to Guide a Restorative Approach

both accountable and supported. Rather than reinforcing shame, restorative practices offer students a path back into the community.

For students who have experienced trauma, the opportunity to repair ruptured relationships can be profoundly healing. It interrupts the cycle of exclusion that often follows behavioural incidents and reinforces the message that they are still worthy of connection. As Amrhein and Sellman (2022) note, restorative practices synergise well with mindfulness, creating conditions where students can attend both inwardly and outwardly – to their own needs, and to those of others. In doing so, they begin to internalise a core belief: that while harm may occur, repair is always possible.

Benefits of Restorative Practices

When thoughtfully implemented, restorative practices offer far-reaching benefits that extend beyond behaviour management. In trauma-informed classrooms, these approaches become relational tools that promote healing, build trust, and foster the social-emotional skills students need to thrive. By centring voice, reflection, and repair, restorative practices help create a classroom culture where every student feels seen, heard, and valued. The following section outlines three key benefits: enhanced accountability, improved relationships, and increased empathy.

Enhanced Accountability

Restorative practices reframe accountability not as punishment, but as a meaningful opportunity for growth. Rather than isolating or shaming students who have caused harm, restorative approaches invite them into a process of reflection and repair. This process supports trauma-informed principles by helping students feel safe enough to take responsibility – without fear of rejection or retribution (Amrhein & Sellman, 2022).

Through structured dialogue, students are asked to consider the impact of their actions, how others were affected, and what steps they can take to make things right. This emphasis on relational accountability moves students beyond simple rule-following and towards a deeper understanding of their role in the classroom community (González, 2015). It also affirms that while behaviour has consequences, those consequences can be restorative rather than punitive.

For trauma-affected students, who may be highly sensitive to shame or accustomed to punitive responses, this approach offers a powerful shift. They are supported to see themselves not as "bad" but as capable of making amends and contributing positively. Over time, students internalise a model of accountability that is grounded in reflection, integrity, and repair – key life skills that extend well beyond the classroom (Lodi et al., 2022).

Improved Relationships

At its core, restorative practice is about relationships. By creating regular opportunities for students to speak honestly, listen deeply, and engage in repair when harm occurs, restorative practices help to build stronger, more authentic connections within the school community (McCluskey et al., 2008). This is especially significant for students who carry relational wounds – those who have experienced rejection, betrayal, or neglect. In restorative classrooms, every interaction becomes a chance to strengthen the fabric of community.

Circles, peer mediation, and restorative conversations create moments where students learn how to navigate conflict without resorting to blame or disconnection. These experiences reinforce the idea that relationships are not disposable but worth investing in – even when they become strained. As students witness and participate in relationship repair, they begin to trust that conflict does not have to mean rupture, and that reconnection is always possible (Schumacher, 2014).

Teachers, too, benefit from this approach. Restorative practices allow educators to respond to challenging behaviour in ways that preserve rather than damage their relationships with students. By approaching conflict with curiosity and compassion, teachers model the very relational skills they hope to cultivate in their students – mutual respect, emotional attunement, and a commitment to repair. As these relationships deepen, classroom dynamics shift. Trust grows. Behaviour improves. And the classroom becomes a safer, more connected space for all (Fronius et al., 2019).

Increased Empathy

One of the most profound outcomes of restorative practice is the development of empathy. When students are invited to reflect on how their actions have affected others – not through lectures, but through dialogue – they begin to see beyond themselves. They hear the emotions in their classmates' voices. They listen to stories of hurt, disappointment, or fear. And in doing so, they start to connect behaviour with impact (Lodi et al., 2022).

For trauma-affected students, developing empathy can be a transformative experience. Many have learned to suppress their emotions or operate in survival mode, where concern for others is eclipsed by the need to feel safe. Restorative practices gently guide students back into a relationship with themselves and others. By participating in structured conversations, they learn to name their own feelings and recognise the feelings of others – core components of social-emotional learning (Amrhein & Sellman, 2022; Morrison et al., 2005).

Empathy, once awakened, becomes a protective factor. It reduces aggression, increases prosocial behaviour, and strengthens the social bonds that buffer against the effects of trauma. More than that, it gives students a sense of shared humanity. In a restorative classroom, empathy is not a lesson to be taught – it is a culture to be lived. And it is through this culture that students come to understand that their actions matter, their voices are powerful, and they are part of a community where everyone's well-being counts.

Section 4: Case Study and Practical Strategies

Case Study: Implementing Restorative Practices in a Year 8 Classroom

Ms. Thompson, a Year 8 teacher in a diverse urban secondary school, had become increasingly concerned about escalating tensions in her classroom. A recent verbal altercation between two students, Lily and Ava, had disrupted a group project and left the class divided. Friends had taken sides, group dynamics had fractured, and the emotional climate of the room had noticeably shifted. Rather than reverting to punitive measures such as detention or removal from class, Ms. Thompson chose to approach the incident through restorative practice.

She began by consulting with the school's well-being coordinator and identified a framework for a restorative circle that would involve the two students directly affected, as well as several peers who had witnessed the conflict. She carefully planned the session, ensuring that students understood the purpose and that participation was voluntary. A talking piece was used to ensure equity in speaking time, and the circle was guided by key questions:

What happened? What were you thinking and feeling at the time? Who has been affected and how? What needs to happen to make things right?

During the circle, both Lily and Ava shared their perspectives. Initially defensive, each eventually acknowledged the miscommunication and emotional hurt that had occurred. Classmates spoke about how the conflict had made them feel uncomfortable and hesitant to participate in group work. The turning point came when Ava – who had previously been seen as indifferent – openly expressed regret, saying, "I didn't realise how much this upset people. I just felt attacked and reacted without thinking."

By the end of the session, both students had apologised and collaboratively identified steps to repair the harm: a public acknowledgement of their role in the conflict, a renewed commitment to respectful group dialogue, and participation in a peer-led circle the following week to check in on progress.

In the weeks that followed, Ms. Thompson observed notable changes. Group dynamics began to stabilise. Students became more open in discussions, and there was a visible reduction in minor conflicts. Perhaps most significantly, the culture of the classroom began to shift – students were more willing to speak up when something felt unfair, but they did so with an increased sense of care and curiosity rather than accusation.

This case illustrates the real-world potential of restorative practices when integrated into a trauma-informed classroom. Through guided dialogue, students had the opportunity to experience accountability without shame, empathy without forced apologies, and repair without exclusion. Rather than simply "resolving" the conflict, the circle served as a site of transformation – one that strengthened relationships and modelled a way of being together grounded in mutual respect.

Practical Strategies for Fostering Peer Support, Social Connections, and Restorative Practices

Creating a trauma-informed classroom is not simply about responding well to crises – it is about building a preventative, relational foundation where students feel safe, connected, and empowered. The following strategies offer educators concrete tools to cultivate peer support, strengthen social bonds, and embed restorative practices into everyday routines. When applied consistently, these approaches nurture emotional safety and lay the groundwork for community-centred healing.

Peer Support Initiatives

Peer Mentorship Programmes

Assigning older students or peer leaders to mentor younger or more vulnerable classmates can create powerful, trust-based relationships. These partnerships can be structured around weekly check-ins, shared goal-setting, or collaborative academic tasks. Peer mentors provide a relatable source of support, while mentees gain confidence, connection, and a sense of belonging.

Morning or Weekly Check-In Circles

Start the day – or the week – with short, structured check-ins where students can share a word, emotion, or goal. These check-ins don't require personal disclosure but instead create space for students to feel acknowledged and to practise active listening. Prompts might include:

- "What's one thing you're looking forward to today?"
- "What's something that's been on your mind?"
- "How are you arriving today – emotionally, mentally, or physically?"

Peer Support Boards or "Help Hubs"

Designate a space in the classroom where students can offer and request support – for example, through anonymous notes, suggestion jars, or affirmations. Students might write encouraging messages, offer to help with homework, or suggest ways to make the classroom more inclusive. These hubs foster a culture of care and normalise help-seeking behaviours.

Restorative Practice Techniques

Sample Script for Restorative Conversations

When harm or conflict occurs, using consistent language supports emotional regulation and models respectful dialogue. A simple script might follow these steps:

1. "Can you tell me what happened from your perspective?"
2. "How were you feeling at the time?"
3. "Who else was affected and how?"
4. "What do you need right now to feel heard or supported?"
5. "What do you think needs to happen to make things right?"

This script can be used one-on-one, in small peer conversations, or during a larger circle process. The key is tone – curious, non-judgemental, and supportive.

Steps for Setting Up a Restorative Circle

1. **Purpose and Timing** – Determine if the circle is proactive (community-building) or responsive (repairing harm). Ensure there is enough time and privacy for thoughtful dialogue.
2. **Preparation** – Identify participants and gain consent. Outline the purpose, expectations, and confidentiality boundaries.
3. **Physical Space** – Arrange chairs in a true circle. Consider a talking piece to guide turn-taking.
4. **Opening and Grounding** – Begin with a grounding activity such as breathing, a quote, or a brief mindfulness exercise.
5. **Guiding Questions** – Use open-ended prompts to explore experiences, perspectives, and needs.
6. **Closure and Follow-Up** – Summarise key takeaways, thank participants, and identify follow-up actions or check-ins.

Conflict Resolution Guidelines

- **Stay relationship-centred**: Focus on restoring connection, not assigning blame.
- **Validate all voices**: Even when harm has occurred, all parties should feel heard.
- **Agree on shared norms**: Collaboratively define respectful behaviours before conflict arises.
- **Respond, don't react**: Allow time and space before engaging in restorative dialogue if emotions are still high.
- **Model vulnerability**: Teachers who own their missteps set the tone for students to do the same.

Social Connection Activities

Collaborative Goal-Setting

Have students work in small groups to set short-term classroom goals (e.g., "We will complete our project with every member contributing one idea," or "We will greet one another respectfully each morning"). Celebrate milestones together to reinforce shared achievement and mutual investment.

Cooperative Games and Challenges

Games that require teamwork rather than competition can promote laughter, connection, and trust. Examples include building a classroom obstacle course, solving group puzzles, or participating in escape-room-style tasks that demand collaboration and creative problem-solving.

Community Service Projects

Invite students to design and implement small acts of service for the school or broader community – writing thank-you notes to staff, planting a garden, or organising a kindness week. These activities help students shift their focus from internal distress to collective purpose, reinforcing the value of contribution and empathy.

Chapter Summary

In trauma-informed classrooms, relationships are the foundation upon which learning, healing, and growth occur. This chapter has explored how peer support, social connections, and restorative practices contribute to creating a classroom environment that is emotionally safe, inclusive, and empowering for all students – particularly those affected by trauma.

When students feel connected to one another, when they are part of a community that listens, values, and respects them, their capacity for resilience increases. Peer support initiatives – whether through mentorship, group check-ins, or collaborative projects – help students feel seen and supported by those around them. Structured opportunities for social bonding foster empathy, compassion, and belonging. Restorative practices take this further, offering students tools to navigate conflict, repair relationships, and take meaningful accountability for their actions. In doing so, they build not only a stronger classroom community but essential life skills in communication, reflection, and empathy.

Crucially, the role of the teacher in guiding these processes cannot be overstated. It is the educator who sets the tone for classroom culture, who creates the conditions in which trust and safety can flourish. By modelling restorative responses, facilitating connection-building activities, and establishing consistent opportunities for peer support, teachers become facilitators of healing and community. Their daily interactions – both structured and spontaneous – shape how students experience relationships, conflict, and repair.

Trauma-informed education is not just about what we teach; it's about how we relate. And when classrooms prioritise connection, empathy, and repair, they become powerful spaces for transformation – for both students and teachers.

Guiding Questions for Reflection

When does connection show up in your classroom, and how do students respond to it?
Reflect on the moments where students reach for one another – through kindness, humour, or shared effort. What conditions make those moments possible? How might your classroom become a space where connection is not the exception, but the norm?

What does it look like when a student moves from compliance to genuine accountability?
Think about a time when a student took ownership of their actions – not because they were told to, but because they wanted to make things right. What supported that shift? What role did you play in helping it unfold?

How do your responses to conflict teach students about relationship, repair, and self-worth?
Consider the ways you respond to tension or harm in your classroom. What messages do those responses send about safety, community, and redemption? Where might restorative practice deepen those lessons?

Teachers Toolbox

Building Connection And Restoring Community

STRATEGY	DESCRIPTION
MORNING CHECK-IN CIRCLES	Begin each day with a brief check-in where students can share how they're feeling or something on their mind. Use prompts like "What's one word for how you're arriving today?" to build connection and trust.
RESTORATIVE CONVERSATION PROMPTS	Use open-ended, reflective questions after conflict: "What happened?", "How were you feeling?", "Who was affected?", and "What needs to happen to make things right?"

(*Continued*)

(Continued)

STRATEGY	DESCRIPTION
PLANNING A RESTORATIVE CIRCLE	Establish the purpose, invite participants, prepare a talking piece and space, and use respectful facilitation. Follow up with summarised outcomes and support agreements.
PEER MENTORSHIP ROLES	Assign leadership roles to students to support others (e.g., welcome buddy, check-in partner). These roles help build empathy, responsibility, and community.
COLLABORATIVE GROUP GOALS	Work with students to set shared academic or behavioural goals (e.g., "We will show respect during discussions"). Celebrate progress to reinforce group cohesion and shared purpose.
REPAIR AGREEMENTS	After restorative conversations, co-create a simple written or verbal plan outlining how harm will be repaired and what support is needed to move forward constructively.
COMMUNITY SERVICE PROJECTS	Facilitate small student-led initiatives (e.g., planting a garden, kindness notes, peer appreciation days) that promote belonging, purpose, and prosocial contribution.

References

Amrhein, B., & Sellman, E. (2022). Attending in and out: Synergising mindful and restorative practice. In B. Amrhein & B. Badstieber (Eds.), *Impossible perspectives on behaviour: Theoretical, empirical and practical contributions to the de- and reconstruction of the label 'behavioural disorder'** (in press).

Brunzell, T., Stokes, H., & Waters, L. (2015). Trauma-informed flexible learning: Classrooms that strengthen regulatory abilities. *International Journal of Child, Youth and Family Studies, 7*(2), 218–239. https://doi.org/10.18357/ijcyfs72201615719

Brunzell, T., Stokes, H., & Waters, L. (2016). Trauma-informed positive education: Using positive psychology to strengthen vulnerable students. *Contemporary School Psychology, 20*(1), 63–83. https://doi.org/10.1007/s40688-015-0070-x

Darling-Hammond, S. (2023). *Fostering belonging, transforming schools: The impact of restorative practices.* Learning Policy Institute. https://doi.org/10.54300/169.703

Fronius, T., Darling-Hammond, S., Persson, H., Guckenburg, S., Hurley, N., & Petrosino, A. (2019). Restorative justice in U.S. schools: An updated research review. *WestEd*. Retrieved from https://www.wested.org/resources/restorative-justice-in-u-s-schools-an-updated-research-review/

González, T. (2012). Keeping kids in schools: Restorative justice, punitive discipline, and the school to prison pipeline. *Journal of Law and Education, 41*(2), 281–335.

González, T. (2015). Socializing schools: Addressing racial disparities in discipline through restorative justice. In D. Losen (Ed.), *Closing the school discipline gap: Equitable remedies for excessive exclusion* (pp. 151–165). Teachers College Press.

Jones, D. E., & Bouffard, S. M. (2012). Social and emotional learning in schools: From programs to strategies. *Social Policy Report, 26*(4), 1–33. https://doi.org/10.1002/j.2379-3988.2012.tb00073.x

Kaveney, K., & Drewery, W. (2011). Restorative practices that support young people in schools: From theory to practice. In T. McCluskey, M. Hadfield, G. Thomas, & P. Spratt (Eds.), *Restorative approaches in schools* (pp. 113–124). Dunedin Academic Press.

Lodi, E., Perrella, L., Lepri, G. L., Scarpa, M. L., & Patrizi, P. (2022). Use of restorative justice and restorative practices at school: A systematic literature review. *International Journal of Environmental Research and Public Health, 19*(1), 96. https://doi.org/10.3390/ijerph19010096

McCluskey, G., Lloyd, G., Kane, J., Riddell, S., Stead, J., & Weedon, E. (2008). Can restorative practices in schools make a difference? *Educational Review, 60*(4), 405–417. https://doi.org/10.1080/00131910802393456

Mead, S., & MacNeil, C. (2005). Peer support: What makes it unique? *International Journal of Psychosocial Rehabilitation, 10*(2), 29–37.

Morrison, B., Blood, P., & Thorsborne, M. (2005). Practicing restorative justice in school communities: The challenge of culture change. *Public Organization Review, 5*(4), 335–357.

Phillips, R. (2017). Five keys for gaining parent and family buy-in for restorative practices. *International Institute of Restorative Practices*. Retrieved from https://www.iirp.edu/news/five-keys-for-gaining-parent-and-family-buy-in-for-restorative-practices

Reimer, K. (2011). An exploration of the implementation of restorative justice in an Ontario public school. *Canadian Journal of Educational Administration and Policy, 119*, 1–42.

Schumacher, A. (2014). Talking circles for adolescent girls in an urban high school: A restorative practices program for building friendships and developing emotional literacy skills. *SAGE Open, 4*(4), 1–13. https://doi.org/10.1177/2158244014554204

Zins, J. E., Bloodworth, M. R., Weissberg, R. P., & Walberg, H. J. (2004). The scientific base linking social and emotional learning to school success. In J. E. Zins et al. (Eds.), *Building academic success on social and emotional learning: What does the research say?* (pp. 3–22). Teachers College Press.

Integrating Indigenous Perspectives and Understanding Intergenerational Trauma

Introduction

Colonisation is not a distant event – it is an ongoing reality with enduring consequences for Aboriginal and Torres Strait Islander peoples. This chapter explores how the legacies of colonisation, forced assimilation, and systemic marginalisation continue to affect Indigenous students today, particularly through the transmission of intergenerational trauma. It highlights how trauma is not only personal but also social and historical, shaping how students engage with education systems that have long excluded, silenced, or harmed them.

Rather than focusing solely on the challenges faced by Indigenous students, this chapter centres cultural safety, community connection, and resilience. It outlines the critical role of schools and teachers in recognising historical injustices and creating learning environments where Indigenous students feel seen, respected, and supported. From curriculum design to conflict resolution, every interaction becomes an opportunity to affirm identity, build trust, and contribute to healing.

Throughout the chapter, educators are invited to move beyond awareness and into action – by embedding culturally responsive practices, building genuine partnerships with communities, and creating spaces where Indigenous voices are valued. In doing so, they help reposition education not as a site of control or assimilation, but as a platform for connection, dignity, and cultural continuity.

Section 1: Historical Context of Colonisation and Forced Assimilation

Overview of Colonisation and Its Impact on Indigenous Communities

Understanding the impact of trauma on Indigenous students and communities requires a clear reckoning with the legacy – and continued effects – of colonisation. In Australia and other settler-colonial nations, colonisation was not simply a historical moment; it was and remains a systemic process rooted in displacement, cultural erasure, and forced assimilation. The profound trauma experienced by Aboriginal and Torres Strait Islander peoples is not only intergenerational – it is ongoing, reinforced by systems that continue to marginalise and silence Indigenous voices.

Policies of forced removal, the suppression of language and cultural expression, and the imposition of foreign educational systems were key tools of colonisation. The removal of Aboriginal children from their families – now known as the Stolen Generations – sought to sever cultural continuity and re-educate children into whiteness. As documented in numerous inquiries and reports, including the landmark *Bringing Them Home* report (1997), these removals were underpinned by assumptions of Indigenous inferiority and enacted through violent disruption of family, identity, and community.

Residential schooling and institutionalisation played a significant role in this cultural destruction. Indigenous children placed in missions or government institutions were often subjected to harsh discipline, denied their language and traditions, and told to be ashamed of who they were. The suppression of language was particularly devastating – not only because language carries cultural knowledge and identity, but because it is central to intergenerational connection and healing. When a child is forbidden to speak their language, they are also cut off from the stories, values, and belonging that help anchor their sense of self.

As the Australian Childhood Foundation (2010) highlights, these historical traumas are compounded by ongoing experiences of racism, dispossession, and socio-economic marginalisation. The psychological, spiritual, and cultural wounds inflicted by colonisation have had enduring consequences for Aboriginal and Torres Strait Islander communities. These include heightened rates of intergenerational trauma, grief and loss, and systemic disadvantage across areas such as health, education, and justice (Australian Childhood Foundation, 2010).

The trauma caused by these policies is not simply held in memory – it is lived. As educators, recognising this history is essential. Trauma-informed practice, when applied in Indigenous contexts, must begin with cultural humility and a commitment to truth-telling. For many Aboriginal and Torres Strait Islander students, school has not historically been a place of safety. Instead, it has often mirrored the systems of control, surveillance, and exclusion that their families have faced for generations. Without a clear understanding of this legacy, well-meaning educators risk retraumatising students through silences, omissions, or culturally insensitive practices.

Yet alongside this trauma, there is extraordinary strength. Indigenous communities have resisted, survived, and continued to nurture culture, language, and connection despite concerted efforts to erase them. Cultural continuity, community support, and identity pride are protective factors that promote resilience and healing. As noted in Chapter 8, inclusive curriculum design that acknowledges and celebrates diverse cultural perspectives is not a pedagogical add-on – it is a form of repair. When schools affirm Indigenous identities and centre Indigenous knowledge, they become part of the healing process rather than its obstruction.

In moving towards trauma-informed and culturally responsive education, teachers must engage not only with the emotional and behavioural impacts of trauma but also with its structural roots. Colonisation is not just the backdrop to students' lives – it is a force that has shaped the institutions they encounter every day. To teach in a trauma-informed way is, therefore, to teach in a decolonising way: one that acknowledges harm, centres cultural safety, and works alongside communities to build environments where Indigenous children feel seen, respected, and strong.

Lasting Effects on Indigenous Peoples and Communities

The trauma of colonisation is not confined to the past. Its impact endures – etched into systems, policies, and institutions that continue to shape the lives of Aboriginal and Torres Strait Islander peoples. Dispossession, forced assimilation, and the erosion of cultural identity have left deep scars that manifest today in stark and persistent disparities across education, health, housing, and employment. These are not simply unfortunate outcomes; they are the structural consequences of historical injustice (Australian Childhood Foundation, 2010).

The education system remains one of the most visible sites where this legacy continues to play out. Indigenous students are more likely to be suspended, more likely to leave school early, and less likely to access higher education pathways than their non-Indigenous peers (MacGill & Blanch, 2013). These disparities are compounded by systemic under-resourcing, ongoing racism, and curricula that frequently erase or tokenise Indigenous perspectives. As noted by Hart, Whatman, and MacGill (2012), the absence of authentic representation and the dominance of Eurocentric narratives in classrooms contribute to alienation and disengagement for many Indigenous learners.

Within schooling environments, Indigenous students may also encounter daily experiences of cultural marginalisation – whether through microaggressions, lowered expectations, or policies that fail to reflect the collective nature of Indigenous cultural values (MacGill & Blanch, 2013). These experiences cannot be disentangled from broader historical patterns. For families who endured the Stolen Generations or mission schools, education has often been a tool of assimilation rather than empowerment. The mistrust that lingers in many communities is not abstract – it is grounded in lived memory and intergenerational pain (Atkinson, 2013).

Health and well-being outcomes further reflect the lasting impact of colonisation. Rates of chronic illness, psychological distress, substance use, and early mortality are significantly higher among Indigenous populations, closely linked to social determinants of health shaped by structural racism and disadvantage (Australian Childhood Foundation, 2010). These issues are not only systemic – they are embodied. As Atkinson et al. (2010) explain, trauma is passed across generations not only through stories and behaviours, but through biology, attachment patterns, and collective memory.

In schools, this may show up as emotional dysregulation, withdrawal, aggression, or avoidance – all behaviours that are often pathologised or punished without consideration of their roots. As Perso and Hayward (2015) point out, failure to understand these expressions within their cultural and historical context risks reproducing cycles of harm. Trauma-informed education, then, must be both historically aware and culturally grounded. It must make space for Indigenous ways of knowing and healing, and resist the temptation to treat behaviour as detached from story.

Yet amid these challenges, there is strength. Cultural identity, kinship, and connection to Country remain powerful protective factors. Research by Chandler and Lalonde (1998, as cited in MacGill & Blanch, 2013) shows that communities with strong cultural continuity – including language maintenance and local governance – experience significantly lower rates of youth suicide and mental distress. These findings underscore a critical truth: that cultural marginalisation is a risk factor, but cultural connection is a healing force.

The work of education, then, must be reparative. It must acknowledge the damage done – not only historically, but through everyday practices that exclude, silence, or misrepresent. It must elevate Indigenous voices, employ Indigenous educators, and teach the truth about this country's history in ways that honour its complexity. Trauma-informed pedagogy, in this context, is inseparable from justice. It is a commitment to transforming schools into places where Indigenous children and communities are not only supported but celebrated.

Educational System's Role in Past and Present Contexts

Education has long been a contested space in the lives of Aboriginal and Torres Strait Islander peoples – a site of both profound harm and enduring hope. Historically, formal education systems were explicitly designed to assimilate Indigenous children into colonial norms, values, and identities. Schooling was not offered as a pathway to empowerment, but as a mechanism of control – a means to "civilise" and separate children from their families, communities, and cultures.

Mission schools, government institutions, and residential facilities were established with the clear intent of erasing Indigenous language, spirituality, and kinship systems. As Perso and Hayward (2015) explain, these institutions were not neutral spaces; they were enforcers of colonial ideology, often punishing students for speaking their language or practising their culture. The consequences were deeply traumatic. Generations of children were told that who they were was wrong – unworthy of respect, unworthy of learning, unworthy of belonging.

For many Aboriginal families, memories of these institutions are raw and unresolved. This history has contributed to intergenerational mistrust of mainstream schooling – an emotional and cultural inheritance that continues to shape the experiences of students, parents, and communities today

(Atkinson, 2013). Education has been a site of loss, but it can also be a site of healing – if it is reimagined with truth-telling, respect, and cultural responsiveness at its core.

Contemporary education systems hold enormous potential to shift this narrative. Schools can become places of cultural safety, where Indigenous identities are not only acknowledged but affirmed. This begins with educators recognising the historical role schools have played in the oppression of Indigenous peoples – and actively working to disrupt ongoing patterns of exclusion. As MacGill and Blanch (2013) argue, teachers must be more than well-meaning; they must be willing to critically examine their own practices, challenge systemic bias, and centre Indigenous voices in both content and pedagogy.

Embedding Indigenous perspectives into the curriculum is not simply about inclusion – it is about justice. When students encounter truth in their learning – about land dispossession, resistance, survival, and sovereignty – they are offered a more honest and inclusive national story. For Indigenous students, this representation affirms their place within the classroom. For non-Indigenous students, it fosters empathy, critical thinking, and shared responsibility for reconciliation (Hart et al., 2012).

Educators also play a crucial role in fostering trust and relationships. Trauma-informed and culturally responsive teaching requires more than academic competence – it demands cultural humility, relational awareness, and a commitment to ongoing learning. Teachers must understand how trauma presents in the classroom, how it intersects with identity, and how their own actions can either perpetuate harm or contribute to healing (Australian Childhood Foundation, 2010).

Importantly, schools that succeed in supporting Indigenous students are often those that build strong, reciprocal partnerships with communities. As Perso and Hayward (2015) emphasise, culturally safe classrooms are co-created with – not just for – Aboriginal and Torres Strait Islander peoples. This means involving Elders, valuing Indigenous pedagogies, and creating spaces where community knowledge is respected as legitimate and powerful.

Repositioning education as a platform for healing requires courage, reflection, and systemic change. It means holding space for grief and pride, for cultural loss and cultural strength. When educators step into this space with openness and integrity, they become part of a much larger story – one in which schools no longer silence, but elevate; no longer erase, but repair.

Section 2: Understanding Intergenerational Trauma and Its Impact on Indigenous Students

What Is Intergenerational Trauma?

Intergenerational trauma refers to the transmission of traumatic stress and its effects across generations. It occurs when the collective trauma experienced by one generation – such as colonisation, displacement, cultural suppression, and systemic violence – continues to influence the lives, behaviours, and well-being of subsequent generations. For Aboriginal and Torres Strait Islander peoples, intergenerational trauma is not an abstract concept – it is a lived reality shaped by the ongoing legacy of colonisation and its many harms (Atkinson et al., 2010).

Unlike trauma that results from a single, isolated event, intergenerational trauma is cumulative and complex. It is rooted in prolonged exposure to adversity – such as the forced removal of children, the denial of land rights, and the suppression of language and culture. This trauma is passed on not only through stories and behaviours, but through relational patterns, emotional regulation difficulties, and the social systems that continue to marginalise Indigenous people (Atkinson, 2013).

Importantly, intergenerational trauma is not limited to individual psychological symptoms. It is also social, cultural, and structural. It affects entire communities – shaping identity, collective memory, parenting practices, and relationships to institutions such as schools, health services, and law enforcement. As the Australian Childhood Foundation (2010) explains, this trauma is encoded not only in the mind, but in the nervous system, in attachment patterns, and in the very fabric of community life.

Students affected by intergenerational trauma may not always be aware of its source, but they often feel its effects. A young person may carry inherited stories of loss and injustice, even if those stories were never explicitly told. They may struggle with trust, regulation, or belonging, not because of personal failure, but because of the echoes of historical harm. In classrooms, this trauma may manifest as withdrawal, hypervigilance, anger, or disconnection – behaviours that can easily be misunderstood or mislabelled in the absence of cultural and historical awareness.

Understanding intergenerational trauma requires educators to look beyond individual behaviour and recognise the broader social, historical, and cultural context that shapes students' lives. It also means resisting

Integrating Indigenous Perspectives

deficit narratives. While trauma is real and its impacts are significant, so too is the strength that Indigenous communities continue to demonstrate in the face of adversity. The existence of intergenerational trauma does not define Indigenous identity – it highlights the need for relational, responsive, and respectful education that honours both the pain and the resilience that coexist in many students' stories.

Manifestations of Intergenerational Trauma in Indigenous Students

The effects of intergenerational trauma often reveal themselves subtly in classrooms – through behaviours, relationships, and patterns that are easily misunderstood without the lens of trauma-informed and culturally responsive practice. For Aboriginal and Torres Strait Islander students, these behaviours are not simply the result of individual adversity, but often the outcome of inherited and collective wounds carried across generations.

One of the most common manifestations of intergenerational trauma is difficulty with trust. Many Indigenous students arrive at school carrying internalised messages about institutions that have historically harmed their families and communities. School, for some, is not experienced as a safe or welcoming place, but as a space of surveillance and judgement. This can lead to guardedness, reluctance to engage, or resistance to authority figures – responses that are frequently misread as disrespect or disengagement (Atkinson, 2013; Perso & Hayward, 2015).

Social withdrawal and emotional shut-down are also common. Students may avoid peer relationships, retreat from group activities, or present as emotionally detached. These behaviours can reflect a deep-seated fear of vulnerability, shaped by past and inherited experiences of loss or rejection. Similarly, hypervigilance – the constant scanning for danger – is often seen in trauma-affected students. These children may be easily startled, appear on edge, or react strongly to perceived threats, including tone of voice, physical proximity, or changes in routine (Australian Childhood Foundation, 2010).

These signs are not random. They reflect nervous systems that have been shaped by unpredictability and harm. As outlined in Chapter 2, chronic exposure to trauma can disrupt the development of the brain's regulatory systems, leaving students with limited access to the executive functions needed for learning and social engagement. Students may struggle with attention, working memory, impulse control, and the ability to shift flexibly between tasks. These cognitive impacts are often misdiagnosed or punished rather than understood and supported (Brunzell et al., 2016).

Chapter 3 further explored how these disruptions affect learning behaviourally. Students living with trauma – especially intergenerational trauma – may present as defiant, oppositional, or withdrawn. Yet beneath these behaviours lies a nervous system doing its best to survive. When teachers interpret these responses through a trauma-aware lens, they can begin to shift from asking "What's wrong with this student?" to "What has happened – and what do they need?"

Emotional regulation is another key challenge. Students affected by trauma may struggle to identify, express, or manage their feelings. They may escalate quickly when frustrated or become overwhelmed by seemingly minor stressors. This dysregulation is not a sign of poor character or inadequate parenting – it is often a neurological imprint of trauma that requires relational, co-regulatory support in the classroom (Alexander, 2019; Atkinson et al., 2010).

Academic performance, too, is often compromised. Students may appear disinterested or apathetic, but in reality, they may be coping with a constant sense of threat or emotional disconnection that limits their ability to attend, process, and retain information. As highlighted earlier in the book, learning is relational. Students cannot thrive cognitively until they feel safe, connected, and supported – physiologically, emotionally, and culturally.

Understanding the manifestations of intergenerational trauma means recognising that every behaviour is a form of communication. It requires educators to look beyond compliance, beyond surface-level performance, and towards the relational and historical layers that shape how students show up in learning spaces. Only then can we begin to create classrooms where healing is possible – and where Indigenous students are met not with judgement, but with understanding and care.

Implications for Educators

For educators working with Aboriginal and Torres Strait Islander students, understanding intergenerational trauma is not an optional extension of good practice – it is central to building safe, inclusive, and effective learning environments. Trauma does not exist in a vacuum. It is shaped by social, cultural, and historical forces that continue to affect how students experience school, authority, relationships, and belonging.

Recognising these broader socio-cultural factors is critical. Behaviour that might be interpreted as avoidance, defiance, or lack of motivation may instead reflect protective responses developed in contexts of cultural loss, systemic racism, or inherited grief. As Atkinson (2013) and Perso and Hayward (2015) both emphasise, educators must resist deficit-based assumptions and instead develop a deeper awareness of how history and identity intersect in students' day-to-day experiences.

A trauma-informed lens, when applied thoughtfully, allows educators to see behaviour not as a problem to be fixed, but as a message to be understood. This approach involves slowing down, being curious rather than reactive, and seeking to understand what might be underlying a student's disengagement or emotional outbursts. In the context of intergenerational trauma, this means recognising that for some students, simply attending school is an act of courage and persistence.

Empathy is essential – but so too is cultural responsiveness. Trauma-informed practice must be grounded in cultural safety and humility. As the Australian Childhood Foundation (2010) notes, support for Indigenous students must be both relational and contextually aware. This includes honouring cultural identity, involving families and communities, and embedding Indigenous knowledges and perspectives throughout the curriculum – not just during NAIDOC Week or on cultural celebration days.

Importantly, educators must also do their own work. This includes critically reflecting on their own positionality, questioning inherited narratives, and engaging with professional learning that deepens understanding of both trauma and colonisation. As Hart et al. (2012) argue, the act of embedding Indigenous perspectives into educational practice is not simply pedagogical – it is political and relational. It signals to students that their stories matter, and that their identities are valid and valued.

Ultimately, to teach with a trauma-informed approach that takes intergenerational trauma into account is to create space for healing – not just academic growth. It means co-regulating before correcting. It means listening more than speaking. And it means standing alongside students, not above them, as they navigate complex emotional and cultural landscapes.

When Indigenous students are met with compassion, consistency, and cultural respect, they are not only more likely to thrive – they are more likely to see school as a place of belonging and possibility. That shift, subtle though it may be, is how systems begin to change – one relationship, one classroom, one story at a time.

Section 3: Creating a Culturally Safe and Inclusive Environment

Principles of Cultural Safety

Cultural safety is not a checklist or a classroom display. It is a relational and ethical commitment to ensuring that all students – particularly those from historically marginalised communities – feel respected, valued, and protected from harm. For Aboriginal and Torres Strait Islander students, cultural safety is the foundation upon which trust, engagement, and well-being are built. Without it, even the most well-intentioned trauma-informed strategies risk falling short or doing harm.

A culturally safe environment is one in which Indigenous students can be themselves without fear of judgement, stereotype, or exclusion. It is a space where they are not asked to leave their identities at the classroom door, and where their cultural knowledge, language, and experience are acknowledged as assets – not deficits. As Perso and Hayward (2015) assert, cultural safety requires educators to recognise the power imbalances that exist in schools and to shift practice accordingly. It demands more than celebrating diversity; it involves actively challenging the systemic forces that marginalise Indigenous voices.

Central to this is the ongoing work of self-awareness. Educators must examine their own beliefs, assumptions, and unconscious biases about Indigenous peoples and cultures. This includes interrogating the dominant narratives taught in schools – those that centre Western knowledge systems and frame Aboriginal and Torres Strait Islander histories through deficit or trauma lenses alone (Hart et al., 2012). Cultural safety begins when teachers acknowledge that their own cultural worldview is not neutral or universal, and that teaching itself is never a culturally neutral act.

Microaggressions – those subtle, often unintentional messages that communicate exclusion or superiority – can undermine cultural safety just as deeply as overt racism. These may include questioning a student's identity, mispronouncing names without effort to learn, assuming all Aboriginal students know each other, or treating Indigenous perspectives as an "add-on" to the "real" curriculum. Left unchecked, these small harms accumulate, eroding trust and reinforcing messages of inferiority. Cultural safety requires that these harms are named, addressed, and prevented – not normalised.

A key principle of cultural safety is that it is defined not by the teacher, but by the student. It is not enough for educators to believe they are being respectful; students must feel it. As the Australian Childhood Foundation (2010) emphasises, safety in the classroom must be experienced relationally and consistently – not just during cultural celebrations or individual lessons, but as an ongoing part of the learning environment.

This means embedding practices that affirm Indigenous identities, involving families and communities in meaningful ways, and ensuring that Indigenous perspectives are visible and valued across the curriculum. It also means creating classroom agreements that centre respect, challenge discriminatory language or behaviour, and uphold the dignity of every learner.

When cultural safety is prioritised, classrooms become places not just of inclusion, but of belonging. Students can take emotional risks, engage more deeply with their learning, and bring their whole selves into the space. For Indigenous students in particular, this can be transformative. It signals that they are not merely tolerated – they are understood, welcomed, and needed.

Practical Strategies for Cultural Safety

Creating a culturally safe classroom is not a passive act. It requires deliberate, reflective choices – both in curriculum design and in the everyday relationships educators cultivate with students and communities. Cultural safety is made visible through action. The following strategies offer concrete ways educators can embed respect, belonging, and cultural affirmation into their practice.

Representation in Curriculum and Pedagogy

Representation matters deeply. When Aboriginal and Torres Strait Islander students see their histories, cultures, and communities reflected in what is taught – and how it is taught – they receive a powerful message: *You belong here.* Integrating Indigenous perspectives across all subject areas affirms the significance of Indigenous knowledge systems and counters the longstanding marginalisation of these voices within mainstream education (Hart et al., 2012).

This includes teaching truthfully about colonisation and resistance, highlighting Indigenous contributions to science, art, governance, and sustainability, and using texts by Indigenous authors in English and literacy lessons.

But it also requires critically examining the assumptions and silences in existing curriculum materials, and working to ensure that Indigenous stories are not reduced to trauma narratives or tokenistic inclusions (MacGill & Blanch, 2013).

Cultural Protocols and Practices

Acknowledging and respecting Indigenous cultural protocols is an important way of embedding cultural safety into the rhythm of school life. Practices such as Acknowledgment of Country and Welcome to Country ceremonies are more than formalities – they are acts of recognition and respect that locate learning on Indigenous land and affirm the sovereignty of Aboriginal and Torres Strait Islander peoples.

These practices should be consistent and meaningful, not performative. Involving students in Acknowledgment of Country, explaining its purpose, and making it a regular part of classroom routines helps build awareness and deepen cultural understanding. Schools can also explore how other local protocols – such as language use, artefact care, or community invitations – might be respectfully incorporated in partnership with local Elders and knowledge holders (Perso & Hayward, 2015).

Culturally Responsive Teaching Practices

Culturally responsive teaching is not about adding content – it's about shifting practice. Indigenous ways of learning often prioritise relational, experiential, and land-based knowledge. Incorporating group learning, storytelling, visual and oral modalities, and place-based education can help align classroom practice with Indigenous pedagogies (MacGill & Blanch, 2013).

Storytelling, in particular, is a powerful tool. It invites connection, transmits values, and makes space for students' voices and identities. Using yarning circles, local stories, or narrative reflection allows students to engage on emotional and cultural levels, not just academic ones. Likewise, learning through doing – through observation, repetition, and hands-on activity – can support students who may struggle with more linear or abstract methods often privileged in Western classrooms.

Importantly, these approaches benefit all students. They enrich classroom dialogue, expand worldviews, and create a more inclusive and dynamic learning environment. When Indigenous pedagogies are valued not only for Indigenous students but as good teaching for all, cultural safety is woven into the fabric of classroom life.

Building Partnerships with Indigenous Communities

Cultural safety is not achieved through individual effort alone – it is a collective responsibility that requires schools to build meaningful, sustained partnerships with Aboriginal and Torres Strait Islander communities. These relationships must be based on respect, reciprocity, and a genuine willingness to listen, learn, and co-create educational spaces that reflect the strengths, values, and aspirations of Indigenous peoples.

One of the most powerful ways to embed cultural safety is by working alongside Indigenous Elders, community leaders, and cultural organisations to guide curriculum development and inform school practices. These partnerships ensure that Indigenous voices are not merely consulted, but central to educational decision-making. As Perso and Hayward (2015) argue, schools must "work with" communities rather than "do for" them – recognising that Elders and cultural leaders are knowledge holders whose insights enrich both the cultural and pedagogical dimensions of schooling.

Inviting community members to participate in curriculum planning, classroom visits, and school events is a practical and powerful strategy. This might include collaborating on local history units, co-designing cultural programmes, or consulting on behavioural expectations that reflect community values. When done respectfully, these engagements enhance relevance, increase community trust, and demonstrate to students that their identities and cultures are seen and valued (MacGill & Blanch, 2013).

Involving Indigenous storytellers, artists, and speakers is another meaningful practice. Storytelling has long been central to Indigenous cultures as a way of transmitting knowledge, values, and identity. When students hear stories directly from community members – especially those who speak with cultural authority – they gain deeper insights into the lived experiences, wisdom, and diversity of Aboriginal and Torres Strait Islander peoples. These experiences are not just informative; they are transformative. They foster empathy, disrupt stereotypes, and build authentic cultural understanding (Hart et al., 2012).

Importantly, partnerships must be grounded in cultural protocols and approached with humility. This means asking rather than assuming, compensating people for their time and knowledge, and being open to feedback – even when it challenges existing school norms. As the Australian Childhood Foundation (2010) notes, for Aboriginal and Torres Strait Islander communities, trust must be earned. Historical experiences of exclusion, tokenism, or exploitation have led many communities to approach schools with caution. Educators must recognise this history and commit to building relationships slowly, consistently, and respectfully.

Schools that invest in these partnerships not only improve outcomes for Indigenous students – they contribute to broader community healing and connection. They become sites where culture is not extracted but nurtured, where learning flows in both directions, and where students come to understand education as something that affirms rather than undermines identity.

Supporting Indigenous Students and Families

Creating a culturally safe school environment extends beyond the classroom – it also means building strong, respectful relationships with Indigenous families. These relationships are central to student well-being. When families feel welcomed, heard, and respected, they are more likely to engage with the school and support their children's learning journeys. For many Aboriginal and Torres Strait Islander families, school has not always been a place of inclusion. Educators must therefore take intentional steps to build trust and ensure communication is open, reciprocal, and culturally sensitive.

Effective partnerships begin with listening. Rather than relying solely on formal processes, schools can invite families to share insights about their child's strengths, learning preferences, and cultural background. This might include understanding kinship systems, ways of knowing and being, or community practices that shape a child's identity and behaviour. As Perso and Hayward (2015) suggest, these conversations are not about "accommodating difference," but about creating environments where culture is recognised as a strength and foundation for learning.

It is also important to offer multiple, flexible avenues for family involvement. Some families may feel more comfortable engaging through informal yarning, cultural events, or by meeting with trusted community representatives. Ensuring the school environment feels culturally welcoming – from visual cues like artwork and flags to the presence of Indigenous staff – can make a meaningful difference in family engagement and student comfort (MacGill & Blanch, 2013).

For Indigenous students, access to culturally safe spaces within the school can provide a critical buffer against everyday stressors. These spaces might include designated rooms led by Indigenous staff or community mentors, lunchtime yarning circles, or dedicated programmes that affirm identity and provide targeted support. Mentorship initiatives, in particular, can offer relational continuity, cultural affirmation, and guidance for navigating both academic and personal challenges (Hart et al., 2012).

Mentors – whether Elders, Indigenous teachers, or community leaders – can help students make sense of their experiences, build resilience, and strengthen pride in their identity. These relationships also create important bridges between the school and the broader community. As the Australian Childhood Foundation (2010) notes, connection to culture and community is a key protective factor in trauma recovery. When students feel culturally supported and relationally connected, their capacity for learning, self-regulation, and engagement grows.

Supporting Indigenous families and students is not about adding one more programme – it is about shifting the culture of the school to one of deep respect, listening, and shared responsibility. It is about recognising that culture is not a barrier to overcome, but a gift to be honoured.

Case Study: Supporting an Indigenous Student Experiencing Intergenerational Trauma

Liam, a quiet Year 7 Aboriginal student, had been on the periphery since the start of the school year. He rarely raised his hand, avoided group work, and often stared out the window during class activities. His teachers initially described him as shy or "hard to reach." He didn't cause any trouble – he just didn't seem to be fully present.

Over time, a pattern began to emerge. Liam would shut down when asked to read aloud or participate in activities that drew attention. He never came to school events, and he often turned in incomplete work or none at all. During parent-teacher interviews, Liam's mother attended alone. She was polite, but reserved, and spoke briefly about her own school experiences, which had been negative and at times traumatic.

It wasn't a single moment that shifted things, but a series of small observations by Liam's homegroup teacher, Ms. Taylor. She began to wonder whether his reluctance wasn't about ability or motivation – but about trust. She knew that for many Aboriginal students, school hadn't always been a safe place. And while Liam hadn't explicitly spoken about his experiences, Ms. Taylor recognised the importance of building a stronger, more culturally responsive relationship.

She reached out to the school's Aboriginal Education Worker (AEW), who already knew Liam's family. Together, they developed a gentle check-in routine. Each morning, Liam was invited to stop by the AEW's room for a casual chat, some quiet time, or help settling into the day. No pressure, no counselling – just presence and consistency.

In the classroom, Ms. Taylor made subtle shifts. She began embedding Aboriginal perspectives into her English and history units – not as a standalone topic, but as a thread throughout the curriculum. She used visual texts, oral storytelling, and yarning circles to give students more ways to engage, and allowed alternative formats for assignments. Liam slowly started participating – not dramatically, but enough to notice. He shared a story from his grandfather during a class discussion and created a poster on Indigenous plant knowledge for science week.

Later in the term, when a misunderstanding arose between Liam and another student, the school opted for a restorative approach. With support from the AEW, a conversation was facilitated where both students had the opportunity to speak, listen, and repair. It wasn't easy, but it left Liam feeling respected and supported rather than singled out or punished.

By the end of the year, Liam was not only more engaged academically – he was smiling more, joining in peer conversations, and attending school events. His progress was not the result of a single intervention, but of consistent, culturally safe relationships and learning environments that recognised who he was, where he came from, and what he needed to feel safe.

This case highlights the power of relational, community-connected practice. It reminds us that the most meaningful change often begins not with grand gestures, but with small, deliberate acts of care.

Practical Strategies for Teachers

While understanding intergenerational trauma and cultural safety is essential, it is the daily practices of educators that bring this knowledge to life in meaningful, sustained ways. Practical strategies grounded in cultural humility, empathy, and reflective practice can help transform classrooms into places of connection, safety, and resilience for Indigenous students. The following approaches offer teachers concrete ways to build inclusive, trauma-informed environments that honour Indigenous identity and foster student well-being.

Cultural Sensitivity Training

A genuine commitment to cultural safety begins with critical self-reflection. Ongoing professional learning around Aboriginal and Torres Strait Islander histories, cultures, and the impacts of colonisation is essential – not as a compliance activity, but as part of a teacher's ethical responsibility. These trainings should be led or co-designed by Indigenous educators and community members, offering opportunities for staff to confront assumptions, explore bias, and better understand the legacy of colonisation in education (Perso & Hayward, 2015). When cultural competency becomes embedded in the school's professional culture, it strengthens the capacity of all staff to work respectfully with Indigenous students and families.

Integrating Indigenous Perspectives

Including Indigenous perspectives in the curriculum must go beyond special dates or isolated lessons. It involves weaving Aboriginal and Torres Strait Islander knowledge systems, histories, and worldviews throughout all learning areas. This might look like exploring Indigenous astronomy in science, analysing contemporary Indigenous poetry in English, or learning about land management practices through geography. Crucially, these inclusions should be done in collaboration with community members where possible, ensuring that representation is accurate, respectful, and locally relevant (MacGill & Blanch, 2013). When Indigenous students see their cultures reflected and respected in everyday learning, it strengthens both engagement and identity.

Encouraging Student Voice

One of the most powerful ways to foster safety and inclusion is to actively invite and honour student voice. Indigenous students, like all students, thrive when they are given opportunities to share their experiences, perspectives, and aspirations. Teachers can facilitate this by creating classroom spaces where storytelling, reflection, and cultural sharing are welcomed and scaffolded. This might include yarning circles, cultural presentations, or reflective journaling. Importantly, student participation should always be voluntary and respectful – never forced or tokenistic. When students are trusted to speak on their own terms, they are more likely to feel seen and valued in the learning community (Hart et al., 2012).

Restorative Approaches

For Indigenous students who may have experienced schooling as punitive or exclusionary, restorative practices offer a powerful alternative. Rather than relying on traditional discipline methods that can further alienate students, restorative approaches focus on relationship-building, empathy, and accountability. When conflict arises, practices such as restorative conversations or yarning circles provide space for students to express themselves, understand the impact of their actions, and collaboratively repair harm. These methods align closely with Indigenous values of community, respect, and collective responsibility, making them especially appropriate in culturally safe, trauma-informed settings (Schumacher, 2014). By using restorative approaches consistently, educators foster a classroom culture that prioritises healing over punishment.

Taken together, these strategies do more than support Indigenous students – they contribute to a school culture where all students benefit from greater inclusivity, empathy, and respect. When educators are willing to learn, listen, and adapt, they help create a system where Indigenous students can not only succeed academically but also feel culturally affirmed, emotionally safe, and genuinely connected.

Chapter Overview

This chapter has explored the complex and enduring impact of colonisation and intergenerational trauma on Aboriginal and Torres Strait Islander students. By tracing the historical roots of educational inequality – through dispossession, forced assimilation, and cultural erasure – it has highlighted how these legacies continue to shape the experiences of Indigenous children and families in schools today.

The chapter emphasised that trauma for Indigenous students is often collective, relational, and historical. It cannot be separated from the broader systems and structures that have long excluded, silenced, or misrepresented Indigenous voices. At the same time, it highlighted the resilience, strength, and cultural continuity that continue to sustain Indigenous communities, offering powerful foundations for healing and growth.

Central to culturally safe, trauma-informed practice is the recognition that schools have the potential to be either sites of harm or sites of transformation. Through cultural safety, restorative approaches, inclusive pedagogy, and genuine partnerships with Indigenous families and communities, educators can play a meaningful role in breaking cycles of trauma and building stronger, more connected learning environments.

Ultimately, this chapter has reinforced that supporting Indigenous students is not about "fixing" behaviour or offering surface-level inclusion – it is about listening, learning, and creating educational spaces where Aboriginal and Torres Strait Islander students feel safe, valued, and empowered to thrive.

Guiding Questions for Reflection

Where in your practice do Indigenous voices feel present – and where are they still missing?
Consider whose stories, histories, and identities are visible in your curriculum and relationships. What might change if those voices were centred more often?

What does it mean for your classroom to feel culturally safe – not just for some students, but for all?
Reflect on how your current environment supports or undermines cultural connection and belonging. How might cultural safety reshape how Indigenous students show up to learn?

Teachers Toolbox

Creating Culturally Safe and Trauma-Informed Classrooms

STRATEGY	DESCRIPTION
BUILD RELATIONSHIPS BEFORE RESPONSES	Take time to build trust and connection with Aboriginal and Torres Strait Islander students. Relational safety often needs to come before academic engagement or behavioural expectations.
INCLUDE INDIGENOUS PERSPECTIVES ACROSS THE CURRICULUM	Embed First Nations histories, literature, science, and art into regular teaching – not just on cultural days. Ensure perspectives are locally relevant and community-informed where possible.
USE RESTORATIVE CONVERSATIONS	When harm or conflict occurs, use restorative questions to guide reflection and repair. Create space for students to speak and be heard in ways that affirm identity and community values.
CREATE CULTURALLY SAFE SPACES	Establish designated areas or check-in routines where Indigenous students can connect with community mentors or cultural workers. These spaces offer grounding, support, and cultural affirmation.
PARTNER WITH LOCAL ELDERS AND COMMUNITIES	Involve Aboriginal and Torres Strait Islander community members in curriculum planning, storytelling, and school events. Seek guidance on local protocols and build partnerships with respect.
SUPPORT STUDENT VOICE AND CULTURAL SHARING	Invite, but never require, students to share their cultures, stories, or experiences. Value lived experience as knowledge and create opportunities for voluntary storytelling and reflection.
INVEST IN ONGOING CULTURAL COMPETENCY	Engage in regular cultural sensitivity training and personal reflection. Approach this as a lifelong journey rather than a one-time task – and invite challenge and learning along the way.

References

Alexander, R. (2019). *A safe and inclusive school: What does it look like and how do we get there?* Education Department, Northern Territory Government.

Atkinson, J. (2013). *Trauma-informed services and trauma-specific care for Indigenous Australian children*. Closing the Gap Clearinghouse.

Atkinson, J., Nelson, J., & Atkinson, C. (2010). Trauma, transgenerational transfer and effects on community wellbeing. In N. Purdie, P. Dudgeon, & R. Walker (Eds.), *Working together: Aboriginal and Torres Strait Islander Mental health and wellbeing principles and practice* (pp. 135–144). Commonwealth of Australia.

Australian Childhood Foundation. (2010). *Doing nothing hurts: A national report into the experiences of children and young people when accessing help for emotional and behavioural problems.* Australian Childhood Foundation.

Brunzell, T., Stokes, H., & Waters, L. (2016). Trauma-informed positive education: Using positive psychology to strengthen vulnerable students. *Contemporary School Psychology, 20*(1), 63–83. https://doi.org/10.1007/s40688-015-0070-x

Hart, V., Whatman, S., & MacGill, B. (2012). Pre-service teachers' understandings of cultural responsiveness: An investigation into transformative learning. *Australian Journal of Indigenous Education, 41*(1), 18–27. https://doi.org/10.1017/jie.2012.3

MacGill, B., & Blanch, F. (2013). Indigenous education and literacy policy in Australia: Extending learning opportunities and outcome. *International Electronic Journal of Elementary Education, 5*(3), 325–338.

Perso, T., & Hayward, C. (2015). *Teaching Indigenous students: Cultural awareness and classroom strategies for improving learning outcomes.* Allen & Unwin.

Schumacher, D. J. (2014). Talking circles for adolescent girls in an urban high school: A restorative practices program for improving social-emotional wellbeing. *Journal of School Counseling, 12*(21), 1–33.

Trauma-Informed Professional Development and Reflective Practice

Introduction

This chapter explores the critical role of ongoing professional development (PD) and reflective practice in sustaining trauma-informed care (TIC) within schools. While earlier chapters focused on foundational principles and classroom strategies, this chapter shifts the focus to the practices that support educators themselves – ensuring that they have the knowledge, tools, and support to implement TIC consistently and compassionately over time.

By examining how structured learning and intentional reflection strengthen trauma-informed approaches, this chapter emphasises the importance of schools investing in the ongoing growth and well-being of their staff. It also highlights the ways in which educators can embed TIC into daily practice, not as a fixed programme, but as an evolving, relational commitment to supporting all students – especially those affected by trauma. Through case examples and practical strategies, this chapter provides a roadmap for sustaining a compassionate school culture where both students and teachers can thrive.

Section 1: The Role of PD in TIC

Why PD Is Essential for TIC

TIC in education is more than a philosophy – it is a specialised, evolving practice that requires knowledge, skills, and reflective capacity. Teachers who support trauma-affected students must understand how trauma impacts the brain, behaviour, and learning, and this understanding does not develop automatically through experience alone. Ongoing PD is essential for equipping educators with the tools to create safe, responsive classrooms and build positive relationships with students who have experienced adversity.

PD in TIC helps educators move beyond reactive or surface-level responses to student behaviour. Rather than viewing behaviours through a disciplinary lens, trauma-informed training reframes these responses as potential signs of distress, unmet needs, or dysregulation. For instance, students who withdraw, lash out, or fail to complete tasks may not be disengaged by choice but overwhelmed by trauma-related triggers. Without appropriate training, these behaviours are often misunderstood, reinforcing punitive cycles that further alienate vulnerable learners (Cavanaugh, 2016).

Research has shown that effective PD includes training in trauma awareness, empathy, and de-escalation strategies, enabling teachers to identify and respond to student needs with greater confidence and care. Trauma-awareness training introduces the physiological and psychological effects of trauma on the developing brain, helping educators interpret behaviour more accurately. Empathy training supports the development of relational skills – essential for building trust and emotional safety in the classroom – while de-escalation techniques help teachers navigate conflict without retraumatising students (Brunzell et al., 2016).

Moreover, PD is not a one-time event but a continuous process. TIC evolves alongside research in neuroscience, psychology, and education. As new insights emerge about the nature of trauma and healing, PD must adapt to reflect the latest understandings. This includes integrating current models of resilience, understanding the intersection of trauma and culture, and applying whole-school approaches that involve all staff – not just classroom teachers.

Effective PD also plays a protective role for educators themselves. Working in trauma-affected environments can place a significant emotional burden on teachers, especially when they lack tools to process their own responses or manage classroom stress. PD that includes reflective practices, peer support, and emotional regulation strategies can help teachers manage compassion fatigue and sustain their well-being over time (Madigan & Kim, 2021; Miller & Flint-Stipp, 2019). In this way, trauma-informed PD benefits not only students but also those who teach and care for them.

Ultimately, TIC is a skill set – and like any skill, it must be learned, practised, and refined. Schools that prioritise ongoing professional learning foster a culture of safety, growth, and compassion, ensuring that trauma-affected students receive the support they need from confident, informed, and resilient educators. Investing in PD is therefore not an optional extra – it is the foundation of effective, inclusive, and healing educational practice.

Key Areas of Focus for Trauma-Informed PD

To be meaningful and impactful, PD in TIC must extend beyond general awareness and into specific, practice-based domains. Effective trauma-informed professional learning includes four key focus areas that help educators build knowledge, deepen empathy, and sustain their work over time.

Understanding Trauma

Foundational to all trauma-informed practice is a clear understanding of how trauma affects the developing brain, learning capacity, and classroom behaviour. PD should include evidence-based insights from neuroscience and developmental psychology, helping educators understand how chronic stress alters neural pathways related to attention, memory, and self-regulation (Brunzell et al., 2016). When teachers recognise the physiological roots of student behaviour, they are better able to respond with empathy rather than judgement. Training should also support teachers in identifying trauma symptoms – such as hypervigilance, emotional dysregulation, or withdrawal – and offer practical strategies to create predictable, safe classroom environments that support regulation and recovery (Cavanaugh, 2016).

Cultural Competency

Trauma does not exist in isolation from identity. For Aboriginal and Torres Strait Islander students – as well as students from refugee, migrant, or other marginalised communities – trauma is often compounded by systemic exclusion, racism, and historical injustice. PD must therefore include ongoing learning around cultural competency, equity, and anti-bias education. This includes understanding intergenerational trauma, incorporating culturally responsive pedagogy, and building partnerships with families and communities as active collaborators in student learning (Perso & Hayward, 2015). As outlined in previous chapters, culturally safe classrooms are essential for healing – and professional learning must reflect this understanding at every level.

Restorative Practices and De-Escalation Techniques

Trauma-aware educators need more than theory – they need tools to respond effectively to challenging moments. Training in restorative practices provides a relational framework for addressing conflict, harm, and behavioural issues in ways that build trust and promote accountability without shame or exclusion. Rather than defaulting to punitive approaches, restorative methods – such as structured conversations and yarning circles – prioritise student voice and repair. Similarly, de-escalation techniques help educators manage heightened emotional states calmly and constructively, supporting both student regulation and classroom safety.

Self-Care and Compassion Fatigue

Working with trauma-affected students is emotionally demanding. Without proper support, educators are at risk of experiencing secondary traumatic stress or compassion fatigue. Effective PD should therefore include explicit strategies for educator well-being, including self-awareness practices, emotional regulation tools, and peer support structures. When teachers are encouraged to reflect, rest, and seek help, they are better equipped to sustain their work over time (Miller & Flint-Stipp, 2019). A trauma-informed school is not only a safe place for students – it is a safe place for staff.

Taken together, these focus areas ensure that trauma-informed PD is holistic, practical, and grounded in the real-life demands of the classroom. They support educators to not only understand trauma but to respond to it with skill, care, and cultural integrity.

Types of PD Opportunities

PD in TIC must reflect the diverse needs of educators and the evolving nature of trauma research. To build an authentic, sustainable trauma-informed practice, schools must offer a range of professional learning opportunities that are relevant, accessible, and grounded in current evidence. The following formats provide meaningful entry points for building capacity and embedding trauma-aware principles in daily teaching.

Workshops and Seminars

In-person workshops remain one of the most effective forms of trauma-informed PD, especially when they include active engagement and practice-based learning. Educators benefit from interactive sessions that offer practical strategies – such as classroom regulation techniques, restorative practices, and co-regulation models – that can be implemented immediately. These workshops are most impactful when co-facilitated by educators and mental health professionals, and when they allow for role-play, discussion, and real-world application (Cavanaugh, 2016). Schools that offer ongoing workshops, rather than one-off events, foster a shared language of care and consistency across staff teams.

Online Courses and Webinars

With increasing demands on teacher time, flexible learning through online platforms has become essential. Online courses and webinars offer accessible options for teachers to build foundational and advanced trauma knowledge at their own pace. These platforms can cover diverse topics – from brain-based responses to trauma, to self-care, to trauma-informed behaviour supports – and are especially helpful for rural and remote educators who may not have access to in-person training. When online learning includes opportunities for reflection and peer discussion, it becomes not only informative but also transformative (Evans & Coccoma, 2014; Oberg et al., 2023).

Peer Learning Groups

Learning is most powerful when it is collaborative. Peer learning groups – such as professional learning communities (PLCs), study circles, or debriefing sessions – offer educators a space to reflect, share, and refine trauma-informed strategies. These groups can reduce the isolation teachers often feel when navigating complex student needs and provide emotional validation and encouragement. As highlighted in the Rivertown case study, peer collaboration increased teacher confidence, trust, and alignment in trauma-informed approaches across the school community. When structured well, these groups promote consistency in trauma-informed values and foster a strong culture of collective care.

Consultation with Mental Health Experts

Trauma-informed practice benefits from cross-disciplinary input. Regular consultation with mental health professionals – such as psychologists, trauma specialists, or school counsellors – offers valuable opportunities for educators to ask questions, receive case-specific guidance, and deepen their understanding of trauma's impacts. These experts can co-deliver PD, offer debriefing after critical incidents, or provide coaching for teachers managing complex student behaviours. Schools that integrate mental health professionals into their PD structures support both student needs and staff well-being (McInerney & McKlindon, 2014; Oberg, 2025).

Section 2: Reflective Practice and Its Importance in Trauma-Informed Education

What Is Reflective Practice?

Reflective practice is the deliberate process of examining one's own actions, beliefs, and assumptions in order to improve professional judgement and effectiveness. For educators, it involves stepping back from day-to-day teaching to ask critical questions: *Why did I respond that way? What impact did that interaction have? How could I have supported that student differently?* This ongoing self-inquiry is foundational to trauma-informed education, where the needs of students are complex, varied, and often invisible at first glance.

Unlike reactive decision-making, reflective practice is intentional and structured. It might involve journaling, collaborative discussion, supervision, or quiet moments of introspection. The aim is not to find perfect answers, but to cultivate awareness, curiosity, and a willingness to change. As Evans and Coccoma (2014) explain, reflective practice empowers educators to explore how their own histories, biases, and emotional responses influence their approach to students and classroom dynamics.

In trauma-informed contexts, this self-awareness becomes especially important. Educators are often called upon to respond to challenging behaviours, emotional dysregulation, or disengagement – and their response can either build trust or reinforce harm. Reflective practice helps teachers pause and consider the meaning behind student behaviours, evaluate whether their response was culturally safe and emotionally attuned, and consider alternative strategies that might be more effective or compassionate.

Reflective practice also supports teachers in recognising their own emotional responses, especially in the face of distressing or triggering situations. As outlined by McInerney and McKlindon (n.d.), educators who are aware of their own emotional states are better able to regulate themselves, model calm, and remain present with students – even in moments of high stress or conflict.

In short, reflective practice bridges the gap between trauma theory and responsive teaching. It ensures that TIC is not simply a set of techniques, but a relational, evolving process grounded in self-awareness and ethical commitment. As such, it is not an "add-on" to trauma-informed PD – it is the thread that runs through it.

Benefits of Reflective Practice in Trauma-Informed Education

Reflective practice is not only a professional responsibility – it is a source of renewal and growth. In the context of trauma-informed education, it allows teachers to refine their practice, deepen their empathy, and increase their own resilience. Educators working with trauma-affected students face emotionally demanding and complex situations, often without clear solutions. Reflective practice provides a space to step back, make meaning of these experiences, and return to the work with greater insight and intention.

Continuous Improvement

One of the most immediate benefits of reflective practice is its role in ongoing professional learning. By critically evaluating what worked – or didn't work – in a particular interaction or lesson, teachers can better tailor their approaches to support trauma-affected students. Reflection transforms everyday experiences into learning opportunities. For instance, a teacher might consider how a student's emotional outburst was influenced by a sensory trigger in the classroom, or how a change in routine might have disrupted a student's sense of safety. These insights help educators adjust their strategies to better meet students' needs moving forward (Cavanaugh, 2016).

Increased Empathy

When teachers engage in reflection, they are more likely to shift from reacting to behaviour towards seeking to understand it. Reflective practice prompts educators to ask: *What might be going on for this student? What might they be trying to communicate?* This orientation fosters deeper empathy, as it invites teachers to consider the student's story, context, and possible trauma history. As Evans and Coccoma (2014) emphasise, reflective practice is a cornerstone of relational work. It encourages perspective-taking, which is essential in trauma-informed approaches that centre emotional safety and connection.

Personal Growth

Trauma-informed work also asks educators to explore their own emotional landscape. Reflection allows teachers to become aware of their own triggers, assumptions, and stress responses – factors that can shape their interactions with students in powerful ways. This self-knowledge supports professional boundaries, emotional regulation, and authentic connection. As noted by McInerney and McKlindon (n.d.), teachers who reflect regularly are more likely to model calm, compassionate behaviour even in moments of challenge. Over time, this process of introspection fosters both personal and professional growth, strengthening educators' capacity to remain grounded, responsive, and aligned with trauma-sensitive principles.

Reflective practice is not about perfection. It is about being willing to sit with complexity, ask difficult questions, and stay open to change. In trauma-informed education, where no two students are the same and every interaction matters, reflective practice is what transforms good intentions into meaningful, sustained impact.

Reflective Techniques for Educators

For reflection to become a meaningful part of trauma-informed practice, it must be intentional and supported by accessible tools. Teachers need structures that invite them to pause, process, and respond to the emotional and relational demands of their work. The following techniques offer educators practical ways to engage in ongoing self-inquiry, both individually and collaboratively.

Journaling

Journaling provides a quiet, personal space to reflect on daily experiences. In the context of TIC, journaling can help educators explore their emotional responses, assess the effectiveness of their strategies, and identify patterns in student behaviour or classroom dynamics. Writing creates distance and perspective, allowing teachers to slow down and make sense of complex situations without the pressure to immediately act or solve. As Evans and Coccoma (2014) note, structured journaling also supports professional growth by encouraging educators to revisit past reflections and notice how their practice evolves over time.

Peer Debriefing

Teaching is relational work – and reflection is often most powerful when shared. Peer debriefing involves talking through experiences with a trusted colleague, mentor, or peer learning group. These conversations help educators process difficult moments, challenge assumptions, and gain new perspectives on their students and themselves. When embedded into school routines – such as weekly team meetings or reflective check-ins – peer debriefing builds a culture of support, vulnerability, and professional learning (Brunzell et al., 2016). Importantly, it also helps reduce the emotional isolation that often accompanies work with trauma-affected students.

Self-Assessment Checklists

For educators who prefer structured reflection, self-assessment checklists provide a concrete way to review daily practice. These tools prompt teachers to consider specific elements of TIC, such as:

- Did I respond to dysregulation with calm and curiosity?
- *Was my classroom emotionally and culturally safe for all students today?*
- *How did I support student voice and agency?*

These checklists can be adapted to suit different learning environments and used weekly or daily as a quick point of reflection. Over time, they encourage educators to make trauma-informed principles visible in their day-to-day practice (Figure 13.1).

Reflective Practice Cycle

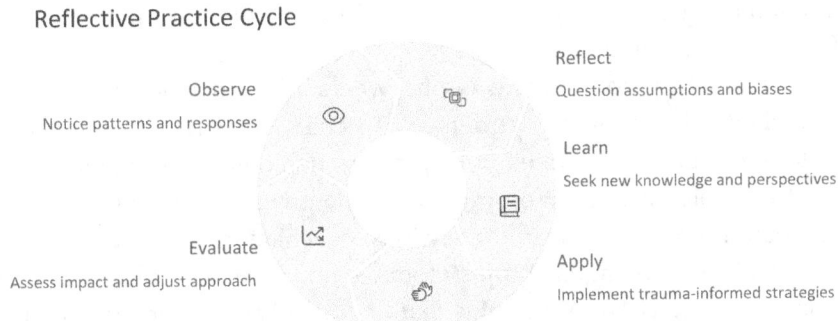

Figure 13.1 Visual Cycle of Reflective Practice for Educators

Mindfulness and Self-Awareness Exercises

Mindfulness is not only a student strategy – it is a powerful reflective tool for educators. Brief mindfulness practices – such as deep breathing, body scans, or moment-to-moment awareness – can help teachers notice their own emotional states and regulate their responses in real time. This self-awareness is critical when working with students who may trigger strong emotional reactions. As McInerney and McKlindon (n.d.) emphasise, when educators are able to pause and ground themselves, they model emotional regulation and create a more predictable, calm classroom climate.

Together, these techniques empower educators to reflect with honesty, humility, and purpose. They create space for learning and growth – not only in how teachers understand trauma, but in how they show up for themselves and their students.

Section 3: Sustaining a Compassion-Focused, Trauma-Informed Approach

Building a Supportive School Culture

TIC cannot rest solely on the shoulders of individual teachers – it must be woven into the fabric of the school culture. When schools adopt a whole-system approach, where all staff share a common understanding of trauma, emotional safety, and relational practice, TIC becomes not just a strategy, but a way of being. Sustaining this approach requires commitment, consistency, and a shared vision of compassion at all levels of the school community.

A supportive school culture is one where PD and reflective practice are embedded into everyday routines. Teachers need regular opportunities to revisit trauma-informed principles, deepen their understanding, and adjust their practice based on evolving student needs. This might include team-based professional learning sessions, coaching from well-being leaders, or collaborative inquiry projects focused on trauma-informed pedagogy (Brunzell et al., 2016). When this learning is collective and sustained, it shifts school culture from compliance to shared responsibility.

Leadership plays a pivotal role in this process. School leaders set the tone for how TIC is valued, prioritised, and resourced. When leaders model relational practice, provide time for reflection and debriefing, and advocate for staff well-being, they create conditions where teachers feel safe to take risks, ask for support, and engage in ongoing learning. As Evans and Coccoma (2014) note, leadership support is one of the strongest predictors of whether trauma-informed approaches become embedded or fade over time.

A compassionate school culture also attends to staff well-being. Teachers working in trauma-affected contexts need to feel that their emotional labour is recognised and that their own needs are not secondary. Providing access to supervision, well-being check-ins, and opportunities for restorative dialogue among staff helps prevent burnout and compassion fatigue. It also signals that emotional safety matters not just for students – but for adults, too.

Ultimately, building a trauma-informed culture is about more than programmes or policies. It is about relationships. It is about trust, shared language, and the daily decisions that prioritise care, reflection, and belonging. When all members of a school community are committed to this vision, TIC becomes not just sustainable, but transformative.

Strategies for Sustaining TIC

Creating a trauma-informed school is only the beginning – sustaining that approach requires deliberate structures, leadership support, and a collective commitment across the school community. Without ongoing investment, TIC can fade into a series of disconnected practices rather than becoming a cultural foundation. The strategies below offer practical ways to maintain trauma-informed principles over time.

Regular PD and Reflection Cycles

To keep trauma-informed practices current and consistent, schools should establish regular professional learning and reflective routines. PD should be built into the school calendar, with sessions that revisit trauma theory, update staff on emerging research, and offer space to practice core strategies. As Brunzell et al. (2016) note, effective trauma-informed PD cycles focus on the interplay between classroom strategies, student well-being, and teacher self-efficacy. Incorporating structured reflection – such as peer discussions or written journals – also supports the consolidation of learning and allows staff to monitor how their practice evolves over time.

Peer Support Networks

Peer learning is a powerful way to sustain TIC in a school. Formal and informal support networks offer educators the opportunity to process difficult experiences, share successful strategies, and learn from each other's insights. According to McInerney and McKlindon (n.d.), collaboration among staff builds resilience, reduces isolation, and ensures that TIC is not left to individual effort but becomes a shared responsibility. These networks can take the form of regular check-ins, structured learning communities, or cross-grade reflection groups, depending on the school context.

Incorporating TIC into School Policies

TIC must be reflected in the core documentation that shapes school life. This includes behaviour policies, well-being frameworks, staff handbooks, and the school's vision and values statements. As Cavanaugh (2016) highlights, policies that explicitly embed trauma-informed principles – such as relational discipline, cultural safety, and student agency – help align expectations and practice across all levels of the school. Embedding TIC in official documents signals to staff, students, and families that compassion, safety, and trust are not optional – they are foundational.

Recognising and Addressing Compassion Fatigue

Educators working in trauma-impacted contexts are often at risk of compassion fatigue and secondary traumatic stress. Sustaining a trauma-informed approach means acknowledging this risk and taking steps to mitigate it. Schools should provide access to counselling, supervision, and well-being supports, while also encouraging staff to use strategies such as mindfulness, emotional regulation, and boundaries around workload. As Miller and Flint-Stipp (2019) explain, schools that care for their staff's emotional well-being are better positioned to care for their students in sustainable, ethical ways. Building awareness of compassion fatigue through PD and regular staff check-ins also fosters a culture of care that includes educators themselves.

Practical Ways to Embed TIC into Daily Practice

For TIC to take root in schools, it must move beyond theory and become part of the everyday rhythm of the classroom. This means translating big ideas – like safety, trust, and emotional regulation – into consistent, relational practices that shape the way students experience school. These daily interactions are where TIC becomes visible, tangible, and most impactful.

Start with Connection

Greeting students by name, making eye contact, and offering a warm welcome at the door are small gestures that build relational safety. These routines communicate that students are seen, valued, and worth pausing for. Regular check-ins – whether verbal, visual (like an emotions chart), or informal conversations – also provide a space for students to express how they're feeling and receive support early in the day (Brunzell et al., 2016). These moments help prevent escalation and support regulation before learning begins.

Establish Calming Routines

Classroom environments that are predictable and soothing support nervous system regulation, especially for trauma-affected students who may be hypervigilant or anxious. Teachers can embed grounding strategies into the school day, such as breathing exercises, movement breaks, mindfulness pauses, or soft transitions between tasks. These routines help create a sense of structure and emotional safety, which are essential foundations for learning (McInerney & McKlindon, n.d.).

Respond with Empathy and Consistency

In trauma-informed classrooms, discipline is relational. When students act out or withdraw, teachers respond with curiosity rather than punishment: *What might this student need right now?* This shift requires patience, but it also builds trust. TIC is not about lowering expectations – it is about understanding the conditions that make learning possible. Responding calmly, validating emotions, and setting clear, compassionate boundaries help students feel secure and respected (Cavanaugh, 2016).

Use Language that Builds Safety and Belonging

The way teachers speak can reinforce or dismantle emotional safety. Using inclusive, strength-based language – such as "Let's try that together," or "You're not in trouble; I want to understand what's going on" – helps students feel supported rather than shamed. Offering choices, explaining transitions, and naming emotions in a regulated tone also foster trust and autonomy. These language shifts, though subtle, powerfully reinforce the core values of TIC: empathy, dignity, and connection (Evans & Coccoma, 2014).

Hold the Bigger Picture

TIC is not a set of techniques – it is a way of seeing students and showing up with compassion. Embedding TIC into daily practice means bringing empathy to discipline, patience to pressure, and presence to moments of stress. It also means recognising that healing happens in relationship – and that every interaction is a chance to restore safety, connection, and hope.

Section 4: Case Study and Practical Strategies

Case Study: Implementing Continuous PD and Reflective Practice in a School

At Willowbank Primary School, a mid-sized public school serving a diverse student population, the leadership team recognised a growing need to support students experiencing trauma-related challenges. Teachers were reporting increased emotional dysregulation, frequent behaviour incidents, and a sense of exhaustion from trying to meet complex student needs without adequate support. Rather than relying on one-off training sessions, the principal, in consultation with the school's well-being coordinator, initiated a whole-school trauma-informed PD initiative that would span the academic year.

The approach began with a full-day staff workshop led by a trauma education specialist. This session introduced the neuroscience of trauma, the impact on student learning and behaviour, and the principles of TIC. Importantly, it also created space for staff to share their own experiences and begin developing a shared language of care. From there, monthly staff meetings were restructured to include short PD modules and guided reflective discussions based on real classroom scenarios.

To embed these practices more deeply, Willowbank implemented a peer coaching model. Each staff member was paired with a colleague to check in weekly, debrief classroom challenges, and offer mutual support. The leadership team also introduced ten-minute reflective journaling at the end of each term, guided by prompts such as, *"What strategies supported regulation in my classroom?"* and *"How did I respond to students' emotional needs this term?"*

By the end of the school year, staff reported higher confidence in responding to dysregulation, greater empathy towards students with complex needs, and increased collaboration among colleagues. Suspension rates declined, and student engagement improved noticeably, especially among those previously identified as at-risk. Most importantly, a cultural shift had taken hold: TIC was no longer a side initiative – it had become part of how the school community understood teaching and learning.

This case illustrates that sustainable trauma-informed practice is built not just on knowledge but on collective reflection, leadership support, and the intentional integration of TIC principles into everyday school life.

Practical Strategies for Engaging in Reflective Practice and PD

Sustaining TIC requires more than understanding – it requires tools that support educators to keep learning, reflecting, and evolving in their practice. Below are three key strategies to help schools and educators embed trauma-informed professional growth into their routines.

PD Toolkit

A range of high-quality, evidence-informed resources can support individual and whole-school learning. Recommended resources include:

- **Online Courses**
    - *"Understanding Trauma in the Classroom"* (Australian Childhood Foundation)
    - *"Trauma-Informed Practices"* (Beacon House UK)
    - *"Trauma-Informed Resilient Schools"* (National Child Traumatic Stress Network)

- **Books**
    - *Helping Traumatized Children Learn* (Massachusetts Advocates for Children)
    - *The Deepest Well* by Dr. Nadine Burke Harris
    - *Fostering Resilient Learners* by Kristin Souers & Pete Hall

- **Expert Organisations**
    - Australian Childhood Foundation
    - Berry Street Education Model
    - The Trauma and Learning Policy Initiative (TLPI)
    - Healing Foundation (for Indigenous-focused PD and support)

These resources support both introductory and advanced learning, enabling staff to revisit trauma-informed practices across the school year.

Reflective Practice Guide

Structured reflection enhances the impact of PD by connecting theory to classroom experience. A reflective guide might include prompts such as:

- *When did I feel most connected to my students this week?*
- *How did I respond when a student was dysregulated? What worked? What might I try next time?*
- *What assumptions did I bring into the classroom today?*

- *In what ways did I support (or challenge) emotional safety in my room this week?*

Educators can journal weekly, use these questions for peer discussions, or reflect at the end of term to track changes in practice. Templates with space for intention-setting and follow-up reflections can help educators build this into a regular rhythm.

Creating a Personal Growth Plan

A personal growth plan allows educators to set clear, meaningful goals around trauma-informed practice. These goals should be specific, measurable, and aligned with the teacher's role and context. Examples might include:

- *"I will integrate two new regulation strategies into my morning routine this term."*
- *"I will engage in one trauma-informed PD session each month."*
- *"I will meet fortnightly with a peer for reflective conversations."*

By tracking these goals across the year – and revisiting them as part of staff development reviews – teachers are encouraged to view their professional growth as ongoing and values-driven (Figure 13.2).

Educator Growth and Reflection

Self-Awareness
Examine personal triggers, biases, and trauma history.

Knowledge Building
Learn about trauma, brain development, and effective practices.

Skill Development
Practice regulation, communication, and intervention techniques.

Community Practice
Collaborate with colleagues for support and accountability.

Ongoing Reflection
Continuously evaluate, adjust, and grow your practice.

Figure 13.2 Framework Showing Stages of Educator Development in Trauma-Informed Practice

Chapter Summary

PD and reflective practice are not just support mechanisms for trauma-informed education – they are the conditions that allow it to thrive. This chapter has explored how TIC requires more than one-time training or isolated strategies. Instead, it calls for sustained, school-wide learning that is iterative, collaborative, and grounded in relational practice.

Continuous PD ensures that educators stay responsive to new insights in trauma research and remain equipped to meet the evolving needs of their students. Reflective practice, in turn, provides the space to examine responses, challenge assumptions, and make thoughtful adjustments. Together, these practices foster growth, resilience, and a deeper understanding of how trauma affects learning, behaviour, and well-being.

At the heart of TIC is compassion – not as sentiment, but as a daily discipline. Compassion-focused practice invites educators to see behaviour through a lens of curiosity rather than judgement, and to respond with empathy, patience, and consistent support. When schools embed these values into routines, policies, and professional learning, they create cultures where both students and staff feel safe, valued, and capable of growth.

Guiding Questions for Reflection

What opportunities exist in your context to strengthen trauma-informed professional learning?
Reflect on whether your school's current PD offerings support sustained learning and relational practice – or whether there is room to grow.

How has your own practice evolved as a result of reflection?
Think about a moment when you adjusted your approach after reflecting on a challenging experience. What changed, and what did you learn?

Teachers Toolbox

Sustaining Trauma-Informed Practice through PD and Reflection

STRATEGY	DESCRIPTION
START EACH DAY WITH CONNECTION	Greet each student by name and check in informally. These small, consistent acts build trust and emotional safety, laying the groundwork for a trauma-informed classroom.
SCHEDULE REGULAR REFLECTION	Set aside a few minutes weekly to reflect on interactions, student responses, and your own emotional reactions. Use journal prompts or peer conversations to deepen insight.
ENGAGE IN ONGOING PD	Participate in trauma-informed professional development at least once per term. Look for workshops, online modules, or readings that extend your understanding and offer practical tools.
DEVELOP A PERSONAL GROWTH PLAN	Identify two or three trauma-informed goals for the term. These might include integrating a new strategy, improving response to dysregulation, or strengthening student relationships.
CREATE A PEER SUPPORT NETWORK	Partner with a colleague for regular reflective check-ins. Use these sessions to discuss classroom challenges, share strategies, and support each other's well-being.
USE A SELF-ASSESSMENT CHECKLIST	At the end of each week, review questions like: "Did I create a calm and safe environment?" or "How did I respond to student distress today?" Use the answers to guide next steps.
EMBED REGULATION ROUTINES	Incorporate simple practices like breathing, movement, or mindfulness into daily transitions. These strategies help students (and teachers) stay grounded and ready to learn.

References

Brunzell, T., Stokes, H., & Waters, L. (2016). Trauma-informed positive education: Using positive psychology to strengthen vulnerable students. *Contemporary School Psychology, 20*(1), 63–83. https://doi.org/10.1007/s40688-015-0070-x

Cavanaugh, B. (2016). Trauma-informed classrooms and schools. *Beyond Behavior, 25*(2), 41–46. https://doi.org/10.1177/107429561602500206

Evans, A., & Coccoma, P. (2014). *Trauma-informed care: How neuroscience influences practice*. Routledge.

Madigan, D. J., & Kim, L. E. (2021). Does teacher burnout affect students? A systematic review of its association with academic achievement and student-reported outcomes. *International Journal of Educational Research, 105*, 101714. https://doi.org/10.1016/j.ijer.2020.101714

McInerney, M., & McKlindon, A. (2014). Unlocking the door to learning: Trauma-informed classrooms & transformational schools. *Education Law Center*, 1–24. https://static1.squarespace.com/static/58867b5ff5e231bde3482767/t/58e7a57c-d1758e667c325c6f/1491576190690/Trauma-Informed-in-Schools-Classrooms.pdf

Miller, K., & Flint-Stipp, K. (2019). Preservice teacher burnout: Secondary trauma and self-care issues in teacher education. *Issues in Teacher Education, 28*(2), 28–45. https://eric.ed.gov/?id=EJ1239631

Oberg, G. (2025). Moral injury in teaching: the systemic roots of ethical conflict and emotional burnout in education. *Educational Review*, 1–24. https://doi.org/10.1080/00131911.2025.2504523

Perso T., Hayward C. (2015). *Teaching Indigenous students: Cultural awareness and classroom strategies for improving learning outcomes*, New South Wales, Australia: Allen & Unwin.

Conclusion
A Compassionate Commitment to Change

Reaffirming the Purpose of Trauma-Informed Education

At the heart of trauma-informed education lies a fundamental shift in perspective – from asking *"What's wrong with you?"* to *"What happened to you?"* As discussed in Chapter 1, this reframing invites educators to see behaviour through a lens of compassion and curiosity. It recognises that students' actions often reflect not defiance or dysfunction, but a response to adversity, stress, or unmet needs. This simple but profound shift alters the way we teach, connect, and care.

Trauma-informed education is not a programme to be delivered or a script to be followed. It is a sustained, relational commitment to creating environments where every student feels safe, valued, and seen. It involves building consistent, trusting relationships; designing inclusive, predictable classrooms; and responding to dysregulation with calm, rather than control. It means understanding that trauma affects how students learn, behave, and relate – and that healing happens in the context of supportive relationships and emotionally safe spaces.

Throughout this book, we have journeyed from theory to practice. We began with an exploration of trauma's impact on the brain, body, and behaviour. We examined the ways trauma intersects with culture, community, and identity, especially for Aboriginal and Torres Strait Islander students. We looked closely at classroom strategies – how to co-regulate, embed restorative practice, build peer connection, and respond with care. And we finished by turning inward, recognising that to sustain this work, educators

Conclusion: A Compassionate Commitment to Change

must engage in reflective practice and ongoing professional development. The path of trauma-informed teaching is one of both compassion and complexity. It asks educators to lead with heart, to hold space for discomfort, and to continually grow alongside their students.

This is not quick work. It is not easy work. But it is meaningful work. And it holds the potential to change not only student outcomes, but the culture of schools – and the future of education itself.

Key Themes Revisited

Over the course of this book, a number of key threads have emerged – threads that are not isolated concepts, but interwoven principles that collectively form the foundation of trauma-informed education. These themes are not bound to specific chapters or strategies; rather, they underpin the entire approach and reflect the values that sustain compassionate, inclusive practice.

Safety and Trust

In the early chapters, we explored the central importance of safety – both physical and emotional. For students affected by trauma, learning cannot begin until a sense of safety is established. This includes predictable routines, calm and regulated classrooms, and relationships built on consistency and respect. Trust is the outcome of safety over time. When students feel safe, they are more likely to engage, take risks in their learning, and develop secure connections with peers and teachers.

Empathy and Compassion

Trauma-informed care is grounded in empathy – not as a vague sentiment, but as a deliberate practice of seeking to understand before reacting. In Chapters 4 and 5, we considered how responding with curiosity and compassion helps educators to see beyond behaviour and recognise students' strengths, needs, and humanity. Compassion invites us to hold high expectations with high support, and to believe in students even when they are struggling to believe in themselves.

Cultural Safety and Inclusion

No trauma-informed approach can be complete without a deep reckoning with systemic inequality and historical harm. In Chapter 12, we turned our attention to Aboriginal and Torres Strait Islander students, highlighting how the legacies of colonisation and intergenerational trauma continue to shape educational experiences. Cultural safety requires more than representation – it demands respect, truth-telling, and an ongoing commitment to listening and learning from community voices. Trauma-informed care must be culturally responsive, or it risks perpetuating the very harm it seeks to repair.

Professional Growth and Reflection

Finally, we acknowledged that trauma-informed teaching is not a static skillset – it is a journey of continual growth. In Chapter 13, we explored the importance of professional development and reflective practice, not only to improve outcomes for students, but to support educator well-being. Teachers need time, space, and support to reflect on their work, challenge their assumptions, and sustain the emotional demands of care. When schools invest in their staff, they invest in the long-term capacity of trauma-informed culture.

These themes are not steps to be completed – they are commitments to be lived. They ask us to show up fully, to keep learning, and to lead with compassion, even when the work is hard. Together, they form a holistic vision of trauma-informed education – one that honours both the vulnerability and the potential of every child who walks through our doors.

The Educator's Role as a Change Agent

Throughout this book, one message has remained clear: educators are not just content deliverers or behaviour managers – they are agents of change. In a trauma-informed school, the role of the teacher expands beyond instruction. It becomes relational, restorative, and deeply human.

Every interaction with a student is an opportunity to either reinforce or disrupt cycles of trauma. When a teacher responds to dysregulation with calm, holds space for emotion, or notices a child's quiet withdrawal, they

Conclusion: A Compassionate Commitment to Change

are doing more than managing a classroom – they are helping to rewire a child's sense of safety, belonging, and self-worth. These are not small acts. They are transformational.

But being a change agent does not mean doing it alone. The weight of this work cannot fall on individual shoulders. Trauma-informed care must be embedded at every level of a school's culture – through policies, leadership, curriculum, and community partnerships. Still, the daily reality is that teachers are often the first line of response. They are the ones who see the tears, the shutdowns, the anger, the silence. They are also the ones who offer reassurance, consistency, humour, and hope.

In this role, educators need to be equipped not only with strategies but with support. They need professional development that is ongoing and meaningful. They need time to reflect, spaces to debrief, and leaders who prioritise their well-being as much as student outcomes. Most of all, they need to know that their efforts matter – that even on the hardest days, the work they do has the power to interrupt trauma and re-establish trust.

To be a trauma-informed educator is to be a steady presence in the lives of children who have known instability. It is to model calm in the face of chaos, to believe in students when they are at their most difficult to reach, and to hold onto hope – even when the system makes it hard. That is the heart of this work. That is the change.

Creating a Whole-School Approach

While individual teachers can make a profound difference, lasting impact requires a coordinated, school-wide commitment. Trauma-informed care is most powerful – and most sustainable – when it moves beyond isolated classrooms and becomes embedded in the culture, policies, and shared values of the entire school community.

A whole-school approach begins with leadership. When school leaders prioritise trauma-informed values, they set the tone for everything that follows. This includes providing time for professional learning, modelling relational leadership, creating space for reflective practice, and embedding trauma-aware principles into strategic planning. Leaders who view staff well-being as integral to student success foster a culture where compassion is not seen as optional, but essential.

Policies must also align with trauma-informed principles. Behaviour management frameworks should move away from punitive models and towards restorative approaches that prioritise relationship, accountability, and repair. School-wide practices – such as positive transitions, regulation spaces, and inclusive rituals – can help reinforce emotional safety and predictability across all settings, from the playground to the staffroom.

Collaboration is key. Trauma-informed care cannot be siloed within one department or dependent on the passion of a few individuals. It requires all staff – teachers, aides, office staff, counsellors, leaders – to speak the same language, share a consistent approach, and support one another through the emotional demands of the work. Peer learning groups, coaching models, and collective reflection help sustain momentum and strengthen shared understanding.

Importantly, a whole-school approach is not static. It evolves over time, informed by feedback from staff, students, and families. Schools that embrace this journey with humility and openness are better positioned to adapt, improve, and meet the unique needs of their communities.

In the end, trauma-informed care is most effective when it is no longer something "some teachers do," but rather "how we do things here." It is a cultural shift – away from blame and compliance, and towards trust, connection, and growth. And it is within reach when the whole school walks the path together.

Looking Ahead: Hope and Resilience

At the centre of trauma-informed education is a simple but powerful truth: healing is possible. Not because trauma disappears, or because hardship can be undone – but because with the right relationships, the right support, and the right conditions, students can learn, grow, and thrive in spite of what they've experienced. And so can the educators who walk alongside them.

This work is not without its challenges. It requires emotional labour, patience, and a willingness to confront discomfort – not just in our students, but in ourselves. But it also offers moments of profound connection: the quiet nod from a child who rarely speaks, the de-escalation that used to end in tears but now ends in regulation, the shift in a school's tone from punitive to nurturing. These are signs of something deeper taking root. Signs that what we do matters.

Conclusion: A Compassionate Commitment to Change

Hope is not passive – it is active. It is something we build, together, one interaction at a time. Trauma-informed educators are builders of hope. They create spaces where students feel safe enough to be seen, known, and believed in. They offer predictability in the midst of chaos, compassion in the face of resistance, and care even when it is not returned immediately. In doing so, they hold a mirror to what is possible – not just for their students, but for education as a whole.

Resilience is not just something we teach – it is something we model. When educators engage in reflective practice, seek support, and return to their classrooms with intention, they are demonstrating resilience in action. When schools commit to doing this work collectively, they are not just responding to trauma – they are transforming the systems that sustain it.

The path of trauma-informed education is not easy, but it is deeply worthwhile. It begins with understanding, grows through compassion, and is sustained by connection. And it ends, not with perfection, but with the promise that every child – and every teacher – deserves to feel safe, supported, and capable of change.

Index

Note: *Italic* page numbers refer to figures.

acting out 30–31
active listening 11, 49–50, 120, 121
acute trauma 4; *see also* trauma
adverse childhood experiences (ACEs) 32, *33*, 41, 106, 108
aggressive behaviours 30–31, 107
Alexander, K. 158, 161, 162, 171
Amrhein, B. 212
anxiety 39, 46, 102, 105, 110
Atkinson, J. 225, 231
attachment theory 44, 62, 107; secure base 45–46; secure vs. insecure attachments 44; surrogate attachment figures 44, 55
attention 25–26
attention-seeking behaviours 32–33
Australian Childhood Foundation 223, 228, 231, 233, 236, 237

Barton, G. 166, 169
Bates, P. 168
Batte, S. 159
behaviours 5, 18, 28, *29*; acting out 30–31; aggression 30–31; attention-seeking 32–33; challenging 29–32, 34–35, 106–109; cognitive impairment in 108–109; disengagement 31–32; in non-judgemental way 50; withdrawal 31–32
Berry Street Education Model 81, 83
Blair, C. 166
Blanch, F. 227
Bowlby, J. 44
breathing strategies 158, 184–185
Brock, S. E. 122
Brunzell, T. 158–160, 164, 168, 169, 172, 180, 181, 184, 187, 190, 192, 202, 206, 255
Bullard, M. 106–109, 120
burnout: compassion fatigue vs. 68; prevention 13–14, 67–68; signs of 69

calming techniques 25, 30, 74, 88
Cavanaugh, B. 78, 255
Chandler, Michael J. 226
change agent 266–267
Chase-Cantarini, S. 182
choice 6–7, 16
Christiaens, G. 182
classroom strategies 110–111; clear expectations 48–49; compassion in 10–12, 69–70; crisis situations in 122–123; empathy in 10–12, 15–16, 49–50, *51*; mindfulness

Index

practices in 19, 179–199; physical aspect 39; predictable and structured environment 46–48; relaxation techniques in 19, 179–199; sense of community and belonging 12; trauma-informed *see* trauma-informed care (TIC)
Coccoma, P. 249, 251, 252, 254
cognitive functions 4, 22, 23, 35; attention and concentration 25–26; deficits in executive function 26; memory and information processing 23–25
collaboration 16, 268; learning activities 206; rationale for 83; school community 7; trauma-informed education 7
colonisation, Indigenous communities 223–227
communication: core techniques for 121–122; and crisis management strategies 119; empathy 121–122; non-verbal 121; trauma-sensitive 120–121; validation 121–122
community-building practices 209
community involvement 84–85
compassion 17, 59–60, 114–115; in classroom 10–12, 69–70; empathy and 265; preventive strategies for 69–70; realistic workload expectations 69; support networks 69–70; in teacher-student relationship 9–10; time management 69; trauma-informed teaching 60, 61, 63–64
compassion fatigue 63–64, 67–68; vs. burnout 68, 69; professional development (PD) 247, 255–256; recognising and addressing 255–256; symptoms 68
complex trauma 4; *see also* trauma
conflict resolution 210–211, 217
consistency 43, 49, 257
cooperative learning 145–146

coping skills 163–164
co-regulation 160
crisis intervention 122–125; balancing safety and compassion 131; case study and practical strategies 132–133; de-escalation techniques 126–127; grounding exercises 124; immediate response strategies 123–124; imminent danger 131; involving support systems 131; offering choices 127; post-crisis support 125; reducing environmental stimuli in 124; student agency and choice in 123; violent/unsafe situations 130
cultural competence 239, 246; professional development (PD) 246–247
culturally responsive teaching 234–235
cultural marginalisation 225, 226
cultural safety 232, 235, 237; and inclusion 266; practical strategies for 233; principles 232–233
cultural sensitivity training 239
curriculum design, trauma sensitivity 17–18, 138–139, 195; checklist for 150–151; differentiated instruction (DI) 141–142; empathy 141; flexibility 139; grounding techniques 150; inclusivity 140, 141; practical strategies 149–150; principles of 139–140; reflective activities 150; relevance 140

Darling-Hammond, S. 209
decision-making processes 16
deep breathing exercises 183
de-escalation techniques 28, 42, 82, 111, 112, 124, *124*, 268; non-verbal 128; professional development (PD) 247; verbal 126–127
deficit-based approach 8, 10
differentiated instruction (DI) 138, 141–142, 144

Index

disengagement 31–32
Dweck, C. 162, 165

educational inequality 241
educator: intergenerational trauma 230–231; to prioritise their emotional needs 14–15; reflective practice for 251, *253*; self-care 12–14, *66*; well-being 12–14
emotional literacy 11, 158–159
emotional needs 14–15
emotional regulation 19, 155, 230; academic engagement 156; breathing techniques 158; case study 172–174; into classroom routines 159–160; co-regulation 160; emotional literacy 11, 158–159; integration with learning 161; mindfulness practices 158; practical strategies 174; self-awareness 158–159; sensory and physical environment 161; skills 155–157; zones of regulation model 157, *157*
emotional safety 18, 39–41, 54–55; building trust 41, 43–44; case study and practical strategies 51–54; classroom environment role in 42, 49–50, *51*; creation 39–55; empathy 49–50, *51*; establishing 46; impact on learning and relationships 41; through predictable routines 51–54
emotional sustainability 71
emotions: numbness *vs.* flatness 102; trauma in 5, 102; well-being 3, 167–172, 176, 256
empathy 59, 231; in classroom 10–12, 15–16; and compassion 265; emotional safety 49–50, *51*; restorative practices 213–214; and self-awareness 123; self-care practices 64; on student security and trust 61–62; in teacher-student relationship 9–10; training 82; in trauma-informed teaching 60, 61;

trauma-sensitive curriculum design 141
empathy-driven interventions 114–115
Employee Assistance Programs (EAPs) 70
empowerment 7, 80
Evans, A. 249, 251, 252, 254
executive function 26, 108, 146, 182

fight-flight-freeze response 4, 28, 104, 107
Flint-Stipp, K. 256
forced assimilation 223–227
Foreman, T. 168

Garvis, S. 166, 169
Gebb, A. 127
goal-setting 165
gratitude practice 14
Greig, J. 78
grounding techniques 124, 150; trauma-responsive teaching 146–147
growth mindset 162, 165–167
guided imagery 187, 188

Hart, V. 225, 231
Hayward, C. 225–227, 231, 232, 235, 236
Howard, J. A. 166
hyperactivity 32–33, 102, 108
hypervigilance 25, 102, 122–123, 229

immediate response strategies 123–124
inclusion 80, 140, 141, 207; classroom norms 207–208; cultural safety and 266; environments 111, 138, 232–237
Indigenous communities: building partnerships with 235–236; contemporary education systems 227; cultural protocols and practices 234; cultural safety 232–237; in curriculum 233–234, 239–240; encouraging student voice 240;

Index

formal education systems 226; impact on 223–224; inclusive environment 232–237; and intergenerational trauma 19, 222, 228–231, 237–238; lasting effects on 224–226; practical strategies 239; restorative approaches 240; supporting students and families 236–237
individual intervention techniques 111–112
information processing 23–25
insecure attachments 44; *see also* attachment theory
intentional breathing 158
intergenerational trauma 19, 222, 228, 237–238; implications for educators 230–231; Indigenous communities and 19, 222, 228–231
intervention strategies 109–113; empathy-driven 114–115

Jennings, P. A. 167, 169, 188

Lalonde, Christopher 226
learning environment: safe and supportive 8; supportive and empathetic 10–12; trauma impact on 18, 22–35
Lopez-Gonzales, L. 182

MacGill, B. 225, 227
McInerney, M. 250, 251, 253, 255
McKlindon, A. 250, 251, 253, 255
memory 23–25
mental health services 69–70, 85, 249
microaggressions 232
micro-practices: mindfulness 193; self-care 171
Miller, K. 256
mind-body regulation 180
mindfulness 13, 19, 65, 72–73, 179; into academic activities 194–195;

benefits 180, 181; brief practices 253; calm and supportive space 191–192; case study and practical strategies 195–197; developmental needs 194; and emotional check-in 174; emotional regulation 157–158, 181–182; micro-practices 193; and relaxation techniques 183–184, *184*; routine for 189–190; scaffolding 194; school-based 182; self-care 169; self-regulation 180–181, 192; stress reduction 182
mindset: deficit-based approach *vs.* strengths-based perspective 10, *11*; trauma-informed care 8–9

National Centre for Trauma-Informed Care (NCTIC) 80
neutral language 127–128
Nicholls, C. 184
non-judgemental approach 70–71, 105
non-punitive approach 114–115; discipline strategies 42, 84
non-threatening language 127–128
non-verbal communication 121; de-escalation techniques 128; eye level positioning 129; neutral and open body language 129; personal space 128; relaxed posture 128; and safety 129–130

open communication 48, 84

partnerships: community 91–92; with Indigenous communities 235–236; with mental health agencies 84
PBL *see* project-based learning (PBL)
PD *see* professional development (PD)
peer support 202–203; benefits 203–204; initiatives 216; networks 65–66, 73; practical strategies 215; structured systems 204–205
Perry, B. D. 110

Index

Perso, T. 225–227, 231, 232, 235, 236
Phillips, R. 206
physical activity 14, 170
positive reinforcement 166, 173
positive teacher-student relationship 3, 18, 39, 43–44, 62, 122
problem-solving skills: collaborative 66; resilience 164; role-playing 26
professional development (PD) 19, 244–246; case study 257–258; compassion fatigue 247, 255–256; consultation with mental health professionals 249; cultural competency 246–247; de-escalation techniques 247; online courses and webinars 248; peer learning groups 248; personal growth plan 260, *260*; practical strategies 258; reflection cycles 255; regular 255; restorative practices 247; self-care 247; supportive school culture 253–254; toolkit 259; types 247; workshops and seminars 248
progressive muscle relaxation (PMR) 185–186
project-based learning (PBL) 144–145

Raver, C. C. 166
reflective practice 12, 14, 65, 72–73, 82, 249–250; benefits 250; case study 257–258; continuous improvement 250; for educators 251, *253*; empathy 251; journaling 169–170, 252; mindfulness 253; peer debriefing 252; personal growth 251; practical strategies 258; professional growth and 266; self-assessment checklists 252; self-awareness exercises 253
relaxation techniques: in classroom 19, 179–199; deep breathing exercises 183; for emotional and physical well-being 188–189; guided imagery 187; mindfulness and 183, *184*; progressive muscle relaxation (PMR) 185–186; routine for 189–190; self-care 169; visualisation 187–188
reliability 43, 107
repair practices 209
resilience 19, 161–163, 269; building pyramid *163*; case study and practical strategies 172–175; coping strategies 163–164; goal-setting 165; growth mindset 165–167; positive reinforcement 166; problem-solving skills 164; significance 163; for students 66–67, 161–167
restorative circle 207, 210, 217
restorative practices 111–113, 208–209; adoption 90, 92; benefits 93, 212; case study 214–215; components 209–210; conflict resolution 210–211, 217; empathy development 213–214; enhanced accountability 212–213; improved relationships 213; Indigenous communities 240; peer conversations 216–217; practical strategies 215; professional development (PD) 247; questions to guide *211*; for rebuilding community 125; relationship repair 211–212; techniques 216–217; types 209; as whole-school cultural shift 209
Rivertown Secondary School 89–93
role-playing 173; exercises 31; interactive scenarios 174; problem-solving 26

safety 6, 15; emotional 18, 39–55; re-establishing 125; and trust 265
scaffolding: mindfulness 194; in trauma-responsive teaching 146
school culture: compassionate 254; supportive *see* supportive school culture
Schumacher, A. 207, 208, 210

Index

secure attachments 44; *see also* attachment theory
secure base 45–46
SEL *see* social-emotional learning (SEL)
self-assessment 174, 252
self-awareness: emotional regulation 158–159; empathy and 123; reflective practice 253
self-care 15, 59–60, 113, 167; classroom culture 168; in daily school routines 168–169; for educator 12–14, 66; emotional well-being 167–172; empathetic engagement 64–65; healthy routines 170–171; integrated classroom routines 172; micro-practices 171; mindfulness 169; on trauma-informed practice 67; pedagogical model 168; physical activity 170; reflective journaling 169–170; relaxation techniques 169; and self-advocacy 167–168; short breaks 171; for students 66–67, 167; in sustaining empathy 64; for teachers 65–66, 66, 168; time management 72
self-expression activities 32
self-regulation 192; and grounding activities 146–147
Sellman, E. 212
sense of agency 16, 133, 157
sense of belonging 12, 62, 86, 93, 140
sense of community 12, 94, 125
social connections: activities 217–218; building 206–207; collaborative goal-setting 217–218; collaborative learning activities 206; community circles/morning meetings 206; community service projects 218; cooperative games and challenges 218; practical strategies 215; restorative circle 207; supportive classroom community 205–206; team-building exercises 207

social-emotional learning (SEL) 31, 78, 206, 214; curriculum integration 90, 161; emotional literacy and self-awareness 159; peer-centred interventions 203–204; policies on 81
somatic symptoms 103
Spence, C. 161, 170
storytelling 234, 235
strengths-based perspective 3, 7, 9, 10, 15–16, 80, 140
stress management 13–14
stress reduction 182
stress response system: chronic activation 4, 30
Substance Abuse and Mental Health Services Administration (SAMHSA) 84
supportive school culture 18, 78–79, 253–254; behavioural and cultural shifts 92–93; case study 89–92; challenges 93; classroom-specific strategies 88–89; communication approaches 87; community partnerships 91–92; effective community involvement 84–85; engagement strategies 85–86; family and community collaboration 82–83; home-school journals 88–89; implementation 89–92; leveraging community resources 87–88; policy and procedural foundations 80–81; policy changes 90; professional development (PD) 253–254; staff training 90–91; take-home resources 88; training and development 81–82; whole-school implementation 80, *80*
Szalavitz, M. 110

teacher: compassion in 60, 61, 63–64; empathy in 60, 61; self-care for 65–66, *66*, 168

Index

teacher-student relationship:
compassion and empathy in 9–10;
positive 3, 18, 39, 43–44, 62, 122
TIC *see* trauma-informed care (TIC)
time management techniques 14, 69, 72
transparency 44, 87
trauma 4; awareness training 81; behavioural indicators 5, 102–103; on brain development *24*; on cognitive development *see* cognitive functions; early recognition 114; emotional indicators 5, 102; impact on learning and behaviour 18, 22–35; neurobiological impact 4–5, 104; physical indicators 103; physiological responses 27–28; recognising 104–106; in students 18, 100–117; symptoms 246; triggers 27, 109
trauma-informed care (TIC) 1–3, *2*; calm spaces 110–111; challenging behaviours 106–109; communication and crisis intervention 18, 119–136; compassion *see* compassion; core values of 257; crisis management strategies 119; into daily practice 256, 257; empathy *see* empathy; empathy-driven interventions 114–115; establish calming routines 256; foundations 3–19; intervention strategies 109–110, 112–113; mindset 8–9; peer support networks 255; principles 6–7, *8*, 15–17; professional development (PD) *see* professional development (PD); relational discipline 257; safe and supportive learning environment 8; into school policies 255; strengths-based perspective 9; structured environment and predictable routines 110; supportive school culture 18, 78–97; sustaining 254
trauma-informed pedagogical environments (TIPE) 180
trauma-responsive teaching 144; case study and practical application 148–149; connecting strategies to 147–148; cooperative learning 145–146; grounding activities 146–147; instructional strategies for 144–147; project-based learning (PBL) 144–145; scaffolding in 146; self-regulation breaks 146–147
trauma-sensitive practices: communication 120–121; curriculum design *see* curriculum design, trauma sensitivity; implementation 8; interventions 8; relaxation techniques and 183–189; school community collaboration 7
trust 6, 15, 79; building 41, 43–44, 48–49, 193; clear classroom expectations 48–49; consistency and reliability 49; empathy on student security and 61–62; open communication 48; safety and 125, 265; student choice and agency 49

Universal Design for Learning (UDL) 138, 140; engagement 142–143; flexibility 143; multiple formats 143; principles 142–144

validation 50, 121–122
verbal aggression 30
verbal de-escalation techniques 126–127; calmness and reassurance 126; reflective language 127; *see also* de-escalation techniques

Waters, L. 182
well-being 13; emotional 3, 167–172, 176, 256; mindfulness practices 13; physical activity 14; practical

Index

strategies 13–14; professional development (PD) 247; relaxation techniques for 188–189; restorative sleep 14; setting boundaries 13; social support 14; time management techniques 14
Whatman, S. 225
whole-school approach: creating 267–268; cultural shift 209; implementation *80*
Willowbank Primary School 257–258
withdrawal 31–32, 102; and social disengagement 108
Wolpow, R. 160, 163

For Product Safety Concerns and Information please contact our EU representative GPSR@taylorandfrancis.com
Taylor & Francis Verlag GmbH, Kaufingerstraße 24, 80331 München, Germany